Nandita Haksar is a human rights lawyer, teacher, campaigner and writer. Her engagement with the people of Northeast India began while studying in Jawaharlal Nehru University in the 1970s. She has represented the victims of army atrocities in the Supreme Court and the High Court and campaigned nationally and internationally against the Armed Forces (Special Powers) Act, 1958. She has written innumerable articles in national dailies and journals and is the author of several books, including *Nagaland File: A question of human rights* (co-edited with Luingam Luithui) (1984); *Who are the Nagas* (2011); *ABC of Naga Culture and Civilization: A resource book* (2011); *The Judgement That Never Came: Army rule in Northeast India* (co-authored with Sebastian Hongray) (2011); *Across the Chicken Neck: Travels in Northeast India* (2013) and *The Many Faces of Kashmiri Nationalism: From the Cold War to the present day* (2015). In her capacity as a human rights lawyer, Haksar has helped to organise migrant workers to fight for their rights and voice their grievances. She lives in Goa, Delhi and sometimes Ukhrul, with her husband, Sebastian Hongray.

I0129448

THE EXODUS IS NOT OVER

Migrations from the Ruptured Homelands of Northeast India

Nandita Haksar

SPEAKING
TIGER

SPEAKING TIGER PUBLISHING PVT. LTD
4381/4, Ansari Road, Daryaganj
New Delhi 110002

First published in paperback by Speaking Tiger 2016

ISBN: 978-93-86338-13-6
e-ISBN: 978-93-86338-18-1

10 9 8 7 6 5 4 3 2 1

Typeset in Adobe Garamond Pro by SÜRYA, New Delhi
Printed at Thomson Press India Ltd.

For Mayori

Contents

Introduction

The Migrant Worker from Northeast India

This book tells the stories of the first generation of migrant workers from the Northeast region, especially Manipur, working in towns and cities in India and abroad. This is the first time that the migrant workers are telling their own stories in such intimate and harrowing detail.

Economic deprivation, insurgencies and deadly ethnic clashes have driven thousands of impoverished men and women to seek a better life in the metropolis, only to find themselves targets of racism, sexual harassment and class exploitation.

Academics complain of the lack of reliable data.[1] There are no dependable statistics on the actual numbers of migrant workers from the Northeast, but some organizations such as the Northeast Support Centre and Helpline have made educated guesses about the number of migrants coming from the Northeast. In a report brought out by the organization in 2011, they estimated that 414,850 people from the Northeast region of India had migrated to various cities such as Chennai, Bengaluru, Hyderabad, Chandigarh, Goa, Mumbai and Delhi during the period 2005–2010. The report also predicted that 50 lakh people would migrate from the Northeast region within five years from 2011 to 2015. Delhi has been the most preferred destination for the migrants.

The one big difference between the migrants from the Northeast and the rest of India is that in the case of the former, unmarried men and women migrate in equal numbers.

---

1. See: Duncan McDuie-Ra, 2012, *Northeast Migrants in Delhi Race, Refuge and Retail*, Amsterdam University Press, and Babu P. Remesh, 2012, *Migration from North-East to Urban Centres: A Study of Delhi Region*, Noida: V V Giri National Labour Institute.

In contrast, migrant workers from other states tend to be male.

The Northeast region consists of eight states: Assam, Arunachal Pradesh, Manipur, Meghalaya, Mizoram, Nagaland, Sikkim and Tripura. In each state there are numerous communities, each with its own distinct language, history and culture. But when migrant workers come to Delhi, Mumbai, Goa or Bengaluru, their shared experience of cultural alienation has helped them forge bonds across ethnic divides, making it possible to speak of the emergence of a Northeastern identity.

Northeast Migrants and Other Indians

Although migration to mainland India has brought migrant workers from the Northeast closer to one another, it has not necessarily brought them closer to other Indians. Many of the migrant workers I interviewed had never been invited to a local Indian home. I asked several of them why they did not try to make friends with the local Indians and they replied that they did not know how to make friends with people from outside their own community.

In part, this is because of their experience with the mainland Indians they have met in their own villages who have not treated them with respect. In the Northeast, almost every tribe has a word for an outsider which is derogative; a tribal from other parts of the region is not included in this category. In fact, even a Westerner, for instance, a missionary, is not included. The word outsider, whether it is the Khasi word dkhar, or the Mizo word bhai or the Meitei word mayang, all denote an Indian who does not belong to the Mongoloid race.

Often, migrants from Bihar, Uttar Pradesh or other parts of India, living in the Northeast are subject to physical assault and even quit notices by the armed groups. Some armed groups have even tried to prevent marriages between their people and the 'outsiders'.

There are many factors responsible for this feeling of alienation from the rest of the country—the difference in cultural practices, the caste system, racism and ignorance. All these factors contribute to making the Northeasterner feel like a stranger in his or her own country.

This feeling of alienation and insecurity has pushed Northeast migrants to ghettoize themselves in specific parts of the city in which they live, whether it is in Humayunpur in Delhi or Kalina in Mumbai. These neighbourhoods cater to the needs of students and migrant workers from the Northeast. Here they have created a world of their own, where one can find shops with vegetables flown in from the Northeast, smoked meats, dry fish, fermented foods such as bamboo shoots, soya beans and the famous ngari (fermented fish). There are small beauty parlours and restaurants that serve spicy delicacies which taste of home. Many migrant workers grow herbs and chillies in pots in any space they can find, even in crowded areas.

Every colony has special fellowships where the workers can gather together for worship; there are get-togethers for people from each village and a network of organizations that maintain the ties between the migrant and his or her community of origin, but also keep them isolated from the rest of the Indians.

Violence and Northeast Associations

Both male and female migrants from the Northeast face physical violence and verbal abuse almost on a daily basis. Here is an account by a Tangkhul woman—who was too scared to allow me to give her name—given to Jagori, a woman's organization in Delhi in 2009. It describes in vivid detail what Northeast migrant workers face:

'On the 11th of October around 00.30 hours, my husband, my niece, my son and I were visiting my brothers-in–law in Humayunpur, Safdarjung Enclave. On our way, four to five locals who were drinking alcohol passed lewd and racist comments (Chinky/Bahadur/Kancha etc.), which we ignored, not intending to get into any argument. After dropping me and the children, my husband and my elder brother-in-law went to park the car outside the locality. They were verbally abused by the same group, which was ignored by my husband and my brother-in-law. This indifference apparently provoked the local goons. Fearing that the vehicle which was parked outside would be vandalized, my husband and my younger brother-in-law went back to inspect the car and saw one of the locals moving away from the vehicle. On inspection of the car, all tires (sic) were found to be deflated. Not wanting to take the matter in our own hands, my husband called the police control room (100), apprising them of the situation. In the meantime, my husband sent my younger brother-in-law to apprise us of the situation. Realizing the delay in the response from the control room and sensing trouble, my husband dialled the control room phone number three times in total. During those moments, a friend of my husband, Mr Chihan Vashum, was returning from work and he stopped to enquire from my husband. Suddenly four to five people from the same group, under heavy influence of alcohol, started to physically assault my husband and his friend, despite the fact that they had not shown any aggression or intention of taking matters in their own hands. My elder brother-in-law, who was in the vicinity, rushed to my husband's rescue on hearing his cries and the scuffle. As he tried to stop the local people from beating them, they beat him as well and in the process of the scuffle broke their glasses, snatched some of our belongings (shirt, a mobile phone, sandals) and some cash as well. We rushed to the spot as soon as my younger brother-in-law informed us of the situation. (My brothers-in-law's house is around 800 metres away from the place of the assault.) We realized that my husband and his friend had been brutally beaten up and were bleeding profusely.

The cops turned up much after the fight. Hearing the commotion, friends and passers-by had gathered, demanding the arrest of the culprits who were in an inebriated condition. The cops, instead of trying to take stock of the situation, came and shook hands with the local people who had beaten up my husband and his friend brutally. On demanding the culprits to be brought forward and be arrested, the cops manipulated the situation and were trying to take into custody another person from the group who was not a part of the scuffle. We identified the culprits to the cops and informed them that they were taking the wrong person into custody, which was responded by physical assault from the cops. Some of our womenfolk including myself were slapped, shoved and pulled by the cops. They dragged in three-four people from the crowd to the PCR van, and in the process, they tried to drag me and my sister-in-law into the PCR van. We were pulled away by my husband, but they forcibly took away four other people from the crowd from the Northeast India sans my husband. All this while there were no policewomen. These unlawful and shameful acts were carried out by the policemen.'

Media reports seldom convey the horror experienced by the victims or their families. But the rage expressed by the Northeast migrants and students did force the Delhi Police to issue Standing order no 383/2009 on Tackling the Problems faced by Students and Others from the North-Eastern States in Delhi (see Appendix). But the standing orders have not made any significant difference and the Northeasterners have mainly relied on their own resources to protect themselves.

The response of the Northeast people to this violence has been to establish Northeast Associations catering to the needs of all members of the Northeastern community living outside the region. One of the first such organizations established in Delhi, the Northeast Support Centre and Helpline, was started in 2007 after a Mizo call-centre employee was raped in a moving vehicle and dumped on the roads of the city.

Although women from the Northeast are particularly

vulnerable to sexual harassment at their workplace,[2] they are not the only victims of physical violence. In February 2014, a nineteen-year-old student from Arunachal Pradesh and the son of a MLA, Nido Tania, was lynched to death in broad daylight by shopkeepers who passed comments on his hairstyle in Delhi's Lajpat Nagar.

The subsequent outrage expressed by students and political leaders from the region forced political parties to take note of the violence against people of the Northeast. As a result, the Bharatiya Janata Party's (BJP) vision document for the Delhi assembly polls in 2015 included a section titled 'North Eastern Immigrants to be Protected'. The document promised:

> 'Special cells in all police stations and special 24-hour helpline numbers to be set up for the protection of the North Eastern migrants. To safeguard the students of NE origin, special guardianship will be arranged with local families for them'.

The Congress Party was quick to react, with its leader Ajay Maken questioning, 'Is BJP trying to say the people from the North East are not Indian citizens?'

However, the political parties did not intervene in any effective way. The Ministry of Home Affairs set up a committee under the chairmanship of M.P. Bezbaruah, a retired IAS officer and member of the North East Council,[3] to 'look into

---

2. The Centre for Northeast Studies and Policy Research MMAJ Academy of International Studies, Jamia Millia, has done a study on violence on women, titled 'Discrimination and Challenges before Women from North East India: Case Studies from Four Metros—New Delhi, Mumbai, Kolkata and Bengaluru', sponsored by the National Commission for Women (NCW), 2012-13.

3. In 1971, the Indian Central government set up the North Eastern Council by an Act of Parliament. The eight States of Northeast India are members of the council. The headquarters of the council

(Contd...)

the concerns of the people of the North East living in other parts of the country'.

The committee noted that there had been a change in the profile of the migrants, which could have been a factor behind the rise in crimes. Earlier, they were mostly students. Now many had come to work in the lower rungs of the service sectors. The preference for workers from the Northeast in certain areas, like the hospitality industry, had caused resentment in some sections of the local population.

The committee also noted that a major problem faced by Northeast workers in the metros was exploitation by their employers and that often it left the worker feeling 'totally helpless to stand up for their rights when they are mistreated and harassed'.

Two years before the murder of Nido Tania, in August of 2012, violence against migrants from the Northeast had become so widespread and so intense that thousands of them converged on railway platforms in cities like Bengaluru and Hyderabad to take trains back home. Special trains were arranged to cope with the rush. The bulk of these people were migrant workers.

The Bengaluru police estimated that 2,50,000 people from Northeastern states were working in the city, in hotels, security agencies, shopping malls and beauty parlours, in addition to students. Vasudeva Adiga, president, Bangalore Hoteliers Association, and owner of the Adiga chain of restaurants, told the media:

(...contd.)

is situated in Shillong and functions under the Ministry of Development of North Eastern Region of the Government of India. The Council is an advisory body and may discuss any matter in which the Northeastern States have a common interest and advise the central government on the action to be taken.

'If the people of the Northeast leave Bangalore in large numbers over the next few days, the hotel industry will be worst affected, as it is very difficult to find replacements. A lot of people from Assam, Arunachal Pradesh and Nagaland are engaged as cooks, captains and waiters in many hotels, especially restaurants serving Chinese and north Indian cuisine.'[4]

According to the Karnataka Security Services Association vice-president, Lt Col (Retd.) Darshan Bal, this exodus also affected security agencies in Bengaluru, since 20 per cent of the around 1,00,000 people they employed were from the Northeast. In Hyderabad the situation was similar.

The reasons for the attacks against Northeast migrants remain a mystery, but that was the turning point when more and more migrants felt the need to have organizations which would represent everyone from the Northeast, rather than representing individual tribes or communities. One of the first such organizations was the Northeast Welfare Association of Karnataka.

In Goa, my husband and I tried to persuade migrant workers from the Northeast to form an organization that would work like a trade union. However, they had never heard of trade unions, labour laws or even human rights. When a Northeast Association was formed in Goa in 2010, the aims and objectives were not drafted in the language of rights but in the language of identity politics with a bit of Christian charity thrown in:

1. For the welfare of the north-east community in Goa
2. To promote the dignity (identity), unity and integrity of the north-east community

---

4. 'Exodus of Northeastern people kits businesses in Bangalore' in *The Business Standard* 17 August 2012. http://www.business-standard.com/article/economy-policy/exodus-of-northeastern-people-hits-businesses-in-bangalore-112081702027_1.html

3. To extend a helping hand to the weak and needy ones among the north-east people living in Goa
4. To bring a living harmony of the north-east community in Goa
5. To promote the true north-east status in India.'

Despite their initial lack of experience and knowledge, Northeast Associations have played a significant role in rescuing men, women and children who have been trafficked. In July 2012, my husband and I, with the Northeast Association, Goa, had helped rescue fourteen men who had been trafficked from Nagaland and Assam to work in the illegal iron ore mines in Goa; in July 2013, the Karanataka Northeast Welfare Association helped rescue two Kuki girls trafficked from Manipur to Bengaluru.

However, these organizations have not been very effective in intervening when the labour rights of migrant workers are violated.

Who Is a Migrant Worker?

So far, scholars have focused their research on issues relating to in-migration, since the Northeast has historically been a migrant-receiving zone. The region has received a large number of migrants from Nepal, Bangladesh and more recently, from Myanmar. The discussions on these migrants have been around the legality of the migrations and security concerns. It is only recently that research has started on the problems relating to out-migration from the region.

Studies suggest that an increasing number of people are migrating from the Northeast. Rough estimates suggest that currently in the Delhi region alone, there are 90,000 to 1,00,000 Northeastern ethnic residences (Indigenous Portal 2010).[5]

5. Babu P. Ramesh, 'Strangers in their own land: Migrants from the North-East in Delhi', *Economic and Political Weekly*, June 2, 2012, vol XLVII no 22. Babu does not clarify what 'ethnic Naga residences' means.

There seems to be confusion about who is and who is not a migrant worker. Often studies on migrant workers from the Northeast include students within their definition. One lecturer from Nagaland teaching in Indira Gandhi Open University in Delhi phoned to ask why I had used the term 'migrant workers'. He wanted to know the difference between 'migrant workers' and students studying in educational institutions outside the Northeast. Several studies have also failed to make a distinction between the two. I think it is very important to make this distinction because the life experiences and expectations of the two groups—migrant workers and students—are very different.

A student is often supported by the family back home or can support him- or herself with a wide range of scholarships meant for members of the Scheduled Tribes; they often have access to reservations in hostels and other facilities such as subsidized food. More importantly, students have very active and strong organizations to protect their interests. These student organizations, for example the Naga Students Federation (NSF) or the All Arunachal Pradesh Students Union (AAPSU), play the role of opposition parties rather than taking up only student issues, and often they have the backing of militant armed groups.

The definition of a migrant worker does not include men and women who have been trafficked: they are modern-day slaves and included in forced labour. A person displaced by development projects is also not a migrant worker, but is called an internally displaced person, while a person who is forced to migrate because of war or conflict is a refugee or asylum seeker. All these are cases of forced migration and not within the scope of this book.

The United Nations Convention on the Protection of the Rights of All Migrant Workers and Members of Their Families defines the migrant worker as follows:

'The term "migrant worker" refers to a person who is engaged or has been engaged in a remunerated activity in a State of which he or she is not a national'.

By this definition, a migrant worker is a person who voluntarily goes to another country in search of paid work. There are a growing number of migrant workers from the Northeast who work abroad in places as far-flung as Dubai, Singapore, London and Oslo. Some of their stories are extraordinary, such as the story of Grace Khamrang, who works on the private yacht of the King of Saudi Arabia, or Wungnaoshung Ngalung who went to Congo as a migrant worker and now owns his own restaurant there. In this book I have told the stories of the internal migrants, the men or women from the Northeast who have voluntarily migrated to other parts of India in search of paid work.

I have also included the stories of those who have been engaged in illegal work, such as in illegal call centres involved in huge scams, as well as alluded to stories about the trafficking of men, women and children from the Northeast to other parts of India.

These migrant workers are not organized; they have to fend for themselves. They also have no reservations for jobs, no security of tenure, not even the basic protection of labour laws. On top of this, they have no financial security. Moreover, they have the responsibility of supporting not only themselves, but also their large families back in the village.

There are absolutely no facilities for training migrant workers so that they may acquire skills and certificates either back in their home state or elsewhere in India. They are a part of the unorganized labour force where mainstream trade unions do not offer any security.

* * *

I have recorded the stories of people from different parts of the Northeast. They all face similar problems, difficulties, prejudices, racism, humiliation and oppression. However, when I went deeper into their lives I realized that each community had very different mechanisms for dealing with these problems. It depended on their specific cultural, religious, social and political backgrounds. I, therefore, decided to tell the stories of only the Tangkhul Naga migrant workers from Ukhrul District in Manipur.

Manipur

Manipur was a princely state till 15 October 1949 when it merged with the Indian Union. Armed Meitei groups politically challenged the merger's legal validity and this grievance continues to be the basis for armed resistance by Meitei insurgents. Meitei Hindus form the majority of the population and they are concentrated in the Valley. In addition, a Manipuri Muslim community also lives in the Valley.

The five hill districts of Manipur are inhabited by tribal communities, which can be broadly divided into Naga and Kuki-Mizo groups. These groups are largely Christian, the majority being Baptists. Although the tribal population is smaller than the Meiteis', the geographical area of the hill districts is much larger and their land is protected by the law from sale to non-tribals.

All these communities—Naga, Kuki, Meitei Hindu and Meitei Muslim—have numerous armed groups, and that is why the clashes between the communities are deadly. It is because of this that Manipur has been called the most dangerous place in India. In a broad sense, all these clashes are based on conflicting demands for a homeland.

The Nagas in Manipur have been demanding that the Naga-inhabited districts be integrated into the contiguous areas of Nagaland, Assam and Arunachal Pradesh. The Meiteis oppose this on the ground that it would break up the integrity of Manipur. In June 2001, a mob of angry Meiteis burnt down the Manipur Legislative Assembly in protest against the Naga demand.

The Kukis in Manipur have also been demanding their own homeland consisting of land which the Nagas claim is traditionally theirs. The Kuki demand for a separate district has resulted in tension and clashes between the Kukis and Nagas. However, when the Meiteis asked for Scheduled Tribe status, which would allow them to buy land in the tribal areas, the Nagas and Kukis presented a united front against the Meiteis.

Most of the migrant workers do not know the cause of the tensions that exist back home in Manipur. In my interviews with them, I found that they may have memories of conflicts but they do not know the history of these political demands.

Away from Manipur, they find themselves overwhelmed by the strangeness of the atmosphere, but the bonds of language[6] and culture (especially food) bring Nagas, Kukis and Meiteis together in a way that is not possible back home. I have noticed that friendships are stronger between the women of different communities than among the men; but I cannot say why. However, these bonds of friendship do not necessarily last when they return home.

At the same time, migrant workers retain their separate tribal or community identities, even if they work at the same place and share the same accommodation. It is interesting to see how these identities are kept alive so far from home.

---

6. Every tribe and community has its own language. For instance, the Tangkhul language is one of the recognized languages in Manipur and is taught up to the graduate level in the Roman script. However, all the tribes and communities living within Manipur speak Meitei-lon (language of the Meiteis) which is the lingua franca of the state. Meitei-lon was included in the Eighth Schedule of the Indian Constitution in 1992 after an intense agiatation in the Valley.

Who Are the Tangkhul Nagas?

The word Tangkhul is of recent origin. Tangkhul scholars have written about the possible origins of the word. One theory is that the word is derived from two Meitei words, tada (brother) and khun (village). In this version, the Tangkhuls and Meiteis were brothers and lived together in the hills, but one day the younger brother went to the Valley in search of fertile soil and started to live there. He referred to his elder brother's village as tada khun. In the course of time, tada was shortened into ta and ta became tang because of phonetic convenience. In the same way khun become khul. The Meiteis still say 'tangkhun' for 'Tangkhul'.[7] Some Tangkhul scholars claim that the original name by which Tangkhuls called themselves was hao, while others say it was wung.

The Tangkhul Nagas are one of the forty or so tribes who collectively call themselves Naga. Each Naga tribe has its own language, culture and history, but they have forged a Naga national identity in part due to historical reasons and largely through a national movement that began in the 1950s under the leadership of Z.A. Phizo and his Naga National Council (NNC).

The Nagas are spread over four states within India and parts of Myanmar. In India, the Nagas live in Nagaland, four districts of Manipur and parts of Assam and Aruncahal Pradesh. The Naga national movement began with the aim of re-uniting all the Naga inhabited areas into an independent, sovereign state.

Every Naga tribe has a well-defined territory that they claim to be their ancient homeland. Broadly, the Tangkhuls are spread across the Ukhrul District of Manipur right up to the Somra tracts in Myanmar. Despite the international boundary, Tangkhuls cross over to Myanmar and there is a lively trade between them.

In 1919, the present Ukhrul District was a subdivision.

---

7. Sothing W. A. Shimray, 2000, *The Tangkhuls*, self-published.

It was upgraded to a full-fledged district in 1969, named the Manipur East District, of 8,200 sq. kilometres. The size was reduced to 4,544 sq. kilometers when, in 1983, Chandel District was carved out of it. The East District was renamed Ukhrul District, with Ukhrul town as the headquarters. The Tangkhuls call Ukhrul town by its Tangkhul name, Hunphun.

Ukhrul District is bounded by Myanmar in the east, Chandel District in the south, Imphal East and Senapati districts in the west and the state of Nagaland in the north. The terrain is hilly, with heights varying from 913 metres to 3,114 metres above sea level (MSL). The district headquarters, Ukhrul, is approximately 80 kilometres from Imphal, the state capital. The total Tangkhul population, according to the 2011 census, is 1,83,998, living in 198 villages.

Ukhrul is portrayed as *the* tourist destination for people visiting Manipur: glossy tourist pamphlets invite visitors to go to Ukhrul, 'the home of the colourful Tangkhul Naga tribe' and climb up the Shirui peak to witness the glory of the unique Shiroy[8] Lily, which blooms on top of the mountain. From there, on a clear day, one can see the Irrawaddy River flowing through neighbouring Myanmar.

However, most people in India hear of Ukhrul in the context of the ongoing Naga insurgency, especially after 1980 when the National Socialist Council of Nagalim or the NSCN emerged as the strongest of the Naga armed groups.

The Emergence of the NSCN (IM)

The Naga insurgency was led by the Naga National Council (NNC) from 1949, when the organization was founded. In 1975, the NNC signed a peace accord with the Government of India after years of deadly conflict. However, some members of the NNC looked upon the accord as a betrayal of Naga

---

8. Shiroy is the Anglicized spelling of Tangkhul Shirui

aspirations and, in January 1980, they formed the National Socialist Council of Nagaland. The name was later changed to National Socialist Council of Nagalim to distinguish it from the state of Nagaland which came into being in 1963.[9]

The Chairman of the new organization was Isak Chichi Swu (1929–2016), a Sumi Naga from the present Zunheboto District of Nagaland; the Vice-Chairman was S.S. Khaplang (b.1941) from Burma; Thuingaleng Muivah (b.1935), who is from Somdal village in Ukhrul District, continues to be the General Secretary.

When I went to Ukhrul for the first time in 1982, it was as a part of the first fact-finding team investigating the atrocities being committed during counter-insurgency operations by the Indian army in East District (now Ukhrul). The army had tortured many men and some had died, women had been raped and the villagers had been terrorized.

The immediate provocation for the army's counter-insurgency operations was the ambush at Namthilok, a few kilometres from Ukhrul town, on 21 February 1982 by the newly-formed NSCN in which soldiers of the 21 Sikh Regiment and a major had died.

When I arrived in Manipur in August 1982 I felt I had just stepped into a Latin American country under military rule. The presence of the armed forces, the deathly silence in the nights and the stories of torture could have been right out of a Costa Gavras film. It was the first time I heard of the notorious Armed Forces (Special Powers) Act (AFSPA), 1958, and how it was used to justify the use of military force to suppress Naga aspirations for independence.

By 1988, the NSCN had split into two groups, one led by

---

9. For a detailed history of the NSCN (IM) see A.S. Atai Shimray, 2005, *Let Freedom Ring: Story of Naga Nationalism*, New Delhi: Promilla and Co Publishers.

Isak Swu and Th. Muivah, the NSCN (IM); the second led by S.S. Khaplang called the NSCN (K). Other armed groups have also emerged in Ukhrul besides these two.

The migrant workers whose stories are told here were all born after 1980, so they have more memories of clashes between the different armed groups rather than between the Nagas and the Indian armed forces.

In 1997, the NSCN (IM) began a peace process which culminated in the widely publicized Framework Peace Accord on 3 August 2015. An overwhelming number of Nagas are hoping that the Indo-Naga peace process will bring an end to the conflict; not only between the Indian state and the Nagas, but also between the Nagas themselves. This longing for peace does not mean that the Tangkhul migrants I interviewed do not feel a strong sense of Naga nationalism, but that feeling does not translate into an uncritical loyalty to any particular armed group. As one of them told me, 'I do not want to live under any army rule, either Indian or Naga army.'

Everyone who lives in Ukhrul is impacted by the presence of the NSCN (IM) and some splinter groups in their daily lives. Despite the ceasefire in place since 1997, there are skirmishes between different armed groups, as well as bomb blasts. The insurgents collect taxes, but often the taxes imposed by the underground groups are seen as unjust and as extortion. The NSCN runs a parallel government called the Government of Peoples' Republic of Nagalim or the GRPN. There is a Town Commander to whom the people may go to with any problems or complaints.

Since the peace talks are held in Delhi, the Government of India has provided a safe house for the NSCN (IM) in the capital. That is why many migrant workers in Delhi are in touch with members of the NSCN (IM) at a personal level.

Tangkhul migrant workers keep abreast of the latest developments in the peace process or other news through social media. Facebook and WhatsApp have linked them to their society back home.

Tangkhul Society and Gender Equality

Tangkhul society is conservative and well organized. A Tangkhul migrant worker may often feel alone, but he or she is always linked to the Tangkhul society back home through a network of organizations, both secular and church based. However, none of these organizations have so far taken up the issue of migrant workers' rights.

The apex body of the Tangkhuls is called the Tangkhul Naga Long. It began in 1929 as a student organization, but from 1936 it has functioned as a body consisting of the Headman and Secretary of every Tangkhul village. It has powers to settle disputes and enforce Tangkhul customary law.

Tangkhuls, like most other Naga tribes, have elaborate rules and regulations to regulate relationships within the family or between villages, and administer criminal law. The Tangkhuls also have representation in the Naga Hoho, which is the apex body of the Nagas and includes Nagas from Manipur as well. Neither the Tangkhul Long nor the Naga Hoho have expressed any opinions on the question of migrant rights.

In addition, there is a separate body called the Tangkhul Maya Ngala Long (TMNL) or the Tangkhul Youth Association. This does not have units outside the district. At one time this organization was given the task of recording the names of the youth who were planning to migrate.

The organization which is most involved with the migrants is the apex body of the Tangkhul students, the Tangkhul Katamnao Sak Long (TKLS or TKS), with representatives from all the villages. In addition there are units in every town where Tangkhul Naga students are found. The TKS is affiliated to the All Manipur Naga Students Association (ANSAM) as well as the Naga Students Federation.

It is the TKS that has been taking up cases on behalf of migrant workers, since there is no separate organization to represent them. However, with the growing number of students studying in various towns and cities in India, TKS has its hands full and it cannot take up the grievances of migrant workers full-time.

The TKS was the first to try to estimate the number of men and women who have migrated from Ukhrul. In 1981 there were only 787 Tangkhul migrants in Delhi; the number increased to 1,266 in 1991 and 5,481 in 2001. A survey conducted by the Tangkhul Students Association in 2004–05 revealed that migrant workers in Delhi had come from ninety-nine different villages of Ukhrul District.[10] The figures available are unreliable and often include students who are not migrant workers.

All these organizations are headed by men, and women have no decision making powers. The apex body for the Tangkhul women is the Tangkhul Shanao Long or the Tangkhul Women's Association which has representatives from every village. It has a unit in Delhi.

Tangkhul women's organizations were formed in response to the atrocities being committed on women by the Indian armed forces in the 1970s and '80s. However, today the problems facing Tangkhul women are of a very different nature. There are cases of violence and even rape within the family.

Tangkhul women do not have equal rights to immovable property. Migrant women who are supporting their families find they have little control over the assets they buy with their hard-earned money. Many have helped build a home for their families, but after their parents die, the house will go to their brother.

---

10. Marchang Reimeingam, 2011, 'Migration from North-East to Urban Centres: A Case Study of Delhi Region', *Eastern Quarterly 7* (III and IV) pp.128-139

The women do not have a perspective on women's oppression within their own society. In fact, they do not always acknowledge the patriarchal basis of Naga society in general, or Tangkhul society in particular. Naga men and most women believe their society is based on gender equality.[11]

Even when women or children are trafficked, Tangkhul society, and even the Shanao Long, have not condemned the people involved because they are Tangkhuls or because they are church leaders. For instance, in 2012, when the Delhi Unit of the Shanao Long rescued fifty children who were trafficked from the Northeast, many of them from Ukhrul, the women were criticized by various sections of Tangkhul society for bringing shame on the community. Tangkhul leaders did not want to criticize the person arrested for running the racket because he was a pastor (from Kerala) and his brother was married to a Tangkhul. The village from where the woman came thought it was more important to protect her than to protect the children. After rescuing, the children were sent back to their families without counselling, so the crime was made invisible.

Migration has had a different impact on men and women. Women often find better-paid jobs and feel a sense of independence, while men feel emasculated and despondent, especially when they do not find jobs. One way the male migrant workers make up for the loss in control is by organizing themselves into tribe-based organizations and re-asserting their lost power. These organizations reproduce the same patriarchal power structures of the traditional organizations with the leadership and control being entirely in the hands of the Tangkhul men. One such organization is the Tangkhul Welfare Union in Goa.

---

11. See R. R. Shimray, 1985, *Origin and Culture of Nagas*, New Delhi: Somsok Publications, p.246

Tangkhul Welfare Union, Goa

The Tangkhul Welfare Union in Goa was set up by Tangkhul migrants in May 2009. However, since they had no precedence before them they began by organizing themselves along the line of the Tangkhul Students Association or the TKS, even having a Freshers' Day every year to welcome new migrants.

In reality the Union has to deal with problems that are very different from the ones handled by most students' organizations. A major problem migrant workers face is the absence of identity papers, without which they cannot open bank accounts, or avail of various schemes or even get married.

Then there are the range of problems that migrant workers encounter at their workplaces, from exploitation by the employer who makes them work overtime without paying wages, to the deprivation of their right to health benefits, provident funds and social security cards.

In addition, there are cases when migrant workers have died or been badly injured in the course of their work. For instance, two Tangkhul waiters, K.S. Lucky and Thotshang, working in Club Fly Lounge on Baga beach in Goa, died on 29 October 2006. They had just come back to their room after a long shift and were frying eggs when a wall collapsed on top of them, killing them instantaneously. Two other Tangkhul workers were injured as well.

The accommodation had been given to them by the employers. The Tangkhul Welfare Union was helpful in organizing the funerals and sending the bodies back home, and arranging for hospitalization of the injured, but it did not have the skills or knowledge of labour laws to negotiate with the owners for compensation. The Welfare Union has not been very successful in protecting migrant workers' rights under labour laws or instilling in them the dignity of labour.

The Welfare Union, however, does play an important role in providing support in emergencies. For instance, in July

2016 one of the workers had twins and both the babies died. The Union had to find a place to bury them, which is not easy in Goa where the majority of the Christians are Catholics, whereas the Tangkhuls are Baptists.

The Tanghul Welfare Union also indulges in moral policing, which has brought about some discipline among the members. This has reduced alcoholism and prevented some women from going into prostitution. When cases arise, the Union arranges to send the erring men and women back home to Ukhrul.

The reason for this moral rather than political approach to social problems is that most of the leaders of these associations are from a theological background, many having graduated from Bible colleges.

The Role of the Church

The majority of the Tangkhul Nagas are Christians. The first missionary to work among the Tangkhuls was an Englishman, William Pettigrew, who landed in Ukhrul on 27 January 1876. Today an overwhelming number of Tangkhuls are Baptists, although there are a significant number who belong to other Christian denominations, and are Catholics, Seventh-Day Adventists, etc.

With the coming of Christianity, the traditional institutions were undermined and abandoned. For example, the morung, which was a dormitory for young boys, worked to build tribal solidarity. It was there that they learnt all about the culture and values of Tangkhul society, the rules of war and peace, and skills such as hunting. The girls too had a dormitory, but it was not such a powerful institution. With the coming of Christianity, the morung disappeared, although the institution of yarnao still survives.

Yarnao, or more formally yarthot, is a group comprising youth of the same age from the same village or locality, who help each other in the paddy fields, especially during sowing, weeding and harvesting. The basis of this institution was to exchange labour and work together in each other's fields since there was no separate class of agricultural labour. Moreover, the youth were expected to find their partners among their yarnao.

Today, Tangkhul society, like other Northeast communities, is becoming highly individualistic. Many are ashamed of their pre-Christian culture: I found that some Tangkhul migrants in Goa have decided not to speak to their children in Tangkhul because they felt the language had no value. There were others who were ashamed to admit they ate certain foods such as dog meat. With the increasing loss of culture and cultural heritage, the only institution that provides the migrants with some sense of belonging and comfort is the church.

The church has helped instill a sense of self-respect and discipline in many of the men and women, but the fundamentalist nature of Baptist theology prevents migrants from a better understanding of their situation. As a result, their oppression is seen more in moral terms than as a part of political oppression.[12]

Religion plays a significant role in defining the identity of the Tangkhuls and other Christian communities from the Northeast. As one research scholar has observed:

'Simply put, global Christian networks outwardly orient the world views of ethnic and tribal communities. They may be citizens of India, but the dominant faith directs their identity outward, especially during periods of overt expressions of Hindu nationalism in mainstream Indian society. While there are strong connections with other Christian communities in India... They gaze outward towards a global religious

---

12. Several books have analyzed the role of the church in the Naga national movement: A.S. Atai Shimray, 2005, *Let Freedom Ring: Story of Naga Nationalism*, New Delhi: Promilla and Co Publishers; and more recently John Thomas, 2016, *Evangelizing the Nation: Religion and the Formation of Naga Political Identity*, New Delhi: Routledge.

community… When they migrate to Delhi, this outward orientation affirms the cosmopolitan elements of their identity.'[13]

In the cities, the migrants often work in places which Duncan McDuie-Ra calls 'de-Indianized spaces'. He writes:

'By this I mean that these spaces seek an aesthetic that transports consumers away from the city, and even the nation, outside and into the global world of fashion, food, and brand-name consumer goods. This has served the interests of Northeast migrants. Migrants from the Northeast have Tai, Tibeto-Burman or Mon-Khmer lineage, and thus their features are similar to those of East and Southeast Asian peoples. Their labour is in demand because they reproduce the de-Indianized aesthetic without the need to import foreign labour.'[14]

Many of the Tangkhul migrant workers I interviewed from the hospitality industry voiced their pride in the fact that their employers preferred people from the Northeast to people from mainland India because they could handle guests better, especially foreign guests.

The beauty and wellness industry also depends on migrants from the Northeast. But the employees I interviewed in Goa, especially the women working in the spa industry, felt no pride in the fact that 80 per cent of the employees in some of the best spas are from the Northeast. The women expressed the feeling of being humiliated and exploited, especially those working as therapists, at having to massage men and sometimes being sent to the homes of ministers, MLAs and friends of their employers.

---

13. See Duncan McDuie-Ra (2012) p. 171

14. Ibid

Globalization

The world of the Tangkhul Nagas has changed. When I went to Ukhrul for the first time in 1982, people had barely heard of the names of towns and cities in India, let alone the world. Today not many Indians have heard of Ukhrul, but the Tangkhuls have travelled to far corners of India and abroad in search of jobs.

Globalization has meant the opening up of opportunities and the linking of Ukhrul with the world. With the promotion of the Look East Policy, the government has built roads and railways to link India with Southeast Asia. The general liberalization of the Indian economy from the 1990s has meant that a number of Tangkhul Nagas were able to study in prestigious educational institutions in India and abroad and get lucrative jobs as lecturers in various colleges and universities. Others have made their mark in the fashion and music industries.

However, the bulk of Tangkhuls have found jobs in the poorly-paid service sectors in India and abroad. They work as waiters and hostesses in hotels and restaurants; massage therapists, hair dressers, beauticians at salons and spas; some have found jobs in casinos in Goa and others have been all over the world in cruise liners. These migrant workers send back money to their families but there is no record of the amount of remittances sent.

Globalization has created a growing gap between the rich and poor Tangkhuls. The middle class has less and less of a feeling of solidarity with the poor; often they see the poor as sources of labour. Poor Tangkhuls from interior villages are migrating to Ukhrul town and working in the homes of the rich; some are employed in Tangkhul homes in cities all over India and abroad. These class divisions, coupled with a breakdown in traditional institutions, have undermined tribal solidarity.

In traditional Naga culture, the primary value was 'each according to his or her ability, each according to his or her need.' The most honoured couple in Naga society was the one who had given a series of feasts of merits, by which they had given away all their wealth by feeding the entire village.

Now the most honoured people in Tangkhul society are those who have money and political power. The impact of rampant consumerism leads to further alienation; the youth deal with cultural loss by turning to video games and Korean culture, which they see as more akin to their society than Hindi movies and songs. There is nowhere for the energies of the youth to be channelized for creative work, neither any movement nor any organization.[15]

Almost without exception, Tangkhul migrant workers dream of returning home. They feel that the only place they belong to is Ukhrul. And this sense of belonging has become stronger with greater connectivity between Ukhrul and migrant workers through Facebook and WhatsApp. But the people back home do not understand the world of the migrant worker. This book is written in the hope it forms a bridge between the two worlds.

Writing This Book

When I first thought of writing this book about the migrant workers of the Northeast, I had thought it would be composed of first-person accounts. I wanted the reader to be able to directly listen to their voices. However, when I began conducting formal interviews in 2009, I discovered the task was far more difficult than I had anticipated.

In the cultures of the Northeast communities there is a great emphasis on self-restraint and enduring hardships with

---

15. I have examined the problems of consumerism in my book, *ABC of Naga Culture and Civilization: A Resource Book* (2011), Chicken Neck Publications.

a smile. Thus talking about one's own suffering is considered bad manners and a sign of weakness. Many years ago, when I was representing Nagas in court, one village elder told me that he did not disclose the details of torture because he thought it would impose a burden on me, even though I was their lawyer.

It is in part this sensibility that makes Northeastern migrant workers hesitant to share their experiences of hardship even with their own families and friends.

The hesitation to talk about their work is also rooted in a feeling of shame about the work they do. When asked where they work they use euphemisms: 'in retail' (in a showroom), in the 'hospitality industry' (as a waiter or hostess), or in 'a US company', (in a call centre).

I have seen photographs of the big, glittering white homes in Dubai that some Tangkhul migrants had posted on their Facebook pages. When my husband phoned them to ask whether we could come and spend a night at their place to do some interviews for this book, we discovered that although they had rented a big house for one lakh rupees a month, they had sublet all the rooms and were actually living in just one room.

Some migrant workers post pictures of themselves standing on the Goa beaches, but they do not say that they hardly ever enjoy the sea because they work such long shifts.

But some of them did want to tell their stories. And when they do, they are faced with another difficulty—they just do not have the words to express their emotions, describe their new experiences. For instance the word 'shim' in Tangkhul means a house or building; it covers a modest home in the village as well as gargantuan cement structures such as a shopping centre or a five-star hotel. Many words do not exist in their languages, words such as depression, opulence or racial discrimination or even 'migrant worker'.

For instance, when I asked Atim to describe her work, she could not find the words to convey how orders are taken and given; how a waitress handles six tables at a time; what are the demands made on her and what the technical problems are. Since I had no idea about the work, I read accounts by waiters and waitresses in the West, some of who had written their memoirs. One of them, Debra Ginsberg's book *Waiting* (2000), on the true confessions of a waitress, was helpful for Atim and me to find the words to describe her work as a waitress.

The Exodus Is Not Over

The title of the book and the chapter headings are mostly taken from songs and poems written by Nagas. The first three chapter titles are from a song written by a Lamkang Naga poet, Shelmi Sankil. Chapter 11 is the title of a song written in 1976 and sung by the Swedish pop group, ABBA. The headings of Chapters 5, 7, 9, 10 and 12 are from poems by Easterine Kire, the first Naga to publish her poems. The heading for Chapter 7 is a line from her poem called 'Kelhoukevira', published in 1982; and the rest are from a poem written many years later, which I reproduce here:

> '*And now poetry is dying in us, even as the spirit of man,*
> *flickering like a candle, is blown out again and again.*
> *There are gunshots deep in the night.*
> *There is blood on the streets still.*
> *But in our hearts is a dull deadness.*
> *Words fail to define despair.*
> *Silences have usurped speech.*
> *We're waiting for silence to scream.*
> *So that the guns may be silenced and fear obliterated.*
> *A nation has been waiting fifty-seven years to be born.*
> *The exodus is not over.*
> *This is not the destiny of the Naga people.*
> *What we have now is not what we want.*'

Esterine's poems were written in a different context, but the words are relevant in the new battles being fought in different fields; the warriors this time are men and women whose bravery goes unrecognized and there are no songs yet written to sing their praise.

It has taken enormous courage for the three migrant workers whose stories are told in this book: Ngalatim Hongray, her brother, Yaokhalek Hongray, and Livingstone Shaiza. Never before has any migrant worker from the Northeast told his or her story, revealing their innermost feelings or the humiliation and helplessness they have to face; nor has anyone dared to speak out about their resentments within the society at home in Ukhrul. Equally courageous is the account of R.S. Mayori, whose story is about how a woman with an indomitable spirit has lived on the edge in trying to avoid becoming a migrant worker.

All four know that they would be the first in their community to speak out and they know they could face censure from family and tribe; but they know that their truth needs to be told if another generation of youth is to be saved from the kind of problems they have had to face. They also want their children to understand their struggles and the sacrifices they have made, as well as the contribution they are making to their society and the Naga nation.

None of these people have ambitious dreams. All that Atim wants is to have a nice home and a loving family; Yaokhalek wants to earn a living through music; Livingstone wants to find space to run a good restaurant. And Mayori wants a society where she can feel accepted and safe. The fact that Indian democracy cannot accommodate such simple dreams speaks volumes about our country; in that sense this book is as much about the development model India has chosen and where it is leading.

These migrant workers, far from home but linked by modern

technology to Ukhrul, still feel a pride in being Nagas. And in many ways the Nagas are unique in the way their nationalism binds them with ties of solidarity. For example, when Goa got a Naga governor, S.C. Jamir, Naga migrants had direct access to the Raj Bhavan. This access included the Nagas from Manipur. When a migrant died, or was injured or thrown out of his job unjustly, they would ring up his secretary and the problem would be fixed. And every year all Nagas would be invited for a Christmas celebration at the Raj Bhavan. Migrants and the governor sat together and enjoyed a dinner of pork and rice.

The migrants' experiences in the wider world are re-defining the meaning of nationalism in a globalized world. Their stories are a celebration of the human spirit and its capacity to survive in all conditions. These men and women are, like the Naga warriors before them, above all survivors. And this book is an ode to them.

Chapter One

From a Land Afar I Come

Ngalatim Hongray does not remember the exact date of her momentous move to Delhi in October 2005, but she remembers vividly her last moments in Ukhrul before she set off. It was so long ago, but the memories of her first train journey are as clear as if it was just yesterday.

It was early in the morning. Ngalatim was the first in the family to wake up. She put some water to boil in a saucepan and then added some tea powder; she poured the tea out into three mugs. She carried out the phika chai for her parents, who had woken up and were sitting outside their one-room house, where the other six children slept in a heap. The air was crisp and cool; the three of them enjoyed the view of the distant mountains in silence.

Atim (the diminutive by which she was called) had finished her eleventh standard from Alice Christian Higher Secondary School in 2004.[16] She still had a year of schooling left but had chosen to give it up because she could not bear the constant deprivation and poverty.

Atim decided to find work in Delhi. She had no idea what kind of work, just as long as she could earn and send money back home. Her father Ramyo was nearly eighty years old, and her mother Shimthrala was some thirty years younger than him. Ramyo had married her after his first wife, Ningmacham, had died.

Atim was the oldest child from the second marriage and she felt it was her responsibility to support her family. She felt angry that her parents had seven children, especially since her

_____

16. Alice was the wife of Reverend William Pettigrew (1869–1943), the first Christian missionary to work in Ukhrul.

father had had nine children by his first wife. Of course she had not voiced this anger.

Atim wanted to go to Delhi because two of her nieces, Lemyaola and Mayori, were already working there. They were the daughters of Ramyo's eldest daughter by his first wife. Mayori was older than Atim, but Lemyaola was her age and had promised to help find her a job in Delhi.

Lemyaola's third sister, Hongreiwon, was a doctor practising in Ukhrul. Hongreiwon had promised to buy Atim tickets to Delhi on the condition she work at her older brother Khangam's home in Ukhrul. Khangam and his wife Leena lived with their two small children; his wife was pregnant and so they needed help with the housework. For the past three months Atim had been living and working in Khangam's home. She used to wake up early and make tea for the family, and then by nine in the morning she had Hongreiwon's lunch of rice and curry ready, so she could eat before rushing off to the hospital where she worked. After that, Atim swept the three-room house, and washed the clothes. It was not hard work and she was treated well, but somehow she always felt somewhat diminished.

Atim had decided to come away for the night and be with her parents, her own family, where she felt she belonged. She took a sip of the tea and heard someone call out her name. It was Hongreiwon and she was in a tearing hurry.

'Pack your clothes. I have booked your tickets on the morning bus tomorrow. We have found two girls going to Delhi. You can go with them.'

Atim had been waiting for this moment, but now that it had arrived she was overwhelmed by feelings she could not describe in words. But her father was calm. He handed her the money he had kept for the occasion. Several weeks ago, Ramyo had sold one of his goats for Rs 1,500, which he gave his daughter. He had been trying to speak to Atim in English, as Hongreiwon had instructed, so that she would be more prepared for Delhi, but it did not seem natural. However, he was confident she would pick it up once she started work.

Atim packed her bag. She would be sleeping in Hongreiwon's place that night and would take the bus early next morning. Her sisters and brothers were asleep, but she decided not to wake them up. It would make it even more difficult to leave. As she was going out of her home, her mother burst into tears.

Hongreiwon took Atim to meet the two young women who would be travelling to Delhi with her. They were two sisters who had studied in Jawahar Navodaya School[17] with Lemyaola, Hongreiwon's younger sister. The older sister was Glory and she was a nurse; Jacinta was working in a showroom in Lajpat Nagar.

Atim could not believe that it was finally happening. She could feel her heart beating fast. She had seen such wonderful photographs of Delhi in magazines; the one she remembered most was an advertisement of a posh restaurant with lots of people and a beautiful woman pouring coffee. Her stepsister, Lily, who was looking at the pictures, had told Atim that her daughter Masowon too worked in a place where she poured coffee for guests. It had sounded so grand.

Lily had shown her photos of Masowon dressed in her black uniform with a bright red collar and matching red lipstick. Just the thought that she could soon be wearing such a uniform had kept Atim awake.

Then Atim remembered the time when she had gone to wash clothes in her neighbour's pond. They had no running water supply in their home. The neighbour was there and they had started chatting. She told Atim that her daughter Angel had told her that those girls who stay in Delhi only go out at night and that is the reason why they have such wonderful complexions.

---

17. Jawahar Navodaya schools were established under the National Policy on Education in 1986. There are 589 such schools across India.

'But how do they go out in the dark?' Atim had asked. Her home had no electricity. The older woman had told her that Delhi was all bright and lit up every night.

Atim did not sleep the night before she left. She had never experienced such excitement in her entire life of twenty years. She kept thinking of the photographs she had seen in Leena's albums. Leena had worked in Delhi before she got married. There were photos of her outside the posh Benetton showroom in Connaught Place. It looked really out of this world. And then there was the magical world of the beauty parlour. Leena's sister's daughter had returned from Delhi looking like a model. She had dyed her hair burgundy and wore lots of make-up. Her skin was so smooth and fair. It was rumoured that she was earning Rs 5,000 a month!

Next morning, Leena pressed Rs 300 into Atim's hand and bade her a safe journey. Atim hurried to the bus stop and found the two sisters waiting for her. It was early in the morning and the bus was already crowded. It took less than four hours on a winding road down the hills to reach Imphal, the capital of Manipur. From there they got a bus for Dimapur in Nagaland, another seven-hour journey.

On the bus, Glory recognized two Tangkhul men, one of whom was a journalist. Atim's excitement had made her speechless. She was startled out of her stupor when Jacinta shook her shoulder and said, 'Take a last look at the mountains. Later you will miss them.' Jacinta had been in Delhi for three years.

Dimapur was a crowded town. But Glory's friends shepherded the three young women and booked them into a hotel and later in the evening invited them to dinner. Atim felt she was living her dream when she found herself in a restaurant, sitting at a table with a tablecloth, and knives, forks and spoons laid out. The restaurant was called Skylark and she was served by waiters.

The journalists had started eating with their hands, enjoying the hot beef curry and steaming rice. Atim picked up the spoon and felt proud that she managed to eat her meal with it.

The next day, the three women went to Dimapur's famous Hong Kong market. Atim gaped with amazement when she saw the variety of footwear. All three women bought sandals; Atim chose a red pair. Jacinta assured her that the other things would be cheaper in Delhi's Sarojini Nagar Market.

At night they caught the train to Guwahati. When they reached Guwahati station they bought Tinkle comics and settled down in a corner to wait for their train to Delhi, which would arrive late in the evening. Atim asked Jacinta to tell her about Delhi.

'Delhi is full of people and buildings.' Atim had seen cities in Jackie Chan movies and imagined Delhi would be full of tall, white, gleaming buildings over which helicopters flew, and broad clean streets.

'Many Koreans come to my showroom. They find it difficult dealing with our money.'

'Foreigners come to your showroom!'

'Yes. I have a friend called Grace. She is very good at bargaining. She fights over every rupee but when we go to restaurants she gives big tips.'

By the time the train to Delhi pulled into the station, Atim's excitement had reached its peak. She was going more than 2,000 kilometres away from Ukhrul, the only home she had ever known. They settled into the train. A Punjabi man in a turban was in the seat opposite Atim. He ate bananas and lotus fruit almost continuously and the women commented on his appetite in Tangkhul.

On the train, Jacinta taught Atim how to use Yahoo Messenger. She had a mobile phone which Lemyaola's older sister Mayori had gifted her.

After a while, Atim asked Jacinta the question that had troubled her sometimes, 'Is it safe for us in Delhi?'

She had heard a story from Tharayo, a friend from her yarnao[18] about a girl from Nagaland who had gone to a shop in Delhi to have her pressure cooker mended. There she noticed that some men had followed her. They tried to molest her but she swung the pressure cooker and hit one of them before running out of the shop.

On another occasion, Atim had overheard a conversation between Hongreiwon and Mayori about how unsafe Delhi was for girls from the Northeast. Mayori had said girls should not wear shorts and wander around at night. Atim could not really understand all this talk, but she felt a nagging fear that she had not known before.

The movement of the train made Atim feel nauseous and she went to the toilet, but the smell made her feel even worse. The constant shaking and noise began to get unbearable. It was only the excitement of reaching her destination that kept her going for two nights. When Jacinta said Delhi was nearing she peered out of the window but could not see any brightly lit buildings.

The Old Delhi railway station was crowded and Atim could barely walk in a straight line. 'This is Delhi,' Jacinta called out to her as she made an effort to keep up with the other two. It was late in the evening and they took an auto-rickshaw.

As they drove through the streets of Delhi, Atim felt a deep disappointment; it was so dark and smelly. Finally, when they arrived at Kotla Mubarakpur and the auto turned into a narrow alley, it seemed even darker than Ukhrul. They lugged their bags up the steep staircase to a small room on the first floor. The room was bare; there was a fridge but it had nothing in it and they had to go downstairs to buy vegetables and cook their

---

18. Yarnao, or more formally yarthot, is a group for youth of the same age group living in a village. This traditional structure has continued in towns, where a yarnao is formed in each neighbourhood. It acts as a support group throughout a person's life.

dinner. There was not even a cupboard. Everything was piled on open cement shelves. There were no beds, and the three flopped down on mattresses and slept. This was not the Delhi Atim had dreamt about.

The next day, Lemyaola turned up with a cousin and another Tangkhul guy. She and Mayori were living in Munirka with their cousin; the accommodation turned out to be much more spacious, even though it was on the third floor. There were two rooms; as they entered Atim noticed a computer table with a computer and a chair. Inside the bedroom there were two foldable camp beds. But the kitchen was dirty and Atim found herself cleaning it while Lemyaola and her friends drank beer. Mayori was away in Bangkok.

Suddenly one of the men felt sick and he got up and tried to jump down from the corridor. The cousin held him down and Lemyaola ran to find help. Atim rushed out and saw that the man was in a strange state. She realized that he had been possessed. She ran back into the kitchen and found some garlic and turmeric. She crushed them together and tried to make the man eat it. She knew that some spirit or lai must have taken possession of him. She had been told that the spirit hides in the armpits or in the groin.

Swallowing her embarrassment she pressed her thumbs into the man's groin and he screamed. And she heard the spirit say, 'I am leaving.' She called out, 'Are you sure?'

The man regained consciousness and went to the bathroom. He came out looking normal. Atim was feeling very embarrassed. The man explained that when he was studying in Shillong he had had a Khasi girlfriend and she possessed him from time to time.

A few days later, Mayori returned from Bangkok with a friend, Angam. It was Diwali and she told Lemyaola and Atim that in the evening they would all be going to Aunty Nandita's for a Diwali party.

When Atim stepped into Nandita's home, she was amazed by the number of people. They were from so many different parts of India; she was introduced to a young Kashmiri couple, Bismillah and Anjum. There was a lot of singing and food. Mayori introduced her to Nandita as Atim, her little aunt.

* * *

I remember the Diwali party. It was in the first week of November 2005. I also remember that Mayori had come, but I did not remember Atim.

As for Mayori. Yes, I remember how she had burst into our lives in Goa in February 2002. A few months earlier our friend, Sonia Muivah,[19] had contacted my husband and me and asked whether we would be willing to take into our care a young woman and teach her whatever we thought would be useful to her. I did need help in transcribing tapes of interviews with Naga national leaders, but I was hesitant to commit myself to looking after a young woman without even knowing her.

Besides, I was not sure how a young Naga woman would adjust to our quiet life in Chorao, an island in the middle of the Mandovi river in Goa. But the young woman had persisted and kept sending us messages and finally I relented and agreed to take her in for a year. We did not hear from her for some time and then one day she arrived in an auto with her baggage.

Her grandfather was Ramyo Hongray (Atim's father), the oldest member of the Hongray clan, and she was distantly related to Sebastian, my husband, since he too belonged to the same clan. But he did not know Mayori, so she was as much a stranger to him as she was to me.

At the time, I did not really know what had motivated her

---

19. Sonia Muivah's husband, Grinder Muivah, had been appointed as a go-between in the Indo-Naga peace talks. He had been arrested in 2000 and I had worked on his case. Grinder died in 2016.

to want to work with me. But as I sat down to write this book, I decided to ask her and she sent this email:

> Dear Aunty,
> It was in 2002 feb, that I landed up in Charao, I was suppose to come in december, but I cant make it in 2001 as my father passed away. I was kind of attracted to you, when I saw your interview for the first time in TV during the June uprising of the meiteis.
>
> It was also the June uprising of the meiteis motivated me politically, I was not able to understand fully why and how of the politics of those days but I felt the hatred towards the Tangkhul in the june uprising and I met Sonia, when we were talking casually ask me if I would want to stay and work with you, learn new things politically etc, though she didnt put it that way.
>
> One main attraction was that which I came to understand year after I left was, the woman part, a woman who is independent, a woman among man talking of politics and issues etc attracts me at that very moment as you know we dont have space or platform for woman to grow, within the society as well as within the boundary of customs and religion.

The Manipur Legislative Assembly had been burnt down on 18 June 2001 by an angry mob of Meiteis who were furious at the demand for integration of the Naga areas of Manipur with Nagaland. The immediate provocation came after the National Socialist Council of Nagaland Isak-Muivah (NSCN-IM)[20] and the Government of India declared a ceasefire in July 1997. The NSCN had demanded that the ceasefire cover all Naga-

---

20. When the NSCN mentions 'Nagaland' they include all the Naga inhabited areas, including the state of Nagaland, four districts of Manipur, parts of Assam and Arunachal Pradesh. Later the NSCN changed its name to National Socialist Council of Nagalim instead of Nagaland to ensure there was no confusion about their intention.

inhabited areas; after all, that was their area of operation. The Manipur Government said this was a ploy to include parts of Manipur into Greater Nagaland.

At the time, the ceasefire was extended every six months. When it was time for an extension, the NSCN (IM) threatened to withdraw from the peace process if the ceasefire was not extended to all Naga-inhabited areas. The ceasefire was to end on 31 July 2001 and so once again the issue of territory had come up.

After much tough negotiation, the interlocutor and former Home Secretary, Padmanabhaiah, announced in Bangkok[21] on 14 June 2001 that the ceasefire had been extended for one more year, commencing 1 August 2001, and that, henceforth, the truce would have no 'territorial limits'. A joint statement issued in the Thai capital said that the ceasefire agreement was between the 'government of India and the NSCN as two entities without territorial limits'.

This triggered the biggest-ever mass uprising in Manipur by the majority Meiteis in the Valley. Up to 50,000 Meiteis took to the streets of Imphal on 18 June 2001, opposing the extension of the NSCN (IM)–Government truce to territories in Manipur. Rampaging mobs burnt the Manipur Legislative Assembly building and a dozen other government offices. Eighteen protestors were killed that day when security forces eventually opened fire to quell the frenzied mob.

A massive civil disobedience movement followed, and Imphal was under curfew for nearly a month. Finally, on 24 July 2001, after a meeting with the chief ministers of the Northeastern states in New Delhi, Prime Minister Vajpayee announced that the ceasefire would once again be restricted

---

21. The talks were in Bangkok because according to the 1997 agreement between Government of India and the NSCN (IM), the talks would be held anywhere outside India. They were held in various places including Amsterdam, Bangkok and Zurich.

only to the state of Nagaland, as had been the case ever since the truce first came into force on 1 August 1997.

At this time, Nagas like Mayori who were living in Imphal began to feel very unsafe there. The Tangkhuls felt especially vulnerable and many had left their homes and returned to the safety of Ukhrul. Mayori, at the time, was confused by the political developments and blamed the NSCN for causing the tension.

Besides, there was a personal reason for Mayori's confusion and anger: in 2001 when the Manipur Assembly was burnt down, Mayori was fully occupied looking after her father who had diabetes. She had taken him to Guwahati for eye treatment and when they returned, the Valley was in turmoil. It was dangerous for Tangkhuls to stay there. They had gone up to Ukhrul, but her father needed dialysis desperately and there was no facility there. Nor could she take him to a hospital in Imphal because of the tensions. This made her angry with the Naga underground. Her father went into a coma. Finally, he died in the December of that year. Her mother had already passed away in 1997 in tragic circumstances and now Mayori felt completely alone.

Throughout that period, the media failed to report the Naga point of view. I was called by NDTV to give my opinion. I knew I was entering into very controversial terrain, but I felt the Naga point of view needed to be stated. Since I was involved in the peace process, it was my responsibility to represent them.

There was a panel discussion. The panelists were the two chief ministers of Assam and Manipur and myself. We spoke politely, without interrupting each other. But in Manipur the programme created real fury and my effigy was burnt along with the effigies of the NSCN leaders and the Indian prime minister. On seeing this, one of my Meitei friends, Yambem Laba, told me how his daughter had asked, 'Why are they burning Aunty Nandita?'

It was this interview that Mayori had seen and which made her decide to work with me. She, like many of her generation, did not know Naga history and was confused by the conflicting identities being imposed on them by various forces. Mayori felt a conflict between her identity as a Tangkhul Naga and her identity as a Manipuri.

She said that when she heard me on television, it helped her to clarify her political stand. It was then that she decided to find me. This way, I also got a chance to hear her story.

* * *

Mayori was born in November 1976. She was a bright student and had a talent for singing and dancing as well. She was in the third standard of St Thomas School when she was selected to be the chief guest at the Children's Day function organized by the district authorities. It was the principal of her school, Mother Blessedia, who gave her the news. She remembered Sister Veronica dressing her up in the school uniform and she even gave her a new pair of earrings. Then, she was taken in a jeep to the Tangkhul Long grounds and Mayori found herself sitting proudly next to the deputy commissioner. Mayori gave a speech (written out for her) with aplomb and distributed prizes.

Mayori was so moved by the kindness of the nuns that she converted to Catholicism in defiance of her Baptist family. She had been a rebel from the beginning.

In 1991, she was selected for admission into the Jawahar Navodaya Vidyalaya, one of the special schools for bright and talented students from disadvantaged families. The school was located at Lambui village near the Assam Rifles camp. The education was good, but there were some problems. A few months after she joined the school, there was a clash between the students and the principal that led to the Assam Rifles being called in to intervene.

The principal was from Uttar Pradesh and unfamiliar with

the culture of the Nagas. He insisted that on Sundays the children watch *Ramayana*, a TV serial based on the Hindu epic. But some of the children wanted to attend church services. The principal did not allow it.

There were other problems as well. Since the electricity supply was irregular, the school had provision for a generator, which also did not always work. The children were given candles. On one occasion, perhaps to make a little money, the principal handed out one candle that had to be shared between four students. The students were angry and demanded one candle each. The principal called them stupid and slapped one boy. The boys retaliated by beating him up. The PT teacher, Raghu, tried to intervene but he was beaten up too. The students knew he was hand in glove with the principal in the corruption.

It was dark and the students could not see who they were punching, and sometimes hit each other. The girl students protected Raghu's wife, who was pregnant. The villagers rushed to the school and stopped the fighting. Matters would have settled down, but the principal's wife came out and started calling the students kutte (dogs) and kaminay (low, base, belonging to a low caste).

The principal called in the Assam Rifles. In the meantime, the students had quickly put on their uniforms and come out, hoping the Assam Rifles would realize they were children. The Assam Rifles asked the students to identify the leaders, but they said they were all involved. The Assam Rifles beat the students with bamboo sticks meant for fencing and tried to force them to give up their leaders, but the children refused. Finally the principal identified fifteen boys who he said had led the attack on him. That day the children did not have their evening meal but the villagers gave them food late at night. The school was closed down for several days.

The fifteen boys returned, having been scolded and given tea and biscuits. After the school re-opened, a Parents Association was started for the first time in the school.

What Mayori remembered most was the time she was sent to the Navodaya in Muzaffarnagar near Meerut (this was a part of the government's efforts at national integration). There she saw the festival of Raksha Bandhan in which sisters tie colourful rakhis on their brothers and are given presents. She envied the sister-brother relationship among the Indians.

Looking back, she felt that Navodaya had given her a good education. Many from her class had joined the civil services, while some had become college teachers and doctors.

In 1997, Mayori finished school, passing her twelfth standard. She decided she wanted to study law in Allahabad, but her father opposed her decision. I asked her how she got this idea and she said she could not recall how she had thought of it. As an alternative, she gave her entrance exam for the local college for a BA course in physics, mathematics and computer sciences.

After the entrance examination, she had some months before the classes began. She had always been a rebel and she decided to go off to Delhi to make some money. She hated being dependent on her father or brother.

In Delhi, she got a job in a beauty parlour where her friend Achan worked. Achan was married to an Indian. There was a gym next door. Mayori worked as a receptionist, but she learnt threading and waxing from the girls. She had learnt how to cut hair in school.

Then one day a man who ran a private vocational college in his basement invited her and Achan to teach dancing. In the beginning, they had small children as students, and then men who wanted to learn to dance in disco clubs joined. Achan and Mayori had no formal training, but they had learnt steps by watching videos.

When she came to Goa, my husband and I would watch

Mayori dancing around our kitchen as she busied herself making tea or washing up. It was a true delight. Then one Christmas, we watched her on stage at a restaurant where we had gone to eat. She won the first prize.

* * *

By the time she came to us in Goa, Mayori had worked in different capacities. She had helped a friend sell encyclopedias to schools in Nagaland; she had sold cosmetics; and had taught mathematics at the Kids English School in Dewlahland, Imphal, when a teacher had gone on leave. She was delighted when she was paid Rs 3,000. Occasionally she had coached school students in maths.

Mayori said she was always aware of the discrimination between girls and boys in Tangkhul society and she resented it very much. That was why she was attracted to me when she watched me on television. For her, I was a woman who could stand up to men, that too powerful men, like the chief ministers. She wanted to be with that woman. Thus, with no clear idea about what she would do, she set off from Ukhrul soon after her father died. She came via Mumbai and, in Goa, she did not bother to phone us but took the ferry across the Mandovi to arrive at our house in an auto.

I heard the auto one day in February 2002 and went to see who could have come. In the village even the sound of an auto aroused curiosity. I saw a diminutive woman in a massive straw hat carrying large bags climbing up to our flat. My heart sank and I wondered what I would do with her. I showed her around the house and told her to put her shoes on the rack outside. She stared at me as if she did not comprehend.

'What's the problem?'

'I cannot.'

'Why can't you put your shoes outside?'

'Because there is no space?'

'Space?' I nearly shouted.

'I have twelve pairs of shoes.'

The next morning she came out wearing bright red lipstick. I told her that feminists of my generation thought cosmetics and beauty pageants objectified women so we opposed them. She was silent and then blurted out, 'That's because you are old. You don't need make-up.'

'But old women need more make-up, don't they?'

She had never heard these arguments and I had no idea how I would cope with her. It was a challenge.

She stayed with us for the year and now she has become a permanent part of our lives.

* * *

Mayori read this chapter in January 2016 in our new home in Goa and remarked: 'Oh, you put that in about my shoes. Now I have nine pairs!'

Chapter Two

I Live Each Day Remembering Guns and Tears

Atim stood dumbfounded. She had just stepped right into her dream and it was even more fabulous than what she had seen in the movies. It was truly a massive building with huge spaces. She saw the shining floor which stretched for miles; and at the entrance was a fountain flowing like the cool streams in the hills. And then she set her eyes on the shops full of amazing clothes. If only she could spend more time looking, just staring at it all. But everyone was rushing ahead to a moving staircase. She too stepped onto the metal step and was carried up to heaven.

Aunty Nandita had brought them to a shopping mall to celebrate Mayori's birthday. Lemyaola asked Atim what she was thinking and she replied in Tangkhul, 'It is like when Somra people come to Ukhrul.'

Atim was referring to the Tangkhuls who lived across the border in Myanmar. They were considered more backward and they came across to Ukhrul for medical treatment or to buy provisions. For them Ukhrul was a beautiful city with shops full of marvellous goodies.

Aunty Nandita gave them all money and told them to choose whatever they wanted to eat. Atim was stunned by what she saw. There was such a variety of food. She and Lemyaola chose a Chinese meal and returned to the table. After the meal, Mayori insisted on going to the bowling alley in the basement.

Atim watched as Mayori picked up the ball and threw it, knocking over some sticks. The man handing over the ball turned out to be a Tangkhul from Humpum village.[22] This was

---

22. The village is officially known as Hundung which is a Meitei word; Humpum is what the Tangkhuls call their village.

his first job and he had to sleep right there next to the bowling alley; he said he missed the silence of the nights in his village.

Lemyaola nudged Atim and took her to inspect the public toilets. They were bigger than her home in Ukhrul. And then she discovered the small machine that was used to dry the hands. Lemyaola remarked that Aunty Nandita must have spent at least Rs 5,000 by now!

A few days later, Mayori announced to Atim that they would all be shifting to a small flat in Vasant Enclave owned by Uncle Sebastian, Aunty Nandita's husband. It had two rooms and a verandah with a toilet, bathroom and a kitchen.

By January 2006, Atim had settled down in Vasant Enclave and Mayori and Lemyaola had started preparing her for her first job interviews. Before coming to Delhi she had been worried about speaking in Hindi, but the real problem was going to be English.

Lemyaola typed out a short biodata and told Atim she should say that she was 'pursuing graduation from Delhi University by distance education.' She learnt the line by heart but was not at all sure what it meant.

Before moving to Vasant Enclave, Atim had gone to a bistro in Hauz Khas Village. Lemyaola had the owner's business card. Lemyaola had had many jobs, but at that time she was not working. On that day she sent Atim with a young man who seemed to be as poor as Atim; his Tangkhul mother had been killed by the Naga underground because it was alleged she was involved in the sex trade. Now he had come to Delhi in search of his father, a non-Naga. Atim gave him her orange jacket which was too large for her.

The young man accompanied Atim and waited outside while she went to talk to the Sardar owner. But she came out very quickly because he said that there was no vacancy.

Then Lemyaola took Atim to Vasant Continental Hotel where she had worked at the pastry shop. Atim secretly hoped she would get a job at the lovely hotel. Apparently there was a vacancy for the job of hostess. Atim was feeling quite confident in her black sweater, black jeans and a bright red Naga bag. She did not understand most of the questions the man had asked, but one of them was whether she smoked and drank alcohol. The questions made Lemyaola angry; how dare he ask such questions from them. Atim was not sure why, but she followed her niece as she stomped out of the restaurant.

Outside the hotel, Lemyaola announced that she had some work to attend to, so she left Atim to take an auto home to Vasant Enclave by herself. It was a short distance, but it was the first time Atim had ever travelled alone in Delhi and her heart was thumping with fear till she reached home safely.

Lemyaola scoured the advertisements in the newspapers every morning, but could not find any jobs suitable for Atim. Mayori was getting impatient. It was difficult to survive in Delhi and every extra person was a burden. Then the two sisters decided to take Atim to a placement firm and on the day of the test, Mayori sat Atim down and helped her practise for the interview.

Mayori told her that if she was asked why she had come all the way to Delhi, she should say it was because the corruption and insurgency in Manipur made it difficult to get jobs in the state. Then she told Atim to say she was from Manipur, but to add that she was a Naga from Manipur. This was the beginning of Atim's political education.

Once Mayori thought that Atim was ready for the interview, she taught her how to apply make-up so that she would look more grown-up. Atim was twenty years old, but her birth certificate said she was born two years earlier. This was the normal practice in Ukhrul and a way parents found to help their children make up for a lack of good education.

Finally, the day arrived. Atim borrowed a black skirt from Lemyaola to go with her black sweater. Mayori applied the make- up: foundation, eye shadow and a bright lipstick. They arrived at a place in Okhla where Atim saw some 150 young women and men holding their biodata sheets and waiting for the written test for a call centre.

Atim sat in a large hall looking at an examination paper she barely understood. And the interview was even worse. She did not get a job at a call centre. Atim was getting desperate; her money had run out and she had asked her father to send her some more, knowing well that he could not afford to support her. However, he managed to send her Rs 1,000 and Hongreiwon sent Rs 300.

Then one day Huimila came to visit them. She was Mayori's mother's sister's daughter and so was a niece to Atim. She said there was a vacancy in a restaurant in Connaught Place. The two women took a bus to Connaught Place and walked into Bercos. A man called Karma interviewed her. He offered both the women jobs and a salary of Rs 5,000. But then he said they would have to pay for their uniforms and they would have to go back on their own at night. Huimila knew that public transport was not reliable and that it would not be safe for them to travel alone at night and so they refused the job.

Atim was feeling despondent. She was doing all the housework because she could not contribute any money; even the little money she had was spent in getting beer for Lemyaola's friends. Atim did not always understand the heated discussions she heard in the house, but she picked up bits of conversations. One of the men who often visited their flat was a research scholar from Jawaharlal Nehru University (JNU) called Yaronsho Ngalung. He was standing for the post of president in the elections for the university's students' union. He knew he did not have a chance of winning, but he thought that it gave him an opportunity to reach out to students and make them more aware of the problems of the Nagas.

Another person who visited their flat was a young woman

who stayed with them for several weeks. She was studying medicine in Australia. Lemyaola informed Atim that the woman's father was General Wungmatem, a legendary officer in the Naga army who had carried out the ambush at Namthilok in 1982. Now he was involved in the peace process. Atim was thrilled when the woman presented her with a Versace Medusa pink top. Atim could not remember when and how she had learnt the names of such high-end fashion labels.

* * *

Atim had not thought of herself as a Naga. She knew she was a Tangkhul and she also knew that her people were fighting for freedom. While she was studying in Holy Spirit School in Longpi,[23] near Kalhang, her mother's village, the girls exchanged stories about the heroic tales of the Alungpashi or the people who live underground, sometimes known as Ishipashi or 'our people'. Atim had assumed 'our people' meant Tangkhuls, rather than the Nagas as a whole.

There was a senior student called Rachael. She would tell the younger girls about the valour of the underground. She said there was one man called Yarchung who was identified by the Indian army by the mole on his cheek. But when they caught him, he jumped down the hills from a moving jeep and escaped. Rachael said that three Tangkhul freedom fighters could kill a hundred Indian soldiers. Her audience listened in awed silence.

The girls would practise Kung Fu moves that they had seen in the movies and were absolutely enthralled by a Tangkhul

---

23. Longpi (pronounced 'long-pee') is a general reference to two villages, Longpi Kajui and Longpi Khullen in the Ukhrul District of Manipur. Longpi is about 37 kilometres north of Ukhrul town, connected by NH150. It is flanked by Nungbi Khullen in the east and Sihai in the southeast; Lunghar in the south; Phungcham, Paorei and Peh in the west, and Kalhang in the north. It is a forty-five-minute walk from Longpi to Kalhang.

movie called *Ramchoramrin*. It had scenes of real ambushes carried out by the underground.

Except for one incident, Atim had not personally encountered the Indian army. That had happened when she was with her mother's elder sister in the paddy field in Kalhang. When the other women started running away because the army was coming, her aunt was not scared. She stood in the field and the soldiers called out to them. The aunt told Atim to ask for roti and the little girl called out, 'roti dedo'. A soldier gave her two rotis which she ate hungrily.

Atim had childhood memories of hearing shots at night in Ukhrul when the Indian army exchanged fire with the Naga militants, and on one occasion two people had hidden in their house for several days. One of them was injured. That was the day when they heard that one of the underground had worn a Haora Tangkhul shawl and calmly walked to the army post and shot some officers. Another time, when there was curfew in Ukhrul town and one of her mother's friends needed to go somewhere urgently, she had put ash in her hair and pretended to be a madwoman.

Later, when she was older and living in the Greenland locality of Ukhrul town, she used to see a very well-dressed young man. It was whispered that he was in the movement and had a reputation for his acts of daring. He even tried to get Atim and her friends to join the organization, but they were not willing to leave their families. Later, they heard he was killed. Atim had also heard of a legendary Naga freedom fighter called Livingstone who, it was said, could turn into a fly and enter the Indian army camps. Atim's father used to tell her about how he had secretly met Muivah[24] himself at Shirui village.

24. Thuingaleng Muivah was born in 1934 in Shongran village. He went to school in Ukhrul and later did his graduation from Shillong

(Contd...)

Sometimes, when Atim was angry with her parents, she would threaten that if they did not listen to her she would join the underground. At the same time, she knew that the life of a freedom fighter was not easy. She had also discovered that there were divisions among the underground. Her mother had told her a story that made Atim's spine tingle with fear.

Atim's mother's friend, Thing Thing, was in the NSCN and living in a camp deep in the forests on the India-Myanmar border. Once, when the women had gone into the forest to collect banana leaves to use as plates, they heard their camp being attacked by the Khaplang faction. All the men, mostly Tangkhuls, were killed.[25] The women ran deeper into the forest. They had no food to eat. One of the women, Ngalangam from Khangkhui village, did not have boots and her feet had started to fester so she could no longer run; she told the others to leave her. They put her under a tree and managed to reach a village to fetch help. When the villagers reached the spot where she had been left, they could not find her body and they assumed that wild animals must have attacked and killed her.

(...contd.)

and post-graduation from Gauhati University. He joined the Naga National Council in 1964 and led a group of Naga insurgents to China for arms training. He is a living legend for Nagas. He is a veteran of many battles and a revolutionary of the old school, which has won him respect from Indian leaders. Successive Indian prime ministers have personally met him.

25. S.S. Khaplang was born in 1940 in Watkham village near Pangsau Pass in Myanmar, bordering Arunachal Pradesh. He is a Hemi Naga and in 1988 he broke from the NSCN to form his own organization called NSCN (K). He had a ceasefire with the Indian government in 2001; but the Indian government did not negotiate with him since he is a citizen of Myanmar. He broke the ceasefire in April 2015. It was while the NSCN was splitting that the Khaplang followers killed more than seventy senior Tangkhul cadres, as described here.

Atim had seen with her own eyes how the Indian armed forces treated the underground. One day, sometime around 1996, when she was a student in Savio School in Ukhrul, she had gone to the bazaar with a cousin to buy henna. Suddenly, the Assam Rifles swooped down and shot several times in the air. And then she saw him, a maikhumbi, a dreaded informer. His face was entirely covered and he was wearing gloves. He pointed to someone, and the entire bazaar froze with fear.

Atim heard the Assam Rifles call out for Star. She knew he was her cousin Yerimayo's mother's tenant. She saw a woman crying, and later saw a sack in which they had put a man. They were beating him. She turned and ran all the way home.

Atim had grown up with tales of the bravery and valour of the Naga nationalists and as a child she had an admiration for these brave men and women. But then in 2005, a year after she left school and few months before she came to Delhi, an incident happened that made her angry with the NSCN.

Every year her family, like everyone else, willingly paid the house tax collected by the Naga national workers. But that year her family was going through an exceptionally bad time and when the 'boys' came to collect the Rs 300 as house tax they just did not have the money. However, the young men would not listen or heed their pleas, and insisted that it was their duty to support the movement. When her parents did not pay, they took away her father at gunpoint.

Atim's mother had rushed to her village, Kalhang, which is thirty-nine kilometres from Ukhrul, and somehow raised the money and managed to free her husband. When her father returned from captivity, Atim had clung to him and asked how he had been treated. Ramyo said he was not treated badly. The Naga army boys had spent their time praying and singing. But Atim found it hard to forgive them for this act of humiliation.

Atim remembered these stories when she heard the animated political talk between Mayori and her friends, and many questions came to her mind, but she did not dare ask them. She pushed them away and focused on trying to get a job.

* * *

Huimila phoned Atim to say she was going for an interview at a posh hotel in Connaught Place. Perhaps both of them would be given a chance. They took a bus and walked to the Metropolitan Hotel. The security guard refused to let the two women enter. When they said they had come for a job, he called the owner and Huimila was asked to come in. She came out and announced that she had been selected. Atim was not even summoned.

The two women were very hungry. When they looked at their monetary situation they realized that between them they had Rs 15. They walked to the Central Park in Connaught Place and sat there. Atim was enchanted by the flowers. They bought Rs 10 worth of channa masala from a man selling them in paper cones. The two then proceeded towards India Gate. It was warm and they felt really thirsty. At India Gate, they went to the bus stop. Just then four or five men came along. They turned out to be Meiteis and they spoke to each other in Meitei-lon; when the men heard about their plight they gave them their half-finished bottle of water.

Atim and Huimila started walking towards Vasant Enclave. On the way, a bus came and they got on. But the conductor threw them out when he discovered they did not have money for the fare. They finally reached Vasant Enclave late in the evening.

Huimila then announced that she did not like the job, and Atim said she wanted it. Mayori, ever resourceful, phoned a Tangkhul IAS officer and asked for his help. He said he would speak to the owners of a boutique in the hotel.

Atim found herself at the Metropolitan Hotel again. This time she went inside. And from afar she saw the brilliant blue of the swimming pool. It took her breath away. She did not know words like ritzy, stylish or even luxurious; in Tangkhul one word described all these qualities—khamatha or beautiful. All she could think of was how beautiful it all was. And she could not help comparing the vast space with the small, cramped, dark room in a big field that she called her home back in Ukhrul.

Atim looked very attractive, though she may not have known it. She was wearing a blue shirt given to her by Mayori's friend, Angam, and black trousers and she had borrowed black shoes from Lemyaola. She carried herself with dignity and had a brilliant smile which made up for her lack of experience and knowledge of the English language. She got her first job!

Atim discovered that she was to work in a shop selling handicrafts. The owner said she could wear the clothes she was currently wearing. She would be paid Rs 5,500 but she would have to bring her own food. There were two shifts; if she were on the night shift she would be dropped home.

The owner of the shop told her to open a bank account, but Atim had no identity card. She, like most migrant workers from the Northeast, did not have a voter's card, a ration card or any other proof of identity. The bank asked for her appointment letter, but the other women working in the shop had told her that they were not given appointment letters. Atim turned to Mayori who once again phoned the Tangkhul officer, who phoned the owner and Atim found herself with an appointment letter and a bank account! It was almost five months since she had come to Delhi and she could now begin her life as a migrant worker, although she did not know what a 'migrant worker' meant. There was no such word in the Tangkhul language.

The work at the shop was very confusing. Atim spent the first few days learning the names of the things that were being sold. She discovered that the shop sold many varieties of organic tea. She had no idea what 'organic' meant. When she found out, she suddenly realized why the vegetables in Delhi tasted so awful in comparison to the vegetables grown in the kitchen gardens in Ukhrul.

She was surprised to learn that there were so many kinds of tea, each with its own qualities and benefits. She had to learn to package these teas in lovely wooden boxes, then wrap them in handmade paper and put little green dot stickers to indicate that they were pure vegetarian products. It felt like being back in school with lessons to be learnt every day.

Then there were confusing types of soaps and cosmetics, and incense sticks in a variety of fragrances. And she learnt to distinguish between different kinds of precious stones such as rubies, amethysts and others whose names she could no longer remember.

In addition, there were the pashmina shawls that were ever so soft. Atim could not believe that the cheapest cost Rs 25,000. Her co-workers had shown her how the entire shawl could be passed through a finger ring—it was like magic.

Just a few days after joining, as she entered the hotel lobby, she was distracted by a commotion. She stopped and stood quite still. Right in front of her was Dino Morea, the actor she so admired. Atim had seen a film of his in Ukhrul called *Raaz*. It was a horror film in which Dino Morea acted with Bipasha Basu, the sexiest actress in Bollywood. Atim even knew the songs from the film, especially '*Main agar samne aabhi jaya karon*'.

Atim pulled herself together and walked past the filming crew. She heard the actor tell someone to let her pass. She saw that one of her co-workers had gone red in the face with the excitement. That evening she returned home bursting with enthusiasm. When she told Lemyaola about the incident she was shocked by the reaction.

Lemyaola was with another young man, also a son of a senior NSCN leader. She said it was 'a useless story'. Thereafter,

Atim learnt to keep her experiences to herself. But she still remembered the hurt and humiliation she had felt.

Every day Atim was learning something new. She learnt how to add bling to the pashmina shawls and scarves with Swarovski crystals. It was a delicate task and she had to be careful while applying the iron. But with this one act, the price of the shawl went up several times. Atim's greatest achievement was when she sold a shawl costing Rs 35,000.

A large number of customers were from Japan and they loved to buy elephants. One of them asked her where she was from and when she said Manipur, he expressed his pleasure at meeting someone from there. He said he knew that the Japanese army had gone up to Imphal.[26] Atim told him that her father had said it had come right up to Ukhrul and the people had found the Japanese to be very polite.

But not all customers were pleasant. One day an Indian couple came into the shop and looked at copies of the *Kamasutra*. Then they made all manner of lewd remarks and started behaving in sexually explicit ways. The manager told the women to stop them but none of them knew how to deal with such a situation.

Atim decided to move out of Mayori's flat. She did not feel comfortable and felt that she was not entirely welcome in Vasant Enclave. She shifted to the third-floor flat in Humayunpur where Huimila was staying. Huimila's roommate had left for Ukhrul so there was space.

* * *

26. The Battle of Imphal took place between March and July 1944 between the Japnese army and the Allied Forces. It is considered one of Britain's greatest battles in World War II. The role of Nagas in the British victory was crucial. Many Nagas remember Japanese soldiers with respect and say they were well disciplined, never took things without paying and were very polite. There were some Nagas who supported the Japanese because they admired Netaji Subhas Chandra Bose and his Indian National Army (INA).

Atim looked at me and asked, 'Did you ever go my mother's village, Kalhang?' She was surprised when I told that I had visited the village in 1982, before she was born.

We were sitting in my home in Goa. I took out my old files and showed her a typed copy of the Report of the Women's Fact Finding Team, which had been compiled after our visit to Ukhrul in February 1982, following the first major ambush carried out by the newly formed NSCN. Atim looked through my file with my notes and her eyes fell on a statement of S. Mahuiri, former pastor of Kalhang village.

'I met him. His field was next to my grandfather's field. When I was in Kalhang I saw him walking with great difficulty. He could not speak properly and my parents told me he had been tortured.'

She informed me that Mahuiri had passed away the previous year, in 2014.

Atim read the note describing how the man was tortured. He had been beaten continuously for several days, subjected to electric shocks from 23 February to the first week of April. The army had taken away the land on which his house stood to expand their camp without giving him any compensation.

That had been my first visit to Ukhrul, and it was the first time I had talked to men and women who had been tortured. Those encounters had left a deep impression on my mind and many years later when *Outlook* asked me to write 'My India Story', I wrote about that visit:

> 'The realisation did not come all at once. At first I thought incidents of torture, rape and murder were isolated human rights violations by Indian security forces. I realized much later that what I witnessed 26 years ago was in fact the dark, ugly side of nation building in our country.'[27]

---

27. Nandita Haksar, 'Democracy, Hang Down Your Head And Cry', *Outlook*, January 14, 2008

It was that experience that compelled me to engage with the question of Naga nationalism.

For Atim, those stories of torture are a part of her parents' memories, not hers. For her it is no longer simply a conflict between Indians and Nagas, it is also a conflict between Nagas themselves.

She told me that she had faced this problem in Delhi with her co-workers. For instance, when she worked in Q'BA, Keto, an Angami[28] Naga woman, had asked where she was from and when Atim replied (just as Mayori had instructed her) that she was a Tangkhul Naga from Manipur, Keto's spontaneous reaction was, 'Oh are Tangkhuls also Naga?'

Atim was furious and she had retorted, 'Have you heard of Muivah? Is he not a Naga? Well, he is a Tangkhul!'

Keto had been silenced; she could not possibly deny that the General Secretary of the NSCN was not a Naga. But Atim's rage was boiling over and she phoned Yaronsho and reported the incident to him. He too felt outrage and had used some choice expletives for Keto.

Then there was another time when Atim's co-worker was a Konyak[29] Naga from Nagaland. She held the firm view that only the Tangkhuls staying in Nagaland were Nagas, not those who were in Manipur. Only Lily, a Sema Naga girl, acknowledged that Tangkhuls were very much Naga.[30]

---

28. Angami Naga settlements are in Kohima District of Nagaland. A.Z. Phizo, widely regarded as the Father of Naga nationalism, was an Angami.

29. The Konyak tribe is found in Myanmar, Tirap and Changlang District of Arunachal Pradesh where they are called Wancho, and in Nagaland where they are the largest of the sixteen officially recognized tribes in the state. Many of them have not been converted to Christianity and follow their old customs and religion.

30. Sema is an anglicized name for the Sumi Naga tribe whose settlements are concentrated in Zunheboto District of Nagaland,

(Contd...)

While telling me these stories, Atim reflected that Tangkhuls themselves exhibit prejudices against other Nagas, such as Konyaks. Her own mother had told her that when a Konyak dies they dry the corpse and eat it.

Atim complained that the Indian workers were very ignorant about the Nagas and the people from the Northeast. She invariably calls the Indians mayang, which is a derogatory term for outsiders in Manipur. It is also a racist term, because other Mongloid people, even though they are not from Manipur, are not referred to as mayang.

Atim's Naga nationalism expressed itself in strange ways. For instance, once she had gone to a Diwali party at Q'BA, the restaurant she was working in, wearing her Tangkhul shawl and the manager had admired it. When he asked her to get one for his wife, she told him it was very expensive but he insisted.

'Did you get him a shawl?'

'No. He is not a Naga, why should I give him our shawl?'

I reminded her that I am a mayang. She laughed.

(…contd.)

although they have spread to other districts. The Chairman of the NSCN (IM), Isak Chishi Swu, was a Sumi Naga. He died in 2016.

Chapter Three

I Carry Dreams in My Heart

Atim found the job at the handicraft shop tiring and she left it after five months in September 2006. She bought newspapers and looked at job advertisements and found a job in a showroom of an international brand of shoes. She was very pleased that she had found the job for herself and gone for the interview on her own.

It turned out to be a very unpleasant experience. Atim described it as 'torture'. First of all, the timings were really bad; she had to be at the showroom in the morning at ten sharp and could not leave till nine at night. The company did not provide transport, even though they expected her to work till after it was dark. The manager offered to drop her home, but she refused because she felt uncomfortable with him. The manager then started what Atim termed as 'giving me pressure'. This is the expression Tangkhul women often use to describe propositioning by their employers.

The manager made Atim's life very difficult in the hope that she would give in to his advances. He would not allow her to sit and made her work in such a way that she found she was standing for twelve hours every day without a break. The staff was not given even a cup of tea. After two weeks, Atim had had enough and she strode into the head office in South Extension and resigned. When she went to collect her dues, Huimila was with her. She received a princely sum of Rs 3,800.

The two women immediately went out to celebrate. They went to Yo China and had Manchurian chicken with noodles, which they sprinkled with lots of chilli powder, and they washed it down with Coca-Cola. Then they spent the rest of the afternoon roaming around the Vasant Vihar market, enjoying their freedom.

When they got back home they had to face the reality of their situation. Both of them had no jobs and no savings to fall back on. Most important, they had no rice.

* * *

Atim remembered the time when her family in Ukhrul had no rice. They had never been very rich, but till then they always had enough to eat for two meals a day. Then her father fell ill again in 1996 and the expenses for his medicines and diet forced the family into dire poverty. They could not afford even one square meal a day. It was then that her mother had sent her to family members and to neighbours to borrow rice. At that time Mayori's mother had been very kind and generous, but her stepbrother Ninghor had not helped at all. He was her father's eldest son and Mayori's mother's older brother. He had graduated from Shillong and was a schoolteacher at the Government Higher Secondary School in Ukhrul. His wife, Panamla, was also a teacher in another government school. Atim resented the fact that despite being the eldest son and employed with a good salary, he had not taken up the responsibility of looking after his father when he fell seriously ill and hence her family had become so impoverished that she had to beg for rice.

Her father had first taken ill in 1994 when Atim was just ten years old. It began with him urinating blood. The family had consulted the traditional doctors. Some suggested giving him dog's blood; others said chicken's blood would cure him. All this cost money and Atim's father's pension at the time was barely Rs 7,000.

Ramyo kept losing weight and the family watched helplessly. A time came when he was too weak to get up to go outside to urinate and Atim's mother kept a bucket for him in the room so he did not have to walk at night. Atim remembered how frightened she had been when she had seen the bucket filled with red urine in the mornings. Ramyo's skin had become yellow and his body had swelled up. The local priest or magician, as Atim called the traditional medicine man, failed to make him well.

In 1995, Atim's mother was pregnant again with Sinhuila who was born in March 1996. After the baby was born, her parents decided to go to Imphal for her father's treatment. They left Sinhuila with Atim, as there was no one else who could help look after the baby. This meant that Atim had to miss school for a year between 1996 and 1997. In any case, she did not have money to pay for the school fees.

Even after all these years she remembers how nervous she felt when she was compelled to go to Ninghor's home to ask for money. She found him playing chess. She told him she needed a little money to buy a notebook for school and he had handed her a fifty-rupee-note without saying anything and gone back to his game. Atim bought the thinnest exercise book so that she could use the remaining money to buy a kilo of sugar.

In Imphal, the doctors did an ultrasound and discovered that Ramyo needed an urgent operation. Atim still does not know what exactly it was that her father suffered from. She does remember the month when her parents were away in Imphal and she was left looking after three children as the worst time in her life.

Atim was, of course, relieved to see her parents return but their troubles were not over. Her mother was grief-stricken because the baby did not recognize her, and so Atim had to continue looking after Sinhuila. And, although her father was better, he needed care, expensive medicines and a good diet, which according to Tangkhul beliefs meant that he had to be given soup made with country chicken to revive his strength. The expenses kept piling up.

Atim was angry with her father's eldest son Ninghor, who had done little to help throughout those three years; he had seen how Atim's parents had to sell the home they had built in Ukhrul after coming from Kalhang. Then they had to sell their field, in which her mother had planted cucumbers and Atim had put snails in the pond so that they could have some protein. Now it was all gone. That was also when Atim's parents were forced to sell their eighteen cows for the paltry amount of Rs 30,000 to give as a bribe for a government job for one of her father's sons. He did not get the job and the family no longer had fresh milk to drink.

* * *

In Delhi, the situation was not that desperate. Friends came to their rescue. Huimila's friends brought some meat for them. It was quite a large amount, so Atim kept it on the verandah to dry it as she would have done back at home. The next day when she went to fetch the meat she discovered that the children from the neighbouring flats were having a feast with it. The moment they saw her, they ran away.

Once Rose,[31] Atim's friend and a member of her yarnao, dropped in. She had brought a brick of ice cream, but since they did not have a fridge, it had all melted and most of it had to be thrown away. But the friend noticed that they did not have rice so she brought a bag for them.

There was a small shop around the corner from them. The owner was quite friendly and gave Atim some rations on credit. Then there was a young man in the NSCN who was posted in Delhi for the peace talks. He had taken a liking to Atim and came to the flat with his friends. He too brought rice.

One day, Huimila told her that she was going for a job interview at a photo studio in Sarojini Nagar Market. The photo studio was managed by a Tangkhul woman. Huimila was selected, but as usual she was choosy and did not take the job. But that was the day when Atim first set eyes on the market which would provide all her needs and dreams for the rest of her time in Delhi.

---

31. This name has been changed to protect the identity of the friend.

Atim stood gaping at the shops full of clothes. There were really trendy tops and kurtas, and when she asked the prices she was amazed at how cheap they were. Later, she would buy clothes and learn to bargain hard and get branded garments for one-fourth of the price. But on that day, her first in Sarojini Nagar, she did not have money.

All she could do was to feast her eyes on the clothes, very much in the same way she had stood staring at the biscuits in the village shop in Kalhang while on the way from her school to the pond where she and the other girls washed their clothes. The biscuits were very big and each of them was shaped like an animal—a frog, tortoise, or crab. They were brightly coloured and very hard and sweet. Even then, she very rarely had money to buy them.

However, Atim was soon to get her first proper job. Huimila's friend Ngami dropped in one day. She was working in a restaurant called Veda, which was owned by the famous fashion designer, Rohit Bal. Ngami told Atim there was a vacancy in a swanky restaurant in Connaught Place called Q'BA. She gave Atim the mobile number of the captain who had worked with her in a restaurant in Hauz Khas Village.

Atim felt no hesitation in punching in the number and talking to a complete stranger, that too a mayang! After her experience at the Metropolitan Hotel she had the self-confidence to speak in English over the phone. She was immediately given an appointment. But she was not quite so confident about locating the restaurant on her own, so she invited Elvina, a friend who had studied with her in Holy Spirit School in Longpi. Elvina was now in Delhi looking for a job.

The two women took quite some time to locate the restaurant. They found themselves walking all the way around the inner circle of Connaught Place twice before they could find the lift to take them up to the first floor. The restaurant advertised itself as having designer interiors and a casual terrace with a menu of eclectic global dishes, music and cocktails. Atim did not know what a cocktail was but the lounge impressed her greatly.

As Atim and Elvina waited in the lounge, Atim took in the decor, the huge bar with shining glasses and strange bottles, a small fountain and the high stools around the bar. They were seated on a plush sofa that went right around the room. Looking up, Atim could see a staircase going up two storeys. Later, she went up the stairs to the two massive open terraces with breathtaking views of Connaught Place. It all looked absolutely magical. If only they would take her. Give her a chance to prove herself.

'Ngalatim, please come.' She saw a young woman with a warm smile asking her to follow her. She looked as if she was from the Northeast and Atim felt reassured.

Atim found herself perched on a high stool being interviewed by the manager who introduced himself as Sunil Tikku. He was sitting opposite her with an arm on the bar right next to the small fountain. Tikku asked her about the work she had done at the handicrafts shop and she found herself answering the questions with élan, something that was totally new to her.

The manager looked at the young woman and he must have liked her professional attitude even though she was obviously new to Delhi. And she looked very presentable: not very tall but she carried herself well and had a charming smile. He looked at her and asked, 'Would you agree to work for Rs 4,000?"

Atim surprised herself when she said, 'No.'

'Then will Rs 8,000 be alright?'

'Yes.'

The manager did not explain that the basic salary would be Rs 4,000, but with tips and the service charge she would earn Rs 8,000. He did assure her that she would be dropped home after the night shift and that she would get one day off a week.

She went excitedly to tell Elvina. Then she waited for her friend's interview, sure that she would get a job too. Elvina was far smarter and more fluent in English than her. But the manager rejected Elvina who felt really disappointed. They went from the restaurant to where Elvina lived and Atim was surprised when her friend proudly announced to everyone that Atim had just found a job with a salary of Rs 8,000.

It was on 1 December 2006 that Ngalatim started working at Q'BA. She was given an appointment letter stating that she had the designation of Hostess.

On the first day when she arrived for work she was greeted by a young woman, Preeti. Preeti took her to a room where she was asked to try out the uniform. The skirts were all far too long and went down to her ankles. The purple blouse, too, was big for her petite frame and Atim did not have the right kind of shoes. The manager told Preeti to buy Atim a pair of uniform shoes and then he noticed that her stockings were laddered.

Tikku warned Atim never to come to the restaurant with laddered stockings; if she did not have any new ones, it was okay not to wear them at all. Then he told her to wear make-up, especially lipstick and kajal in the eyes. Atim protested that she did not usually wear make-up, but he told her it was a must for her job. Later, on one occasion, he rubbed lipstick on her cheeks when he thought she had not put enough rouge. It made her really angry.

After work on the first day, Atim gave the skirt for alteration to a tailor who sat in a kiosk near her flat and bought herself purple lipstick. The next day, Preeti taught her how to wear the make-up; she had been trained as an airhostess. Atim thought of the time when she was a very little girl and how she had tried putting on her mother's lipstick and how it had smeared all over her face. Then her dad had taught her how to apply lipstick properly after which she did not eat all day so that the colour would remain in place.

Preeti covered Atim's hair with a net and inspected the young woman. She looked really pretty. Then Preeti gave Atim her first lessons on the duties of a hostess.

Every morning when she came for work, Atim had to wipe all the menu cards one by one so that they were not sticky or stained. Then she had to clean the candle stands with hot water.

Preeti then went on to explain that Atim had been appointed as a hostess and that the hostess is the first person guests see on entering the restaurant; she welcomes them with a smile and then takes them to their seats. Atim learned that this was not as easy as it sounded. She had to ask the guests whether they had prior reservations; if they did not she had to allot a table and write down the table number in a register. Sometimes the guests could be fussy and demand to be seated at a table that had already been reserved. It required tact and patience to give explanations and soothe their ruffled feathers. She then had to hand over the menu card and return to her station by the front door.

Atim was also taught how to attend to calls. The first time the phone rang she panicked. Preeti told her to say, 'Kindly please hold on' to the client waiting for the reservation. And then she had to press the hold button and transfer the call to the manager. Later, she learnt to take calls. She would answer the call with, 'This is Atim, how may I help you?' If the guest wanted to make enquiries about reservations she would transfer the call to a manager.

She learnt the importance of 'promotions' which the guests were encouraged to take advantage of. These were special offers, usually of alcoholic drinks on discounted prices. She remembered the first time a couple had asked her for a Screwdriver. She had blushed and just ignored them. It was Valentine's Day. When they repeated their order, she had to ask her colleague, Damyanti from Manipur, what a Screwdriver was. This was the first time she heard the word.

Speaking of cocktails, one of the drinks that the bartender made that never ceased to fascinate Atim was the Flaming Lamborghini.[32] She had not tasted it, but had watched fascinated while he made the cocktail with different shaped glasses and a variety of coloured liqueurs, which he poured into the glasses. Then he dramatically set the concoction on fire. Atim watched the guests quickly drink the cocktail with a straw, making sure their hair did not go up in flames. It looked like they were drinking fire and Atim wondered how it did not burn the lips.

The manager had told the staff that they would get 'incentives' if they were able to sell certain kinds of alcohol. He cited the example of Marina, a Kuki woman who had worked as hostess and was very good at marketing. She had sold a record number of bottles of expensive wines. Marina had left by the time Atim joined, but those who had been with her spoke highly of her skills. She had been very charming and Atim discovered she had been Miss Kut.[33] Atim could never learn to talk to customers. She said the Kukis were much better than the Tangkhuls at this.

While Atim was working at Q'BA one of her co-workers, Ruth, managed to sell a huge number of expensive vodka bottles and was presented with a bottle of Smirnoff by the management. Ruth wanted to share it with the girls so they trooped into the washroom. Atim took in some lemons and others carried the small shot-glasses. There, they poured out the vodka, squeezed a bit of lemon and added a pinch of salt and drank the shot in one gulp.

---

32. A cocktail made with Kahlua (coffee liqueur), Sambuca (elderberry liqueur), Blue Curacao, orange liqueur and Bailey's Irish Cream.

33. Kut is the main festival of the Kuki-Chin-Mizo group of tribal communities. It usually takes place in the autumn, around August-September which coincides with the end of the maize harvest; one of the highlights of the festival is the crowning of Miss Kut.

Although Atim did not have to serve food, she sometimes had to serve the drinks. She was taught to hold the glasses from the stem and never the goblet. On the third or fourth day of her job, Atim tripped and broke twelve glasses. The shards lay all around and she just stood there transfixed, waiting to be shouted at. But the manager did not say anything, not a word. However, the captain passed some remarks to humiliate her.

Soon, she was allowed to work in the evenings. That was when everything got exciting. She saw huge platters of all kinds of food being carried up and down. They would be sent from the kitchen in a dumbwaiter, which was a lift for food service. They called it the dummy, and it was hidden from public view by a wall. The dirty plates were also stacked near the dummy. One day, one of her co-workers beckoned her towards the dummy. It was the dirtiest part of the restaurant, and Atim's colleague stood there with a plate of what looked like noodles.

'Come and taste Spaghetti Carbonara.'

Atim looked at the long pasta and the white sauce and it did not appeal to her, but when she sampled it the taste of bacon and cheese exploded in her mouth. If only she could have added a little chilli powder!

In contrast to the delicious aromas of the roasted meats, fried chicken and other dishes, the staff's food was tasteless and never varied. It was rice, dal and a vegetable curry made of potatoes or nutrella. The chefs said they had no time to cook anything better. She could not swallow it. She asked a chef for some chillies but he refused. She took the matter up with the manager, who called the chef and instructed him to give Atim as many green chillies as she wanted.

Atim saw so much food being wasted; just thrown away at the end of the day. She could not understand why the staff was not allowed to take home the leftovers. The security checked their bags every day just to make sure they were not carrying home food. This, however, did not prevent the staff from tasting the leftovers; that was how Atim got a taste of Indian food. She loved the tandoori potatoes stuffed with pomegranate seeds, but not the paneer or even the roast leg of lamb, though she quite enjoyed the pizza. Since she was a hostess, she did not learn much about the ingredients in the dishes or about the different kinds of wine. That was what she missed most, the opportunity to learn more about culinary secrets.

The most difficult part of her job was handling the guests when they came in large groups for a party in the private dining area. It was Atim's job to check the guests against the list given by the person hosting the party, and often she found that ten to fifteen extra people had sneaked in. The management did not embarrass the guests, but they charged for the extra food. The host of the party would sometimes challenge the manager and the manager would call Atim and she would have to show the register. She noticed that often the guests were allowed to get away with their lies.

In fact, guests seemed to get away with so much. Once a manager told the children of a guest to be careful because they were dangerously near the stairwell. The father got up and slapped the manager. Then the family walked out without paying their bill.

The restaurant had many celebrity guests. One morning when she came for work, Atim found a huge crowd outside the entrance and when she went upstairs she was told there was going to be a film shooting. She found herself opening the door and wishing good morning to Sonam Kapoor and Abhay Deol.[34] They had booked the entire restaurant for the morning. The actors went straight to the private dining room. Atim also saw designers and musicians. She was shocked to see a famous designer wearing pink, with his hair coloured a golden yellow.

---

34. Sonam Kapoor is a Bollywood actor, a style icon and daughter of Anil Kapoor; Abhay Deol is the nephew of Dharmendra and known for playing complex roles.

It was the first time she had heard of gay men. Atim feasted her eyes on beautiful women like Celina Jaitly who had once been Miss India and marvelled at the way all these beautiful women maintained themselves.

Some days there was live music and Atim could not believe her eyes when she saw Nikhil Chinapa, the MTV star, close up. On such days Atim, the simple Tangkhul girl from Ukhrul, felt she was living on another planet.

Atim did not dream of becoming a film star or Miss World. All she really wanted was to save money to help her family build a nice house with a vegetable garden.

It was also the first time Atim had been around so many foreigners and she noticed how some of her co-workers flirted with them. One of them hung around a Frenchman. He was much older, but he found her attractive and one day he presented her with a huge bouquet of flowers and proposed to her. They got married and she went to France. Atim heard that she had even won the Miss India competition in Paris. But later she ditched the man and fell into the hands of traffickers, who raped her. Ultimately, she escaped and went to the Indian embassy. Atim heard that she was now working somewhere in South India as a Food and Beverage Manager.

Atim noticed that on the whole foreigners were more generous with tips than the average Indian customer. There was an elderly Afghan man who was a regular. He took a liking to the smiling hostess who gave him a warm welcome every evening and on one occasion Atim found a fifty-euro-note in her hand. She slipped the note into her bag and did not put it in the tip box.[35]

But there were Indians who could be generous too. On one occasion, a large group of people came in together. As Atim

---

35. Tips have a long history with origins in sixteenth-century England, Some claim that the word stands for 'To Insure Promptness'. In most

(Contd...)

escorted them to the lounge, she could not but help admire one particular woman who looked so beautiful that Atim wondered how she maintained her figure. Her eyes fell on the stunning necklace glittering around her neck. The woman, a Sardarni, asked Atim whether she could have a green salad.

Atim asked the chef to make a crispy green salad and gave it to the woman for no extra charge. The woman was so pleased that she gave a tip of Rs 1,500. A little later, Atim found the same woman in the bathroom. This time the woman confided that she was exhausted. Atim picked up courage and asked whether she was a model. Pleased, the woman opened her golden clutch-purse and gave her another Rs 500.

One of Atim's co-workers, Stacy, said a customer had once wrapped up a Rs-500-note in the cork and slipped it to her. Another time, a guest had taken off her Titan wristwatch and given it to Stacy.

As a hostess, Atim had the power to give guests discounts. Once she saw a big group of Nagas, mostly Rongmei Nagas,[36] who were very polite. Atim told the management that they were friends of hers and got them a 15 per cent discount. And then there was a Tangkhul airhostess who had come with her Indian boyfriend; they ordered lobster and Atim got them substantial discounts.

(...contd)

restaurants today, tips are pooled together in one box and shared between the serving staff, with a percentage going to the kitchen staff. This practice ensures that the wages of the restaurant staff are kept low. They have to depend on tips more than any other profession. See: Debra Ginsberg, 2001, *Waiting: The True Confessions of a Waitress*, New York: Perennial.

36. Rongmei or Ruangmei Nagas live in Tamenglong District of Manipur but also have settlements in Assam and Nagaland. It was a Rongmei Naga, Jadonang, who first gave a call for an independent Naga Raj during the British period.

Atim noticed one local young man who often came to the restaurant with different girls, mostly from the Northeast. She had seen him at Mayori's flat at Vasant Enclave. Once, he had come with a Tangkhul woman who had been very active in church activities. Atim was shocked to see her flirting with this man. Then one day, when she had gone to Elvina's home, she discovered that the same man had given her friend lots of chocolates and shampoos. Atim was furious with Elvina; she phoned the man and warned him against flirting with 'our women'.

Atim discovered that the chefs were people she had to be wary of. The head chef in the restaurant never missed an opportunity to make sexist remarks. He would tell Atim she was looking sexy or comment on the large breasts of one of the stewardesses or make other distasteful remarks. Atim asked one of her co-workers about him and discovered that he was married, with a child. The next time he made a comment, she asked him, 'Chef, are you not satisfied with your wife?' After that he stopped talking to Atim and told her senior that Atim was a bit too smart.

The bartender was also in the habit of passing comments on women, both staff members and guests. On one occasion, a guest wrote a complaint in the feedback card and the manager caught the bartender tearing it up. He was dismissed forthwith.

On Monday nights there were few customers and the staff would go to Agni disco at the Park, a five-star hotel nearby. It was open to all hotel staff in Delhi; they were required to show their identity cards and could enter free. This was the first time Atim saw the psychedelic insides of a disco. She enjoyed dancing as it relieved the tension, but none of them could afford to buy drinks or snacks, even though they were given 15 per cent discount.

Every year, Q'BA closed for a day on Diwali and the owners came to celebrate the festival with the staff. There was a big spread at the buffet, but it was vegetarian. One of the owners gave the staff vouchers for Rs 1,500 from his shop, which was well known for branded clothes. The local Indian staff was not interested in buying branded clothes and would sell their vouchers to their co-workers from the Northeast for Rs 500.

Atim bought six Numero Uno jeans[37] with the vouchers by putting in a little extra of her own money. She later gave two pairs to her younger sister, Ramchanphy. The management also had a lottery for the staff. The first Diwali, Atim won a rack for plates and crockery.

Most of the women wore salwar suits for Diwali, but Atim draped her bright red hand-woven Tangkhul shawl over her jeans. The owner's wife admired the beauty of the shawl and one of the managers asked how much it would cost if she was to get one for his wife. This was when Atim deliberately quoted a much higher price of Rs 5,000 to discourage him; in her mind she thought the shawl should only be worn by Tangkhuls and not mayangs.

Every month, the management cut a cake for the birthday of a member of the staff, and on that day they gave a certificate to the best employee of that month. A cash award of Rs 500 went with the certificate. In April 2008, Atim was standing with the rest of the staff during the cake-cutting ceremony when she was shocked to hear her name being announced as the best employee of the month!

The general manager handed her a certificate of excellence which stated that her 'positive attitude, team spirit, hard work and dedication to work have been an asset to our organization'.

Atim had worked hard and could indeed be proud of herself. On an average month ten to twelve thousand people came to the restaurant. It was not an easy job, and Atim was

---

37. Numero Uno is India's first indigenously manufactured denim label.

beginning to feel permanently tired. The standing for long hours made her legs stiff and often she would get cramps in the night. On those nights, she would tie a scarf tightly around her legs. She was also missing home; at the time she had bought a small Fly mobile but her parents did not have a mobile or even a landline. It was with very great difficulty that she managed to speak to them occasionally. She longed to go home.

Besides, she felt she could now afford to support her brother, Yaokhalek, who was two years younger than her. He had dropped out of school and was doing nothing. Her mother wanted Atim to persuade him to go to Delhi and find some work. But she needed to have more money before she went back to Ukhrul. She had not been able to save much because she had been sending money home and the expenses in Delhi did not allow for saving.

* * *

Atim decided to meet Rose, one of her friends in her yarnao, who was in Delhi. Rose was living with a mayang man who was married. His wife had refused to give him a divorce, so Rose lived alone in a spacious three-bedroom flat below the apartment where her lover lived with his family. Atim tried to find time to visit her on her off-days, but would come away feeling sad.

Rose told her she had contacts in Panipat where they could buy very cheap clothes. So one day, the two friends set off together early in the morning on a local train; apart from them the only other passengers at that hour were daily wage labourers.

When they reached Panipat, the two women found their way to the warehouse. Rose knew the owner and he allowed them to pick and choose from the massive heaps of clothes amassed there. The owner used them to make carpets by cutting them into small bits. The clothes were being sold at the rate of Rs 35 a kilogram. Rose and Atim spent the entire morning looking through the piles and Atim picked out bed sheets and blazers. She would later wash and iron the bed sheets and blazers and sell them to her fellow workers in Q'BA for Rs 300 and 250 respectively.

By the afternoon, the two women were hot, tired and hungry. They bought ten brown boiled eggs and ate them with salt and chillies, and washed them down with cold beer being sold in the shop next to the warehouse.

Atim was able to make a quick profit of Rs 3,000 with the blazers and then some extra with the sheets. Now she had Rs 15,000 to take home with her. She was also excited because she would be taking a flight to Imphal. It was the first time she would fly in a plane. She was confident about handling the procedures for checking in the luggage and getting through the security. But she had to ask a friend how to locate her seat number.

Atim saw her parents standing at Imphal airport. The parents and daughter had an emotional reunion. They stayed that night at a small hotel in the town and took a bus the next morning for Ukhrul.

* * *

Atim decided to throw a party to celebrate her father's birthday. He would be eighty-three years old. She called all her yarnao and they came to help cook the dinner. Atim bought pork, chicken and chickpeas for making ooti, a Meitei dish. She also bought cabbage, tomatoes and green chillies for a salad.

Atim invited all of her father's children; all came except for Mayori's mother who had already died. Then she called her father's friends, some immediate neighbours and, of course, her yarnao. There were more than seventy people. Obviously, there was no place for them in their one-room rented home so they got chairs and put them outside. There was a small programme with prayers and songs; then her yarnao presented her father with a shirt. One neighbour gave him a box of cornflakes and the others also brought gifts for him. After the yarnao left, the family sat around a bonfire and Atim told them her stories about Delhi. That evening someone remarked that Atim's younger sister, Ramchanphy, looked radiant.

Her parents looked with wonder at their daughter's photographs: in one she could be seen smiling with Delhi's iconic Indian Gate in the background; in another there she was in front of the Lotus Temple.

Atim had spent Rs 7,000 for the feast. The family felt that their dignity had been restored. No longer would they be seen as people who begged and lived off others.

That night Atim dreamt of the family home her parents had built in her mother's village. In 1991, after her father Ramyo retired from his postiona as an extension officer in the Agriculture Department, he decided to shift to his wife's village, Kalhang. He had some money, and with that he built a small L-shaped house and bought a paddy field that produced 300 tins of paddy annually.[38] There were three rooms and a kitchen. There was a lot of land around the house and her parents had planted fruit trees like peaches, oranges, lemons and even sugarcane on the edges. They had a cowshed with seventeen to eighteen cows and a young Nepali boy to look after them. At the back, there was a big kitchen garden, where Atim's mother had planted cabbages, carrots, mustard leaves, peas, beans and maize.

The entrance to the house had tall eucalyptus and some alder and cherry trees and beds with colourful flowers blooming. Ramyo had painted the house white with black borders. He had put house horns on the roof like in traditional Naga houses and placed Naga spears along with pieces of driftwood in the verandah. At the entrance, the nameplate proudly read: Ramyo Hongray retired EO. The house was near the national

---

38. One tin of rice is around 20 kilograms.

highway,[39] away from the main village.

Those years, from 1991 to 1995, were the happiest in Atim's life. And then her dad's eldest son, Ninghor, had insisted that they move to Ukhrul. He had said it did not look nice that Ramyo should be staying in his wife's village. After all, he was the senior-most member of the Hongray clan. She had been there when her dad and his son had exchanged hot, angry words. But in the end, her father had succumbed. Atim pushed those painful thoughts and promised herself that she would build a beautiful house for her family.

The days in Ukhrul passed quickly and very soon it was time to go back to Delhi. She was happy because this time she would be taking her brother, Yaokhalek. But her mother felt she was losing two of her children and she could not help the tears that flowed down her cheeks. Everyone told her not to cry because it was inauspicious, the children would face obstacles on their journey.

* * *

Atim and Yaokhalek took the bus to Imphal and then another bus for Dimapur, but at Mao Gate, the border between Manipur and Nagaland, they discovered that there was a bandh,[40] and the Manipur buses could not cross into Nagaland. They had no option but to hire a taxi. Even though they shared it with other passengers they still had to pay Rs 600 per person and that was only up to Kohima, a short distance away. From Kohima they had to hire another taxi to Dimapur, which cost them another Rs 1,200.

---

39. Kalhang is on National Highway 150 which connects Kohima to Imphal via Jessami.

40. Atim and Yaokhalek were travelling along National Highway 39, which starts in Numaligarh in Assam and ends in Moreh on the Indo-Myanmar border. Now it has been renamed Asian Highway 1 and will be the longest route connecting Tokyo to Europe. Bandhs or

(Contd...)

Atim had called a friend from her yarnao in Dimapur and was looking forward to meeting her, but the taxi had three punctures on the way and it was night by the time they reached. Atim's mobile had also stopped working and so they went directly to the railway station and were grateful when the train turned up. They found themselves in a compartment with an Indian army soldier, who tried to talk to them. But the brother and sister were too tired for conversation and they slept almost all the way to Delhi.

(...contd)

blockades on the highway are a political tool used by all communities to try and enforce their demands. Bandhs cause tremendous economic loss. The total loss suffered by the Manipur economy on account of economic blockades was Rs 246 crore in 2004–05; it rose to Rs 2,027 crore in 2006–07. See: Sushil Kumar Sharma, 2014, *Dynamics of Bandhs and Blockades in Northeast India*, New Delhi: Centre for Welfare Studies, 2014.

Chapter Four

Things Fall Apart

Atim was a bit worried about bringing her brother into the
flat she was sharing with five other women. She and Huimila
had moved out of their old flat because the landlord refused
to replace the fan that had conked out. The heat had become
unbearable on the third floor and they didn't want to spend
money on buying a fan.

Elvina had found them a spacious flat in Krishna Nagar,
near Safdarjung Enclave, on the second floor. It had two rooms,
a big terrace, a kitchen and a bathroom. Atim remembered
how the women had enjoyed shifting into their new flat. She
had bought a tape recorder and they put on music and danced
around while they settled in. Elvina had invited three other
women so there were six of them sharing the flat.

However, with Yaokhalek it became a little awkward and
cramped. She was keen to take him to Gurgaon where he
was supposed to join a Bible study programme[41] run by
Hangkhami, a woman her mother knew. But she had to wait
for her day off before she could accompany him to Gurgaon.

Atim bought her brother soap, a towel and some new
clothes. She also bought him a mobile so they could keep
in touch. And she gave him Rs 1,500. When she left him in
Gurgaon, she thought that he would be happy with the other
young men.

A few days later, when she returned from Q'BA she was

41. There are hundreds of institutions teaching rudimentary Christian
theology run by Baptist missionaries in India. Although the quality of
education offered is not very high, it does afford the Nagas and other
Christian tribals from the Northeast an opportunity to get some
education, rather like the average Muslim madrasas in India.

shocked to see Yaokhalek. He had phoned to say he did not like it in Gurgaon, but Atim had hoped he would get used to it and was planning to visit him on her next free day. She had not thought he could manage to find his way from Gurgaon to their flat in Krishna Nagar. Yaokhalek said he had left all his belongings behind, so that it would not look as if he was leaving. He had made an excuse of going to the market and had run away.

Now there were seven of them living in the two rooms; soon one of the girls brought her boyfriend, and that made it eight people squeezed into two rooms. Atim found that she was spending nearly all her salary on feeding the others. She was earning the most and so was buying the meat; she had also bought a fridge. On top of it all, she was paying Rs 1,500 for Yaokhalek separately. Besides, the women were squabbling over small things and it was becoming quite unpleasant.

Atim asked Ester, a Kuki co-worker at the restaurant, whether she knew of any vacant rooms; Ester said the room next to hers was vacant. It was in Munirka. Meanwhile, Yaokhalek had found himself a job with a group of potters from Ukhrul and had moved to Vasant Kunj Extension. Atim was now on her own and so she shifted into the room next to Ester.

Atim found that she had not been able to save anything. The expenses of going to Ukhrul, supporting her family and then renting the rooms had left her with no extra money. She began to think about getting a better job; she needed to earn much more if she was to build a home and save something in case of an emergency.

Atim was afraid that if she fell ill, she would not have the money for treatment—she had first-hand experience of dealing with her father's illness. She had seen how an illness in a family could wipe out an entire life's savings. She also knew she had to save money for herself because her parents would not be able to help her. The other option was to get married and have a husband to support her, but Atim could not see herself getting married any time soon. In ninth standard, when she had been studying in Alice Christian School, she had a boyfriend. They never met alone. He would follow the girls as they walked home and he would pluck plums and throw them for Atim and her friends. They giggled and ate them. Sometimes, he offered Atim and her friends some chewing gum and, on occasion, donuts.

Atim and her boyfriend had exchanged letters every day. She had to consult the dictionary in order to reply. She now regretted that she had not kept any of those letters. They had got lost in all the shifting she had done. In those days no one had mobiles so Atim had no means of keeping in touch with him. She had subsequently heard he had gone to Kazakhstan to study medicine. Apparently, someone had sponsored his studies. Later, when she got a mobile she found him on Facebook and he promised to return to India to marry her. But his family opposed their marriage. They did not want a waitress for a daughter-in-law. In any case, she had moved on and even the memory of him had faded.

In Delhi, a young NSCN man had pursued her and had even given her an expensive ring, but she was sure that she wanted a secure and safe future for herself and her family, something that someone in the underground could not guarantee.

Back at the restaurant, things were getting tougher. Many of the women Atim had made friends with had left. It was then that Atim thought it would be good if she could find a job on a cruise liner or perhaps go abroad, either to Dubai or Singapore. She knew some women who had done so and they had made enough money to build nice homes for themselves in Ukhrul. The first thing she needed was a passport and so she started collecting the documents she needed to apply for it. Her friend Rose did not have a passport either. She applied for one as well.

* * *

Rose was very upset because her companion had gone off on a cruise. He said he would have taken her with him if she had a passport. To make up for her disappointment he had offered to pay for a holiday in Goa for Rose and Atim. This was in the late summer of 2009.

Atim was quite excited about the idea of a holiday in Goa. She had never been on a holiday. The closest to a holiday was the time when Rose and she had been together on an excursion to Shillong; someone had sponsored the trip for the youth living in Greenland colony. Atim had been around sixteen years old at that time. It had been great fun; they had gone in a bus and seen Cherrapunjee. She reminded Rose of the quantities of steel wool she had bought in Shillong. Rose could not remember why she had done that. They giggled over those shared memories.

Rose's brother was working in Goa and he had promised to find them a decent place to stay. He said that since it was just before the monsoons, it was off-season and things were cheaper. The women went by train and Rose's brother was there to pick them up. He came with a friend so they had two two-wheelers. Rose's brother said there was a vacant room with a kitchen next to where he was staying, this meant they would be close by. Atim could not remember where they went except it was somewhere in North Goa.

Just after the four of them arrived at Rose's brother's place, he got a call to inform him that his wife had been picked up from the beauty parlour where she worked and was in jail.[42] Atim and Rose were shell-shocked.

The two women decided to find another place and Rose's brother's friend helped them find a nice one in Calangute. They were thrilled with the big beds in the room.

---

42. In fact, she was not in a jail but at a government detention centre for women rescued from prostitution at Merces, Panjim.

The next day, Rose's brother called to say his wife had been released so they went to meet them. His wife insisted that she had done nothing wrong and she did not understand why the police had taken her to a women's home. Atim heard someone mention Aunty Nandita's name, but no one could tell her where she was.

In any case, there was no time to meet Aunty Nandita; Rose and Atim wanted to have as much fun as they could possibly manage. Atim looked at the immense expanse of the water and was wonderstruck by the waves coming in from the ocean to the beach. It was so vast, so thrilling and oh my god so inviting. She and Rose bought themselves some beer and spent hours on the edge of the sea, letting the waves splash them, giggling with delight.

On the beach, Atim bought a pineapple. She sat on the sand and ate it with enjoyment, her eyes fixed on the sea, while Rose had a massage by a woman who was offering her services for Rs 200. Atim got herself photographed with a fisherman and wondered why he had not caught much fish. She did not know that fishermen do not go fishing in the monsoons.

Then the women treated themselves to a seafood platter. They were served by a Tangkhul waiter. The platter had crabs, shrimps, squid and fish. But the two were disappointed because it was all very bland, cooked in butter and wine. They wanted something with chillies or at least some spices. Atim was fascinated to see three women smoke a hookah and they tried one as well.

The two women did a little shopping. They bought themselves wraparound skirts and some seashell jewellery. Atim bought a dress for herself.

Rose's brother's friend invited the two women to his home and they were thrilled to eat beef intestines. The food tasted even better while sitting on the verandah of the house which was right on the beach.

Then another friend of Rose's brother called them for his birthday bash. Atim knew the friend was doing Bible studies. There were two rooms filled with people, mostly Tangkhuls. In one, the men and women were dancing to loud music, while in the other, food had been laid out. The men were quite drunk and the host asked Atim to dance with him. When she refused, he tried to pull her into the room and she slapped him. Atim had heard he was a drug addict. The two women decided to leave the party. As they were leaving, Atim saw some really nice bamboo shoots growing outside and she bent down and pulled them out. They would help make the curry more flavourful the next day.

Another of Rose's brother's friends invited the two women to Riio Da Club (sic). The DJ was a Tangkhul named Peter, and many of the waiters were also Tangkhul. Atim and Rose dressed up; Atim wore the new dress she had bought and both put on their high-heeled shoes. But when they arrived at Riio, they were shocked at how casually the women were dressed. They were even more shocked to see Tangkhul women dancing with strange men. It was rumoured that the owner, Naresh Gidwani, had a Tangkhul girlfriend. One of the women who danced at the bar regularly was the sister of the man who had tried to force Atim to dance with him.

Atim was told that fishermen from Mumbai come to the bar to dance. After some time, the two women decided to go home. This was not their kind of scene.

It had been a wonderful holiday and on the last day, the women found white mushrooms near Rose's brother's house; they picked a bucketful. They took it into his kitchen and made iromba, a hot, flavourful salad.

* * *

Atim came to Goa again in July 2015 when I invited her to spend a month so we could record her story. She said she would like to explore the possibility of finding work in Goa because she had heard it was much less stressful. But she also remembered the raid in which Tangkhul girls had been picked up when she had come with Rose in 2009. She wanted to know whether that happened often.

I told her that there were regular raids on beauty parlours, spas and dance bars by the police, supposedly to rescue women who had been trafficked and were in danger of going into prostitution. However, the women, at least the ones from the Northeast we had talked to, were doing regular work and were hoping to get trained. They were not involved in any form of prostitution.

Atim said that at least such raids did not take place in Delhi and that the migrant workers were not put into detention centres. I told her that it might be true that women were not picked up, but several Tangkhul men had been arrested after they sold their ATM cards for a paltry sum of Rs 4,000 to drug dealers, who used the accounts to transfer their illegal earnings. These were usually men working in call centres that paid salaries by cheque, which meant that the workers had to open bank accounts. When they left the call centre, they did not bother to close the account and some sold their ATM cards. Atim was shocked to hear of these cases, more so when she learnt that many of the men were in Tihar Jail without proper legal help.

Atim wanted to know more about the raids in Goa. I told her that I could tell her a little about the raid that had been conducted on Nippon Beauty Parlour in Arpora in May 2009. She wondered whether it was the same raid in which Rose's brother's wife had been picked when they came to Goa. I said I could not say for sure since I did not know the woman, but there had been several raids that year.

I had met one of the women who had been picked up and put into the Protective Home located at Merces, a village just outside Panjim. The raid had been conducted on the basis of information given by a NGO dedicated to fighting trafficking. The NGO worked in close coordination with the police, therefore it did not challenge the police or state authorities.[43] Often, the police violated the provisions of the anti-trafficking law and wrongly detained women who were not in need of rescuing since they were migrant workers. The NGO did nothing about the horrendous conditions inside the Protective Home and it did not question illegal and humiliating procedures such as the two-finger test[44] in the hospital when the police took the girls and women there.

I had newspaper reports about women trying to escape from the home as a protest against a prolonged stay without legal aid, and one woman had even tried to commit suicide in the home in 2013.

I told Atim the story of Yuimila, who was around twenty-three in 2009. She was, like Atim, the eldest of six children. Her father, V.S. Wunganing, was working as a chowkidar, or watchman, of a village Baptist church with a salary of Rs 1,000

---

43. There has been a long debate between those against trafficking of women, who want a ban on all prostitution and some feminists, who have argued that some women may go into prostitution voluntarily. The latter argue that there is a need to recognize the rights of the prostituted women, rather than putting them into rescue homes. However, in the above context, the NGO had 'rescued' women who were not remotely in need of rescuing. The Tangkhul women who were supposedly rescued were migrant workers seeking skills and needed their rights to be protected under labour laws rather than police intervention. Also, the police and the state-run home were guilty of committing human rights violations which were not even recognized by the said NGO.

44. The Maharashtra Government had by this time already passed a Government Resolution (GR), which stated: 'The procedure [the two-finger test] is degrading and crude and medically and scientifically irrelevant'.

a month. He had a field which he ploughed with the help of a buffalo, to supplement his income.

'They are even poorer than my family,' was Atim's reaction.

Wunganing's brother's son, Raymond, was working in Mumbai and it was on his suggestion that Yuimila had decided to come down to Goa where Raymond's wife's relatives were working. Raymond suggested she work in a beauty parlour and learn some skills rather than in a hotel.

Before Yuimila had come to Goa, her younger sister, Sochanphi, had been there. She had also worked in a beauty parlour. In May 2008, there had been a raid and Sochanphi had been taken into custody. The NGO had insisted that her father come from Ukhrul to take charge of his daughter. The father had to spend Rs 20,000 for the airfare from Imphal to Mumbai and then the bus to Goa. It was the first time he had been away from Manipur and he was completely at a loss.

I told Atim that I had not been able to meet Sochanphi and I did not know the details of that raid. The court insisted that the father take his daughter back to Ukhrul, but what would she have done there? She decided to find work in Mumbai. The father went back to Ukhrul.

Yuimila had arrived in Goa in January 2009. She looked for a job and in March finally got one in the Nippon Beauty Parlour with the help of Ngayinmi, a young Tangkhul man who was training in hair-cutting. He told her that there were two other women, one from Karnataka and the other from Goa, who were involved in 'dirty massaging', but she would not be expected to do any dirty khamkhao (massage in Tangkhul).

Since Yuimila was not going to be doing any massages, she would be paid only Rs 3,500 a month and would be trained in pedicuring and manicuring. Once she learnt the skills, she would be paid Rs 4,000. Yuimila said the owner kept her word and she was never asked to massage clients.

Yuimila told me that a lot of people came to the parlour—

men, women and even grandmothers—for facials. They charged Rs 1,000 to Rs 1,500 for a full body massage with coconut oil, and if it was with aromatic oil it was Rs 3,000. She was aware that some shady things were going on, because taxis would stop by with clients asking 'for extra service' which meant dirty massages.

Yuimila had worked for barely two months when the police raid took place and both she and Ngayinmi were taken in; he was first put in the police lockup and later in jail. She was sent to the Protective Home.

Yuimila did not understand English properly and when Sebastian and I approached the NGO and offered to translate, they refused our help, even though they knew us to be human rights lawyers. Instead, they sent a young law student from the Poumai Naga tribe, who did not know Tangkhul. He spoke to Yuimila in Meitei-lon, which she did not know well. When she complained about the conditions in the home he did not bother to record her complaints. The NGO insisted during the hearing that her father be called from Manipur, even though we told them he could hardly afford the fare.

When Wunganing heard that he had to go to Goa again to rescue his eldest daughter, he felt absolutely helpless. He had no money and it was time to plough his field. He had already borrowed Rs 17,000 at an interest of 4 per cent and was still trying to pay off the loan. This time, he sold his buffalo and came to Goa with that money.

I still remember him sitting in our dining room while I took notes. He felt so confused and so upset. He had turned to Sebastian and asked, 'What is prostitution?' He did not even understand what crime his daughter was being accused of. The NGO people had insulted him and shouted at him, but he could not understand why. Now he had no money to go back and he wanted to know whether he could leave his eldest daughter in Mumbai; if she earned a little, he could pay off the loans.

Yuimila was angry. She had had to spend twenty-five days in the Protective Home where the conditions were filthy. She was angry at the way the media had carried reports and she was angry with the NGO who was supposed to have 'rescued' her. All she had wanted to do was to acquire some skills so she could earn and support her family.

The court order stated that the father had to 'give a report in this regard to the nearest Police station at Manipur, also to the protective home at Merces every three months that his girls are residing at Manipur'. The father asked me whether it was absolutely necessary to follow the order.

Before I could answer, Yuimila asked what the court expected her to do, sitting at home? She needed to work to repay her father's debts. She asked what would happen if she continued to stay in Goa and work. Would the NGO get her arrested again?

To my mind, the order was absolutely illegal. The Constitution of India gives every Indian citizen the right to move freely about the country, the right to profession and the right to live with dignity. Those were the three fundamental rights of every migrant worker. Yuimila had not been trafficked, she was a migrant worker and she needed to work to support her family. The NGO had effectively deprived an entire family of all their rights under the Constitution. But there seemed to be no way of making them accountable.

'What did you do, Aunty?' Atim asked.

I said I felt really helpless. Just as in so many other parts of the country, in Goa too the anti-migrant feelings are very deep. Additionally, there was no group I could expect help from, since the migrant workers from the Northeast had no organization of their own at the time[45] and the Tangkhul Welfare Union had no experience of taking up cases involving both workers' rights and women's rights.

---

45. The Northeast Association, Goa was registered in 2010.

The plight of Ngayinmi was even worse. Since he was a man, he had been put into jail instead of a protective home. One of his relatives had managed to engage a lawyer and get him released on bail. When we talked to him, he said he did not even know under what charge he had been arrested. He was worried because he had no papers to prove he had been employed in the beauty parlour as a trainee. Beauty parlour owners and hotel managers don't usually issue appointment letters; thus, the migrant worker has no way to prove that he or she is working at a particular place. The beauty parlour owner wanted to keep him in Goa so that he could testify in her favour, so she had allowed him to stay in the staff accommodation. But she did not pay him.

Sebastian and I went to the owner of the parlour who gave us her list of woes. She said the police had taken her nice new towels and Rs 74,000. She insisted she did not provide any 'extra service' even though there was a lot of pressure on her to do so; even the sarpanch had come once for some extra service.

'So you really could not do anything?' Atim could not believe that I had been so helpless. But it was true; all I had been able to do was to publicize their plight in the local papers and write an open letter to a famous Goan writer, Damodar Mouzo,[46] who had won a Sahitya Akademi award for his novel *Karmelin* on the conditions of a Goan migrant worker who goes to work as a maid in Dubai. Sebastian and I had also tried to organize the migrant workers into a union, but none of them had heard of labour laws or trade unions.

The raids did not stop and almost every year, women from the Northeast found themselves thrown into the women's rescue home. All we could do was to help get them out and sometimes the articles we wrote had some impact, but it was marginal.

* * *

46. See *Goan Observer*, October 30–November 5, 2010

Atim wanted to know whether I knew about the raid on Riio Da Club, which she had visited on her holiday in Goa. She had heard there had been a raid there in which many women had been arrested.

I told Atim I did know about the raid. It was conducted on the night of 29 June 2013. In that raid, eighteen girls were picked up; most of them were from the Northeast and Nepal. Just a few days after the raid, the president of the Tangkhul Welfare Union, Livingstone Shaiza, contacted us.

He said the raid had most probably been instigated by the local BJP MLA, Michael Lobo, who wanted to close down all dance bars, and that this was a part of the attempt to 'clean' Goa.

I asked Livingstone what happened in these dance bars, were they like the dance bars in Mumbai?[47] He said he could not say about all the dance bars in Goa but in Riio, where his wife also danced, there was no prostitution. The girls earned mainly by getting the men to buy drinks for them. They were given non-alcoholic drinks, but the customer was charged for alcohol. Each woman was given a commission on the number of drinks she could get the customer to buy. However, the customers were strictly prohibited from even touching them while dancing.

At about the same time, the DJ at Riio was Sebastian's nephew, Peter. Peter had invited us to Riio when he learnt that we wanted to study the conditions of the Tangkhul migrant

---

47. Dance bars started in Maharashtra and it has been estimated that 20,000 women were employed in them in that state. In Mumbai alone there are estimated to be 700 dance bars. In 2005, the Maharashtra Government banned these dance bars and at the time many of the women were reported to have moved to Goa. The ban was struck down by the Supreme Court in 2013 but the Maharashtra Government again banned them in 2014. The Supreme Court once again held the ban to be unconstitutional.

workers. We had seen with our own eyes that the women danced keeping a safe distance from the customers.

Livingstone's wife, Ruth, was one of the women who had been picked up from Riio, but he had managed to get her released. Another was the Nepali wife of a distant nephew of Sebastian. The problem was that in the identity papers she had given her Tangkhul name and they did not have a marriage certificate. It took some legal imagination to produce papers to get her released.

Although Livingstone and the Tangkhul Welfare Union were helping all the women, even if they were not Tangkhul, the Northeast Association and the Union could not take up the case officially, partly because the women were from different communities and partly because they were afraid that back in Ukhrul people would think they were helping 'girls with loose morals'. Each family had to engage their own lawyer and pursue the individual case to get their family members released.

Livingstone found it difficult to deal with such cases. He had no experience in coping with courts, police and employers. Until now, the Tangkhul Welfare Union had been involved only with welfare matters within the Tangkhul migrant community. Livingstone said he had found it very difficult to be so confrontationist. In Tangkhul society it was considered bad manners and disputes were always settled by negotiation and consensus. But then, the Tangkhuls were no longer dealing with matters within their own community.

Livingstone showed us the order of the Collector-cum-Sub-divisional Magistrate releasing his wife Ruth. In the first paragraph it said that Naresh Gidwani, the owner of the bar, and his assistant were procuring girls

'under the garb of employing them as a waitress and dancer at Riio Bar and restaurant which is functioning as a discotheque and the accused persons were using the victim lady for the purpose of prostitution…it is further submitted that accused

persons were living on the income of prostitution carried out
in the vicinity of religious place.'[sic]

The court order was outrageous. It made all kinds of charges
against both the women and owner without any evidence
except the word of the NGO—the same one that had initiated
the raid on the Nippon Beauty Parlour.

The women were furious. Ruth refused to undergo the
humiliating two-finger test. She said she was not a prostitute
but a wife and mother of a small baby. Her indignation was
noted by the court which recorded that 'victim is agitated and
is instigating the other girls to fight with the authorities.'

Livingstone said there was no question of the women doing
anything other than dancing because Tangkhul men were
around to make sure they did not face any problems. Even so,
he did not like the idea of Ruth working in Riio. But she said
they needed the money. They had had a baby in May 2012
and she was confined to the house. She had been working as
a receptionist at a beauty parlour in Baga where she had been
getting Rs 15,000. Now that income was not there. In Riio she
could dance late at night while Livingstone could look after
the baby for a few hours. And she could earn Rs 1,000 a day.
'It was a hard life and we had a baby which meant more
expenses.'

* * *

The Tangkhul Welfare Union was formally inaugurated on 12
May 2009 at a function where Sebastian was the chief guest. It
had been formed on the initiative of James Muinao, who was
from Ngainga village. He had a bachelor's degree in theology
from the Tabernacle Baptist Bible College at Horamavu in
Bengaluru. He had come to Goa in 2007.

James began by working as a waiter in various restaurants,
including at the Taj Village at Sinquerim and the famous Tito's
with a salary of Rs 3,500. He enjoyed talking with foreign

customers, but he felt that the employers in Tito's discriminated against the Northeasterners and favoured the Goans.

James wanted his own 'Children's Ministry'.[48] He had brought five small boys from Ukhrul; they were the sons of his relatives. He had hoped to get some foreigner interested enough to donate money so he could look after the kids. There was already a pastor from Kerala called Jason who ran a similar orphanage with his Poumai Naga wife.

James did not succeed in getting any funds and he had had a tough time when his wife Achui got pregnant. Her younger sister, Asingphi, had come from Ukhrul to be with her. Since there was still time before the baby's birth, the sister took up a job with a beauty parlour. The police raided the parlour and the girl was put into the Protective Home. This was in October 2010. She had been in Goa for barely a month and knew no English. James had to run around to get his sister-in-law out of the Protective Home.

In Ukhrul, however, the rumour mill started saying that the girl was involved in prostitution. It was only when Sebastian phoned some people there that the rumour was quashed.

* * *

In addition to the Tangkhul Welfare Union, a Northeast Association had also been formed to look after the needs of migrant workers from all the different Northeast communities, not just the Tangkhuls. Its first president was a Chakhesang Naga from Nagaland. However, the organization had not done much.

We suggested to Livingstone that the Riio raid be taken up by the Northeast Association, especially since many of the women who had been detained at the Protection Home

---

48. Baptists evangelize among children, especially those who are not Christian. In many cases, it becomes a means of livelihood by getting foreign funds in the name of educating orphans.

were not Tangkhuls but from various parts of the Northeast including Sikkim, Nagaland and Manipur.[49] At the time of the Riio raid, the President of the Northeast Association was Wungchipem Pheirim. He worked in Wok and Roll where the owner had given him managerial responsibilities. Wungchipem was a Tangkhul and he immediately agreed to take up the case if we would guide him along the way.

The women wanted their employer, the owner of Riio, to apologize because he had done nothing for them when they were arrested, though he had managed to bribe the police and save himself from arrest. The women had to bear the costs of litigation as well as the humiliation of the medical tests and detention.

On our recommendation, Wungchipem issued a statement to the press outlining the issues that the recent raid had raised. We all sat with the women who had been arrested and formulated the following demands:

- A public apology from the police for illegal arrest, making women sign false statements and giving misinformation to the magistrate, on the basis of which he had dubbed the women 'prostitutes';
- An apology and compensation from the owner of Riio, Naresh Gidwani;
- Guidelines to the police and other public authorities on racial profiling;
- Transparency and accountability on the working of NGOs in the field of trafficking.

We decided to file a complaint with the Goa State Women's Commission, but it did not even bother to reply. The plight of migrant labour was, it seemed, not its concern.

---

49. In fact, one of the women was from Goa, but no one had come forward to help get her out of the rescue home.

While we were fighting the racial profiling and racial branding by the Goa media, other Tangkhuls living in various parts of the country were busy condemning the women caught in the raid. Social media was used to attack even the Tangkhul Welfare Union for promoting prostitution. It was very disturbing how people back in Ukhrul condemned the migrant community, calling the women prostitutes and questioning their morality. I helped Livingstone draft a statement on behalf of the Tangkhul Welfare Union that was put up on Facebook.

Atim felt the people back home in Ukhrul would never understand. She said she could not share so many things with her parents because they had no idea about the reality in which she lived and worked.

I felt this was true to some extent, but I also felt we had not made enough efforts to make them aware of the complexities. It was precisely for this reason that I had thought of writing this book, so that the people in Ukhrul would understand not only the problems faced by the men and women working in distant cities, but also how hard they worked to support their families back home.

* * *

Atim asked, 'What can be done for the women in such cases?'

I said the only thing the women needed to do was to organize themselves and learn to fight for their rights. I gave her the example of the Northeast women working in Tatva Elements Spa. I had been deeply involved in the case, which was why I could tell Atim the story with all the details.

One day, towards the end of August of 2014, Livingstone had brought eighteen women and a Kuki man who had been working at Tatva Spa. They came to our home and told us how their services had been summarily terminated by the owner, Asha Arondekar. She had not paid the women for several months and denied them even the uniforms and other essentials that were part of the package. She had even threatened to frame the

Kuki man in a false case of sexual harassment. On top of that when they went to her home to demand their emoluments, she had called them 'Northeast beggars'. That had infuriated them more than anything else.

What's more, she had even threatened her employees by saying she was from Goa so they could do nothing against her. Later, when I did a search on the Internet, I was shocked to learn that the woman had been invited by the International Centre Goa to be the chief guest for their Women's Day function.

I saw an appointment letter she had given to one of the employees, a Tangkhul woman called Ashim. It had a clause that read:

'AND WHEREAS the Employee has agreed that he/she shall bear all the expenses himself/herself and has requested Tatva Spa to pay the sum of Rs 90,000 as a loan to the employee in the form of training expenses to be incurred by Tatva Spa.'

Ashim was scared that she would have to pay the money if she left the job, but after I had assured her to the contrary, she decided to fight. But throughout she kept getting calls from her employer to hand back the original letter.

I phoned my friend Christopher Fonsesca, the General Secretary of the All India Trade Union Congress (AITUC), and asked for his help. The AITUC helped the Tatva employees to file a case before the labour court against the illegal and arbitrary termination of the service of thirteen Tatva workers.

Of the original eighteen women, five had withdrawn and rejoined Tatva. They were too scared to fight their employer. But among the women who continued to fight were three sisters from the Lotha Naga tribe. The courage of the women paid off when they won their case in the labour court.

They received around Rs 30,000 each and there was wide

publicity in the media. The police had also been extremely helpful, perhaps because the Director General had once been posted in Arunachal Pradesh and harboured genuine affection for the people of the Northeast.

I was hoping that after their victory in the labour court, the women and men would realize the importance of trade unions, so that we could organize them into a proper union. It was the only safety for the migrant workers. Comrade Christopher was more than happy to help and asked the women to become members. But I said it would be better if the Northeast Association could affiliate itself to AITUC, so that Northeastern solidarity should be preserved within a class organization.

But the success and publicity had gone to the head of the then President of the Northeast Association, George Longpinao from Choithar village. He began boasting of his contacts in the police and media; he collected money and did not put it into the bank. The Goa Salon and Spa Association Secretary, Sumeet Bhobe, had offered an apartment to the Northeast Association to run their office. George accepted the offer, and the Facebook page of the association had photographs of Sumeet and Archana Bhobe inaugurating their new office.

I asked Livingstone whether anyone had objected to this move by the spa owners to buy off the Northeast Association. He said the other office bearers had noticed a lack of transparency and accountability on the part of George, but they had not understood that the offer of an apartment by the spa owners was a bribe.

Livingstone was also very disappointed with George. But he said he did not know how to deal with the situation. They did not have a mechanism to cope with a corrupt leader other than wait till his term was over. But Livingstone had another worry. 'Now that I am a manager of a restaurant do I have to give my employees all these rights under the labour law? I cannot afford to do so right now.'

* * *

Livingstone had come a long way from the time he left Ukhrul in 2008 in search of a job in Bangalore. I thought his story needed to be told.

Chapter Five

Words Fail to Define Despair

In the last week of January 2013, Livingstone did not have a single rupee saved up, but he thought he knew enough about the business of running a restaurant to start dreaming about owning one. He had worked as a waiter since 2008 and had been promoted to captain; in his experience the success of a restaurant was largely dependent on keeping the customers satisfied. So when he heard that his boss Henry Pfeifer was thinking of selling his company Eastern Delicacies Private Ltd, Livingstone offered to buy it. It showed remarkable courage because Livingstone knew that the business was not doing as well as it used to.

One day, in October of 2013, Livingstone phoned to say he wanted to meet us. He came with his wife, Ruth. They said there was a possibility that they could become owners of the restaurant because Henry and his Thai wife, Chawee Konking, had decided to leave India. The problem was raising money to buy the company's assets such as the freezer, furniture, crockery and cutlery.

Livingstone said he was thinking of selling a plot of land he owned back in Ukhrul, but I told him that he should not sell it because he would not be able to afford to buy another piece of land there. Prices of land were skyrocketing. I offered to lend them the money, an offer they took happily.

* * *

It had been a long journey for Livingstone from the time when he left Ukhrul in 2008 in search of a job. I asked him to tell us his story and how he had landed in Goa.

Livingstone Shaiza was born on 3 May 1983 in Leinganching village in Ukhrul District. He was the third child of Joyson, his father, and Alungphy, his mother. He had an elder sister, Katawon, and a brother, Donald, who was two years older than him. His parents went on to have nine more children. Soon after Livingstone was born, the family shifted to Ukhrul town and lived in his father's sister's home till they could rent a house for themselves.

His earliest childhood memory was of seeing a bhoot or ghost near the pond by the bamboo grove. The bhoot was very short and it came chasing after the little boy and his friends.

Alungphy, Livingstone's mother, had never been to school but his father had passed seventh standard and could read English and Meitei-lon. He taught his children Meitei-lon. His parents were keen to educate their son and admitted Livingstone into one of the better schools, Scholar Pakshmi School in Viewland.

Livingstone walked about three kilometres to his school in Viewland. He had started taking coaching classes by the time he reached the sixth standard in the hope of getting into the Navodaya School, but he did not get selected. His father enrolled him in the Government Secondary School, but there were more than a hundred children in each section and there was no possibility of getting individual attention; besides, the textbooks were proving to be very expensive.

Livingstone grew up in Ukhrul where there was always some tension and a threat of violence in the air. He grew up knowing that there was an insurrection and he had once heard a loud bomb blast in the Tangkhul Long[50] ground on 15 August, India's Independence Day. He could not remember the year. The Assam Rifles had surrounded the whole town; everyone lay down on the ground and prayed. Livingstone

---

50. Tangkhul Long is the apex body of the Tangkhul tribe. Their office is in Wino Bazar and there is a huge ground in front. Before the ceasefire, the Naga insurgents often disrupted the official Indian Independence Day celebrations conducted on the grounds.

saw the armed forces picking up young men and hitting some people with the butts of their rifles. His father was also dragged away, but on that occasion the women went to the camp and brought everyone back.[51]

He also has a memory of the Naga-Kuki clashes. The clashes began in 1992 and lasted for a whole year. He distinctly remembers his father digging a bunker outside their home and the colony bell ringing at night, calling the men to come out and guard the locality. He also remembers seeing his father and brother make arrowheads by beating pieces of coal tar tin drums into shape. The tins were picked up from the road when it was being blacktopped and were usually used to store water, which was always scarce in Ukhrul town.

Livingstone did not know the origin of the Naga-Kuki clash except that his people were trying to throw the Kukis out of Tangkhul lands.[52]

* * *

In 1997, Livingstone's father decided to send his son to a relatively safer place for schooling. He was sent to Jessami, a small village on the border of Ukhrul District and Phek District in Nagaland state, where he stayed with a distant

---

51. There is a history of women, especially Meitei women, rescuing the men from the army camps by going in large numbers and demanding that the boys or men be handed over to them.

52. The Naga-Kuki clashes started in May-June of 1992 in Moreh, Chandel District, bordering Myanmar. The reasons for them were complex and deep-rooted; in part they were fuelled by the divide and rule policy of the Manipur government and the Centre, which used a section of Kukis against the Nagas. In part, it was an assertion by the Kukis of their demand for a separate Kuki district to be carved out of the Naga majority districts, including a part of Ukhrul. Initially the Kukis had the upper hand, but later they suffered far greater losses. Both communities were backed by armed groups which made the clashes lethal.

relative of his mother who worked in the Excise Department. Livingstone had to cook and clean the house for a salary of Rs 500 and the opportunity to attend the government school. But the teachers were mostly absent and there was no one to ensure that the little boy studied properly, so Livingstone enjoyed his freedom.

The Indian army had a heavy presence in this border town and because of this the inhabitants spoke Hindi. As a result, Livingstone picked up a smattering of Hindi and Nagamese, the lingua franca of Nagaland. He also learnt the Chakhesang Naga language spoken in the neighbouring Phek District.

Livingstone did not pass his tenth standard and returned home to Ukhrul in 2001, but there was nothing very much for him to do. To begin with, he helped his parents in the paddy field and accompanied his father when he went to do odd jobs for people; he would chop wood for firewood, or help in their fields. Soon, Livingstone felt embarrassed to work in the houses where there was a girl he liked and hoped to court.

* * *

He also missed his elder brother Donald, who had joined the Indian army and had not come home for Christmas for the past two years.

Thus, in the December of 2001, the eighteen-year-old Livingstone set off to find his brother and bring him home for the New Year. It was a bold and courageous idea because he had never been out of Ukhrul District except once briefly when his uncle had taken him to Imphal, a three-hour bus ride away. Now he would be travelling absolutely alone and without an exact idea of the route.

He remembers every detail of that journey, his first outside Manipur. His father had given him some money and he took the bus from Ukhrul to Imphal. At Imphal, a Meitei had helped him get onto the bus to Guwahati. Livingstone was heading towards Shillong. He had heard that his brother was posted there.

On the way to Guwahati the bus halted for dinner. Everyone got down and rushed to a hotel. Livingstone followed suit. He found that they did not serve rice, only rotis, and so he had his first taste of them. Even though he had eaten four big rotis he felt dissatisfied and hungry. He walked back to the bus, but found it too smelly and got off again. He strolled around and found another hotel where people were enjoying rice and meat. Livingstone went in and ordered a plate of real food.

He reached Shillong early in the morning and took a taxi to Happy Valley, the regimental centre of the Fifth Assam Regiment. When he reached, the taxi driver demanded Rs 600. Livingstone was astounded. It had cost him Rs 600 to get from Imphal to Shillong by bus and now the taxi was charging the same amount for a short ride. Just then an army officer drove up on his motorcycle and asked what the problem was. He settled the amount with the taxi driver and Livingstone paid only Rs 200.

At the centre, he learnt that his brother had been posted to a small village in Assam, so he set off for the interstate bus station to take a bus back to Guwahati. There he asked a man from Arunachal Pradesh the way to the local bus stop and the man took him to the ticket counter, paid for the ticket and then took him out for lunch. Livingstone remembers, in great detail, the kindness shown to him on that epic journey.

Livingstone could not remember the names of the village or the nearest town he went to while looking for his brother. All he remembers is that he was in an auto with an Assamese man who did not speak a word of Hindi or English and they went on for ages in the dark. Livingstone just prayed silently till they reached a small house where the man invited him in. His family was warm and welcoming and said Namaste to him in greeting; he shook hands with everyone. Livingstone was relieved to learn that his companion's brother spoke English and promised to take him to the army camp. But they were all scared of the Indian army which had been carrying out counter-insurgency operations because ULFA had a strong presence in the area.[53]

That night the Assamese man took Livingstone on his bicycle to the army camp. But Livingstone was not used to riding pillion and his bum hurt, so he preferred to walk.

When they arrived at the camp, Livingstone shouted out in Hindi that he had been given permission to visit his brother. The Assamese man waited patiently till Livingstone went inside. There he was escorted to the mess with one soldier in front and another marching behind him. The captain asked Livingstone whether he should call his brother, but he said he would prefer to meet him in the morning. He was afraid his brother might be drunk and get angry. That night he ate and slept in the Indian army camp.

Livingstone noticed that the soldiers and officer had kept their hair long instead of the usual short army cut. He discovered that it was to protect them from being easily identified by the ULFA when they went out in civvies. There were only thirty men in the camp and the next day he met his brother's friends. They told him that his brother was posted in the town, which was about 14 kilometres away. Before taking him there they shared a meal; he had a mountain of rice and half a kilo of pork. It was New Year's Eve and at midnight they cut a cake.

In the morning they took him in a convoy to the town. Donald was really surprised to see his younger brother and hear about his adventurous journey. Livingstone went to the Commanding Officer and requested that his brother be granted leave and returned home triumphantly with Donald.

The next year, Livingstone proudly escorted his father to

---

53. United Liberation Front of Asom (ULFA) was formed in 1979 with the aim of establishing a sovereign, independent, republic of Assam.

Assam to meet Donald. It was his father's dream to visit Guwahati. He remembers how happy his father had been when the bus went over the Brahmaputra River; he said, 'Now I am happy, even if I die at least I would have seen this.'

* * *

Back from his adventures in Assam, Livingstone tried to find some way of earning a living. He came into contact with some older boys who invited him to join them in their business. They were selling the ganja that grew abundantly in Ukhrul. But he did not make much money.

Then his friends invited him to Imphal, where they all lived together in a rented room. He was the youngest among them. The men were involved in another sort of business—buying bullets from Indian armed forces and selling them to the NSCN. They had permits from the NSCN to conduct such transactions. This licensing policy ensured that they did not sell their bullets to other insurgent groups, even if they were willing to pay more for them.

Usually one bullet cost them around Rs 150 and they sold it for Rs 200. The bullets for AK-47s fetched the best prices. Business was not always good and they took loans to pay for the travel and rent; whatever money they earned went into paying back the loans with interest. There was not enough for their own needs, so Livingstone never sent money to his family. And the parents did not know what their son was up to. Livingstone, therefore, decided to go back to Ukhrul where he lived with his parents in the Seipet Ramlung locality.

Livingstone obviously had leadership qualities, because soon after he moved back to Ukhrul in 2002 he was chosen to be the youth president of his locality.

That year saw the Manipur Assembly elections. As youth president, Livingstone looked to the parties to give money to the youth association in exchange for their support. He worked for the BJP candidate, Danny Shaiza. He was noticed when he suggested some ways of garnering votes and was invited to be the polling agent. Livingstone saw how bogus votes were cast and how rubbing a little Vicks ointment could remove the voting ink. Later, Danny offered him a kerosene agency for his services, but he earned only Rs 2,000 to 3,000 selling the kerosene, which didn't really help the family. However, it did help him get to know some influential people.

For the next few years Livingstone remained in Ukhrul, but could not find any real job. Then in early 2006—he could not remember the exact date—he was contacted by the NSCN (IM). Apparently while he was in Imphal he had caught the attention of some members of the NSCN, and when one of them asked him to help in collecting taxes on behalf of the organization he could not refuse. This would give him the opportunity to earn some commission.

His job was to collect the monthly taxes[54] from the Nagas and in exchange he would get a small percentage. The NSCN man gave Livingstone a letter on the NSCN letterhead stating that he was an assistant lieutenant. Livingstone asked his friends to help him in this new job.

One day he went to Yaingangpokpi[55] to collect taxes from a contractor. He had gone with another person. He remembered that it was 9 June 2006, because it was the first day of the FIFA World Cup. He was looking forward to watching the match

---

54. The NSCN (IM), like every other insurgent organization in Manipur, collects monthly taxes; however, there are increasing incidents of NSCN cadres extorting extra money and pocketing it. There have been strong protests by Naga people against such corruption, warning the Naga national groups to stop the high level of such extortion.

55. Yainganngpokpi is 24 kilometres from Imphal on the Imphal-Jessami Highway. The NSCN (IM) has protested against the inclusion of the village and Tangkhul settlements within Imphal Police Districts.

on television. Instead he found himself and his companion being dragged in full public view and shoved into a car by two or three people. At the time Livingstone did not know that one of them was the Finance Secretary of the NSCN. When he realized that they were NSCN, he asked permission to fetch the letter appointing him as assistant lieutenant. But they said there was no need.

Livingstone found himself being driven through the jungle along a road which was not black-topped. They arrived at the NSCN camp somewhere deep in the forest in Senapati District where he was locked up in a cage that was too small for him to stand in. His hands were tied tightly behind his back. He was frightened because he had heard that sometimes they killed people without sanction of the leaders.

Livingstone remembered his friend, Pamza, who was a black belt in Wushu, the Chinese martial art. A NSCN official's bodyguard had caught Pamza drinking alcohol.[56] The bodyguard told Pamza to bend down; Pamza bent down thinking he would be given four or five whacks. Instead the bodyguard kept beating him with a stick and he counted fifty whacks. When Pamza's father saw what the NSCN had done to his son, he went to the NSCN official and demanded justice. The bodyguard was made to apologize, but what he did not see coming was a forceful sock on the jaw that dislodged two teeth.[57]

The NSCN first took Livingstone's companion who was

---

56. The NSCN Manifesto recognizes only Baptist Christianity as the official religion of Nagalim and in accordance with the Baptist moral code, has banned drinking of alcohol by NSCN cadres and all Baptist Nagas. They allow Catholics and Nagas practising their old religion to have traditional rice beer.

57. There are innumerable instances of Tangkhuls criticizing the NSCN for its abuse of power, but that has not necessarily lessened their support for the cause of Naga nationalism.

much older than him. Livingstone could hear him being beaten and his screams. Then they came for him. Livingstone was blindfolded and led into a room. He was given a resounding slap and then asked to explain what he was doing. He said he had been authorized to collect taxes and been given a letter and he had never cheated the NSCN. After hearing him, they asked him whether he understood Nagamese. He said he did not. Then they discussed his case in Nagamese, but he understood what they were saying because he did know the language. They were convinced that he had not cheated them. However, they found that his companion had tried to cheat them, so he was kept in the lock-up. Livingstone did not meet him again.

It was decided that Livingstone was not at fault, but even so he could not be released unless someone was willing to take him back, or his family members came to fetch him. But how would they know where he was? He was assigned a room belonging to a captain of the Naga army until they could make arrangements for him; the officer had gone on leave.

Livingstone found himself living in the NSCN camp for a month. There was nothing for him to do. He observed their routine and was surprised to learn that they got up very early in the morning. The food was very well cooked. The cooks had to be very careful because even if the chutney was badly made they could be given some hard whacks on their backsides right in the dining room. Livingstone watched a cook being pulled up: he was told to bend and was walloped. Then the man went back to finishing his meal as if nothing had happened.

He enjoyed the masoor dal soup; it was nice to drink something hot in the evenings, which were quite cold. He also noticed that the way the NSCN cut the pork was very different. They did not sear it before cooking as Tangkhuls usually do, because they could not light fires; that would give their location away.

Livingstone watched the NSCN cadres play games; sometimes it was volleyball while at other times they played chess. He joined in sometimes. In the evenings they had their dinner. The only other entertainment was the television which was attached to a generator. TataSky had reached deep into the NSCN camp.

Then one day Livingstone saw a person he recognized; he was from his mother's village, Khamasom Khullen. He told the man about his plight and asked him to take him away. The man agreed and informed the Commanding Officer that he was Livingstone's uncle. The CO agreed to let Livingstone go. It was the last day of the FIFA World Cup, so Livingstone stayed in Imphal to watch the closing match on 9 July 2006. The next day he took the first bus to Ukhrul.

Livingstone decided to give up the business of collecting taxes as well as the other ventures his friends had been involved in. He stayed at home and sometimes helped in the field but there was nothing much to do. He knew he could better himself if he had a proper job. He was not afraid of hard work but there seemed to be no opportunities for him.

* * *

Then in April 2008, a neighbour, Ramtawon Kasar, came back to Ukhrul. She had been working in Bengaluru[58] for some time. When they met, she insisted that he go back with her to Bengaluru. She was a little older and very insistent. She worked as a hairdresser and earned Rs 16,000 a month. She said in Ukhrul a haircut cost Rs 15 while in her salon it could cost up to Rs 5,000 if it included colouring. She managed to persuade Livingstone to leave Ukhrul.

Livingstone's father gave his son Rs 10,000 for the journey and Livingstone set off, feeling confident that he would find himself a job. After two nights on the train from Guwahati, they reached Bengaluru late in the evening. He had never seen such a massive railway station. People were running around in

---

58. Bengaluru was known by its Anglicized name Bangalore till 1 November 2006.

every direction. When Livingstone stepped out of the train, he felt his whole body shaking.

Ramtawon and Livingstone took an auto-rickshaw to her flat in the Neelasundra locality. It was the buildings that he noticed most. He had never seen such huge structures before. Her first-floor flat was spacious. Soon, friends started arriving to take things she had brought for them from home, mostly food that parents had sent for their children.

Livingstone watched the young men and women talk confidently to each other; they all had jobs and they spoke English. He felt everyone was so much better than him. He remembered the exact words that he had said to himself, '*Ngazan meikap kachi.*' I am weakest of them, financially and educationally.

Nearly all the money Livingstone had brought from Ukhrul had been spent. He had been buying food for everyone on the train, and since there was no concept of going dutch, no one realized that he had overspent. That evening he counted his money and found he had just a few hundred rupees left.

Ramtawon shared the flat with her sister and her boyfriend; with Livingstone, there were four people. The boyfriend was working in a pastry shop and her sister in a showroom.

Over the next two or three days Ramtawon and her sister gave Livingstone his first lessons on survival. When he went to the market with the two sisters he heard men passing comments. He turned to see who they were, but the women warned him to keep quiet and not respond. They said they had got used to such things and had learnt to ignore them. Livingstone felt really angry but also helpless.[59]

---

59. Duncan McDuie-Ra has documented how masculinity is most ruptured by migration. Men can no longer play the roles of protectors and providers. Migration removes men from the environment where their masculinity is produced, while women gain freedom away from the constraints of home. See McDuie-Ra (2012) pp. 119 and 126.

Back in the flat, the women warned him not to react when men tried to provoke him. 'Just walk away.' They also told him never to sit on his haunches as men do back in Ukhrul while smoking or chatting. 'They associate it with squatting in a toilet.'

Livingstone began to feel an unease he had not experienced before. It seemed as if he had stepped into a dangerous place. He said, 'Back in Ukhrul I was equal with others, but here I had no rights at all.'

Livingstone had been in Bengaluru for three days and had to begin looking for a job. His flatmates taught him how to face an interview. They said he would most certainly be asked to tell them something about himself. Livingstone found that a very difficult concept. He had never told anyone about himself; he had never needed to introduce himself in this way before.

Ramtawon and the others had started working again, but Ramtawon's boyfriend's brother, Pamreiyo Yangya, had come from Goa where he had been working. Pamreiyo, or Ayo as he was called, said he would help Livingstone find a job.

The two men set off by bus and arrived at Brigade Road, the heart of Bengaluru's commercial centre and busiest shopping area. They literally went from restaurant to restaurant asking whether there were any vacancies. Everyone said they had none and the men returned home disappointed. Livingstone was getting more and more anxious; money was running out and there was no job in sight.

After three or four days of searching, which meant walking for hours and knocking at doors, he found a job in a restaurant in a hotel called Raaga's Raiin (sic) Tree off Brigade Road. The interview was in the basement and not in the restaurant. They were not asked to sit. The two men stood next to each other, and when the manager asked Livingstone a question, Ayo, who was fluent in English, answered. Livingstone got the job with a salary of Rs 2,200. It was his first job in Bengaluru, a city of 8.5 million people.

* * *

On the first day he went to work by bus. Once he was inside the restaurant, he suddenly felt absolutely alone; he had no idea what he was expected to do. He soon found out that his job was to wipe plates and cutlery. Livingstone stood by the cashier and wiped plate after plate after plate.

He would come in for work before the breakfast buffet and make sure that everything was nice and clean before the guests started arriving. And soon the plates would start coming up for wiping. He was not allowed to sit; he had to stand and wipe, wipe and wipe.

Barely had the buffet breakfast finished, when the lunch had to be readied and once again the wiping started. After lunch when the plates were all washed and wiped, he got time off. Finally, he could sit down and rest in the basement. There was no place to lie down.

On his second day he found that the captain was a Kuki who was nice but could do little to help Livingstone. The cashier was a Goan and since he stood next to him, they could talk. The Goan turned out to be friendly and even taught him a little English. Livingstone learnt the names of the different kinds of plates and the cutlery; he learnt the difference between a dinner plate and a saucer, a teaspoon and a tablespoon.

Livingstone had picked up English in Ukhrul by reading whatever he could get his hands on, usually old newspapers such as the *Sangai Express*. As a result he could read even if he did not always understand the meaning of the words. At home he tried asking Ramtawon and Ayo the meaning of some words but they made fun of him. He knew they did it without malice but he felt belittled so he relied on his Goan teacher.

He had taken a bus to work on the first day, but then he discovered that there were shared autorickshaws. He would take the rickshaw in the morning but in the evening he would walk back, a distance of around four or five kilometres.

When Livingstone received his first salary, he gave it all to Ramatwon to pay for his share of rent and food. She gave him Rs 200 for his expenses. The major expense was cigarettes, but he solved the problem by picking up butts from the restaurant and smoking them.

The working conditions were unbearable and Livingstone decided to quit. He was working from nine in the morning till nine in the night with two short breaks. He was not allowed to sit. It was very tiring and his legs ached from standing for nine hours. When the pain was too much to bear he would manage to get a little relief by sitting on his haunches for a minute or two when no one was looking, or by going to the toilet; but the manager would tell him not to take too much time.

Livingstone had discovered that there was a rivalry between the kitchen staff and the serving staff. The chef would refuse to give him an extra onion or tomato to make the lunch more palatable. He found the sambhar too sour and coconut in curry was something he was still not used to. He opted to eat when he got home at night, but that meant he had no food throughout the day.

When he informed the manager that he wanted to leave, he was told that he would have to wait till the end of the month to get his salary.

The night before his last day at Raaga Raiin Tree, Livingstone met with an accident. He was walking home at night when a bike hit him hard from behind and he fell. All he remembered was that he had taken two lightbulbs from the restaurant for his room and when he was hit, he was trying to save them. He woke up in a hospital.

When he opened his eyes, he remembered people asking him who he was. At the time he had no mobile or any identity papers; there was no way anyone could have found his identity.

When he tried to speak, the words did not come out coherently, although he could understand what they were asking him. With great difficulty, he gave them the only number he knew: the mobile of his father's sister's son in Ukhrul. Livingstone heard them say he had given them only nine digits.

Even though he had managed to give his cousin's mobile number, he knew that his cousin did not have Ramtawon's number. His cousin would have to walk to his parents' home, which was quite far. Besides he would not dare go out at that time of the night. It just was not safe. But his words made no sense to the doctors looking down at him. Even if they had understood, would they have understood the reality of Ukhrul?

Livingstone slowly recovered consciousness. He realized he was in a Catholic hospital. He was able to give the name of his employers, but by then the restaurant had closed for the night. He wanted to go home. Then he noticed that the man whose bike had hit him was still there. He apologized and offered to take him home in an auto. When they reached, he gave him Rs 3,000.

The next day Livingstone stayed at home and went to work the following day to collect his salary. They cut one day's wages and gave him the rest. But Livingstone was feeling lucky because he had 'earned' from his accident. He thought he deserved to rest for a few days before setting out to find another job.

It was then that a fellow Tangkhul called Ashang came to Ramtawon's house. He too was searching for a job and they decided to look for one together. Ashang had been studying in a Bible school and knew English fairly well.

* * *

The next day, Livingstone and Ashang went to Pizza Hut where they were told they needed delivery boys. They had heard that they could get good money. They met the general manager. Although there was usually an interview and a written test, on that day they were asked to read out from a newspaper which both of them could do without much difficulty.

The general manager asked a few questions and Ashang answered all of them, while Livingstone stood next to him smiling intelligently; sometimes nodding a yes or shaking his head as a no. Then came the inevitable question: Could they drive? Did they have a driving license? They both had licenses but Ashang did not know how to drive and Livingstone had once got onto a bike, but had never driven it for any distance. They did not get the delivery boys' jobs but were selected for training as waiters.

Livingstone enjoyed the training; it was held in a big building, not in the restaurant. There were around thirty other trainees, many of whom were from the Northeast. He was now employed in a really big company. On the first day, each of them had to introduce the person sitting next to them. Livingstone was worried because he did not know enough English to find out about his neighbour and introduce her or him. Luckily by the time his turn came, he found he had to introduce Ashang and he had no difficulty in doing so.

During the course of the training the manager, who was a young woman, asked whether anyone could sing and Livingstone volunteered. They had been told to be smart, so he walked right up to her and sang 'Girl of My Dreams'.[60] The first verse and chorus went like this:

You are the girl of my dreams, in my heart, I believe
You are the girl of my dreams, baby
Of my dreams

All alone, in my room, wishing that you were here
Without you, in my arms, I'm holding back all of the tears
Without you in my life, I'll never be satisfied

---

60. This is a 1998 song by the Moffats, a Canadian pop/rock band.

He could see that she seemed rather embarrassed as he sang, but since he did not understand the words he was not sure why. Fortunately, she liked his singing and she gave him a chocolate from a basket full of them. Every time a trainee excelled in anything through the seven days of training, he or she was presented a bar of chocolate from the basket. Several trainees had won many. This was the only one that Livingstone had won.

So far the trainees had not been to the restaurant. For the last bit of training they were taken to McDonald's and the whole group was asked to give their feedback in English.

Livingstone's knowledge of English was limited to the sixty sentences they had been told to learn by heart. These ranged from various phrases for greeting the customers to the selling of different kinds of pizza. The one word Livingstone did not understand was 'insist'. Livingstone practised the sixty sentences in front of the mirror and by the time the final exam came, he was ready.

The trainees were told that if they did not pass the examination they would be sent to the kitchen to do the washing. Each of them had to pretend to sell a pizza and were asked questions from the sixty stock possibilities.

Livingstone was not asked too many questions and he did well. He was told he had passed and should report for work the next day and his salary would be Rs 5,000 with Rs 1,000 bonus. The day after the training, the trainees were given their first taste of pizza. Livingstone did not like it; he could not finish even the smallest slice.

But before he could join for duty in the restaurant he got a break. The general manager asked him whether he would sing for the annual Pizza Hut event for employees. Ashang was to play the guitar to accompany him. He was given a month to practise.

It was the best month Livingstone had. He did not have

to report for work and he could sleep, watch television, eat at home and do a little practice. They had chosen two simple songs. Then the day arrived. The event was to be held in a five-star hotel.

The general manager dressed Livingstone appropriately. He sprayed his hair to make it spiky and then sprayed some colour. He wore jeans for a rugged look. Livingstone did not feel nervous; he was just enjoying the excitement of being in a five-star hotel. He had never seen the inside of one. He could not believe his eyes when he saw the varieties of alcohol on display. He confidently went on the stage with everyone shouting 'bring it on'.

Livingstone began by singing the Moffat song he had sung during his training. Then he sang a second song. This time it was a song by Enrique Iglesias[61] called 'Maybe':

Maybe you'll say you still want me
Maybe you'll say that you don't
Maybe we said it was over
Baby, I can't let you go

There was a thunderous applause when he finished and people walked up to him to shake his hand and talk to him. Livingstone received several invitations asking him to sing for various occasions. Ashang did most of the talking; Livingstone created the impression he was a quiet guy—a man of few words.

After this event, Livingstone joined Pizza Hut as a waiter. He wore the uniform and started serving pizzas. Although Ashang had taught him many things, it was Livingstone who got more badges. Sometimes the Pizza Hut people came disguised as customers to check the way they handled clients;

---

61. Enrique Miguel Iglesias Preysler is known as the King of Latin pop and has acted in several films. 'Maybe' was first sung by him in 2001.

even if he made mistakes they did not report him; they warned him quietly. This was because they recognized him as the singer who had entertained them at the annual event.

After a week Livingstone started taking orders independently. He also received individual tips, and on an average earned up to Rs 3,000 in tips. In effect he was earning more than Rs 8,000. The company opened a bank account for him—his very first. Livingstone did not try to save money for himself, he sent it all back to his parents. The money was sent through a Tangkhul private courier service that took a 10 per cent commission.

The work in Pizza Hut was not easy. The waiters worked nine hours a day with a half an hour break for lunch. They were not given lunch, so they generally did not eat. They would just sit in the basement or in the garden in front of the restaurant.

The other employees would ask where he came from: 'What is your native place?' When he said he was from Manipur, they would ask, 'What currency do you use in your country? Show us.' He felt anger at not being accepted as an Indian, but it did not occur to him that he himself had always asserted that Nagas were different.

Livingstone could not bear the smell of the cooking oil because it made him feel nauseated. Like most Tangkhuls, he was used to boiled food. Although they may eat pork fat, the meat was boiled with herbs and chillies, not cooked in oil. The polluted air of Bengaluru was affecting him too, since he was used to the cool, crisp and clean Ukhrul air. On top of that, he had to stand for long hours, without eating.

He soon developed acidity and started getting stomach cramps. But he could not take time off and he did not want to go to the doctor. Sometimes he would just sit behind the counter and writhe in pain while others covered for him.

Livingstone did not want to continue at Pizza Hut. He had heard accounts of Goa from Ayo. He wanted to see the sea. He had seen a map and found that on one side of Goa there was only water—no land at all till you reached Africa. Ayo told him that in Goa he would be more relaxed and could even talk to foreign customers. And he would taste all kinds of fish in the shacks on the beach.

Ramtawon warned Livingstone about Ayo and his addiction to alcohol. But Goa was beckoning and Livingstone told Ayo to go ahead and book their tickets to Panjim on a Karnataka State Transport bus.

Chapter Six

My Sister Is Dead

24 October 2009. That is one date Atim will never forget all her life.

She had returned to work at Q'BA after her Goa trip. On that afternoon, the staff had had their tea and she had gone back to the lounge downstairs. There were a few guests at the bar. Suddenly, her mobile rang. She answered. It was Yaokhalek. His voice was shaking. He just said, 'Come home fast' and put the phone down. He was living in Vasant Kunj Extension with a group of Tangkhul boys engaged in making special black pots.

Atim wondered what could possibly have happened. Once again her mobile rang. 'Something has happened to Ramchanphy. She is not feeling well.'

Ramchanphy was their younger sister. She had just turned nineteen. She had come to Delhi barely a month ago and was perfectly well when Atim had left in the morning. Yaokhalek must have come to meet Ramchanphy. The phone rang once more. It was Yaokhalek again. He said, 'The gas cylinder has exploded.'

Atim told the manager she had to go home. He asked what had happened and she replied, 'My sister has died.'

Atim had no money in her purse. She had left Rs 500 with Ramchanphy. She had expected to be dropped home after work, but now she needed to take an auto. Srilata, a co-worker, gave her some money and she quickly got into an auto. Yaokhalek phoned again and she told him she was in an auto on her way home. Atim asked whether there was anyone around to help him. He said Ester and her mother had gone to Sarojini Nagar, but there was a man listening to music standing just outside the room.

Atim phoned Yaronsho and asked him to be with Yaokhalek. She had kept in touch with him ever since they had met at Mayori's. Atim's mobile rang again. This time it was Ramchanphy's boyfriend calling from Ukhrul to say that she was not answering his calls. Atim blurted out, 'She is dead.' Then she burst into tears.

By now Atim was howling out loud. When the auto stopped at the traffic lights she was aware that people were staring, but she was beyond caring. She was stuck in the evening traffic. She called her friend Rose who assured her that she would go to Atim's flat immediately. It took fifty minutes for Atim to reach Munirka and climb up to her room. By then, many Tangkhuls had already arrived. They were sitting in her room.

Atim looked for the Rs 500 note she had left under her pillow. She also tried to find the mobile phone she had given Ramchanphy, but both were missing. Atim could not make herself go into the kitchen where she knew her sister's body would be lying.

Yaronsho called the police and they came and took the body away. There were perhaps five hundred Tangkhuls gathered together. They were singing hymns and keeping vigil.

Atim went into Ester's room next door and lay down. Ramchanphy had arrived in September full of excitement. Atim had picked her up from the airport. The moment they reached the flat, Atim had asked her sister what she had brought from home. Then the two sisters had taken out the goodies from Ramchanphy's bag: there was thangching or lotus fruit, sakao or dried beef with smoked chilli powder, fresh umrok, the hottest chillies in the world, and, of course, the delectable ngari or fermented fish without which a chutney did not have the kick; and lots of snails.

Atim felt a pang of guilt. She had not been able to take her younger sister sightseeing. Work had kept her busy and she returned late every night. Atim had promised to take her out on her next day off.

Ramchanphy was the most beautiful of the four sisters and many boys were interested in her. Atim's mother had been complaining to Atim that almost every evening young men dropped in and Ramchanphy and her sister Chonsomi would make cups of black tea; this was the traditional courting or the meisum kapam. Atim could imagine the singing and the light-hearted banter and mild flirtation. Later, when the man and woman were more certain of their feelings, they could go out alone together. Ramchanphy had already decided on the man, but her mother did not approve of him and so she had encouraged her daughter to visit Delhi.

The previous night Atim and Ramchanphy had lain side-by-side and chatted the whole night. It was mostly Ramchanphy telling her elder sister stories. Atim felt she could not share her experiences because her sister would not understand the world she lived in, but she was very pleased when Ramchanphy told her that ever since Atim had started sending money they did not have to go begging for rice anymore.

* * *

Ramchanphy had spent some time in Nagaland and she had many anecdotes to share. She had gone there with a woman who was a distant relative and who was married to a man from the Pochury Naga tribe; earlier they had lived in Greenland, the locality where Atim's family was living. When the couple shifted to Kohima they took Ramchanphy with them to help with the housework. After living in Kohima for some time the family had moved to a Pochury village in Phek District.

Ramchanphy told Atim that the family had pork to eat for lunch and dinner every single day! And their barn was full of smoked pork. She used to go to the paddy field and there she saw a lot of fruit trees growing, especially bananas. The Pochury man's mother was very kind to Ramchanphy and had presented her with a chamthei, a valuable bead used in the kongsang, the traditional Tangkhul necklace. While there, she had also picked up the Pochury language.

Then Ramchanphy had regaled Atim with ghost stories. One was about parents who came to pick up their daughter from school after it had closed for the vacations. The girl was in the toilet and the chowkidar had locked it from the outside. The parents went away, thinking their daughter had left without them. When the school reopened, they found her body in the toilet; she haunts the school.

Atim smiled through her tears. She could hear Ramchanphy's voice. How they had laughed together over silly jokes and shared life experiences. Atim had come away to Delhi and so had missed seeing her sister grow up; Ramchanphy was much closer to Chonsomi, but here in Delhi they had become closer.

Atim remembered how Ramchanphy had cooked the peacock meat Yaokhalek's friends had brought for the younger sister. Ever since she had come to Delhi, Ramchanphy would cook for Atim. It had been so nice to come home every evening to a warm meal and a sister to chat with instead of an empty room. Again Atim felt a pang of guilt. She had not taken a single photo of Ramchanphy in Delhi.

* * *

In the morning, Atim forced herself to go to the kitchen; she saw the broken tube and two boiled eggs and rice. She must have been cooking when the gas cylinder burst. She had taken out the old rice and must have been about to cook it for Atim. The tears just flowed down her cheeks.

Yaokhalek took her hand and they went to Safdarjung Hospital. Ramchanphy's body had been taken there and the family members were requested to remove her clothes so that a post mortem could be conducted. Atim saw how badly her sister's stomach had been burnt, and her tongue and neck and hair were also burnt. What a terrible death. Atim did not know what was happening around her; all her thoughts were concentrated on her sister. The burnt clothes were left at the hospital; later the lawyer asked her why she had not kept them. She said no one had bothered to tell her that they were evidence. She had not even suspected that her sister had been murdered.

The doctor called Atim into his room. The police were also there. He was a Meitei and he asked Atim whether she suspected anyone: who could have murdered your sister? Atim could not believe her ears. Murder? Who would want to kill her? She had been in Delhi for barely a month and she did not know anyone.

The doctor told her that his examination of her sister's body showed that the burn marks were not severe enough to have caused her death. It seemed the murderer had attempted to cover the evidence of strangulation by trying to make it look like an accident in the kitchen. The doctor looked at Atim who just stood still like a statue. 'Your sister was strangled to death; not burnt. Is there anyone you suspect? Think.'

Then she remembered the man who had shifted into the room next to theirs. The room had been occupied for a long time by two Nepali women whom she suspected were prostitutes, because different men visited them. They had moved out and a man called Pushpam had moved in just twenty or twenty-five days earlier.

Atim remembered how the man had a habit of staring at the women. On one occasion, Ester had shouted at him. And Ramchanphy had told Atim she was scared of him; one day he had knocked on the door when she was alone. Atim told her to remain inside the room with the door locked. But then their kitchen was on the opposite side of the small corridor.

But could a man who had just committed a murder just stand around listening to music as Yaokhalek had seen him do?

On the evening of the murder, the Vasant Vihar police station had asked Yaokhalek to give his statement. He was in no state to write so Florence, a Tangkhul woman who stayed in the building next door, had volunteered to take it down for him. It was a short and simple statement:

> 'My younger sister Ramchanphy came to Delhi in the month
> of September 2009. I found her dead body in the kitchen
> around 6 p.m. in the evening. At first I enter our room and
> kept my Bag and went inside the kitchen and I saw my sister
> lying on the ground and our gas was leaking. It was smelling
> and light smoke was found. And we don't suspect anyone at
> the moment. And we don't suspect any fault play in the death
> of Ramchanphy.' [sic]
>
> The statement was written by Florence Awunshi as told by
> Yaokhalek on 24 October 2009.

The next day the police phoned Atim to ask whether she would
like to give her statement. Suddenly, Atim's grief turned into
anger. Atim and Yaokhalek went to the Vasant Vihar police
station. This time Atim gave her statement in her writing that
they suspected Pushpam of murdering their sister. He was
the only person present on the floor. She said that on the day
before, her brother and she were in no state of mind to think
matters over carefully.

It was after that the police went to Munirka and arrested
Pushpam Kumar Sinha. He turned out to be a research scholar
from Bihar doing his PhD at Delhi's prestigious IIT. The police
seized his laptop and other items. They also photographed
the slogans written on the wall of his room expressing his
frustration at not finding a woman to marry.

In the evening, there was a condolence service at the
Methodist Church. After the service, the Nagas, mostly
Tangkhuls, congregated at the police station. The police had
brought Pushpam to the station. The anger was palpable. In
front of the entire group, without any pressure from the police,
Pushpam said he had strangled Ramchanphy. Yaokhalek's anger
boiled over and he rushed at the man. The other Tangkhuls
began asking each other whether they should finish the man off

there and then. Sebastian overheard them and restrained them. They were at the police station till ten that night.

*　*　*

Atim and Yaokhalek were worried about the expenses. They had paid Rs 4,000 for the embalming of Ramchanphy's body. And then they had contacted the Funeral and Ambulance Services at Humayunpur. An ordinary polished coffin cost Rs 5,000; the packing another Rs 3,000 and the ambulance charges to the airport were Rs 1,000. The total bill was already Rs 13,000. In addition, they needed to pay the cargo charges for Ramchanphy's coffin and buy their own airline tickets.

Atim could not remember any more how the money had come. But looking through her papers she saw that the Tangkhul Katamnao Long, Delhi, or the Delhi branch of the Tangkhul Students Union, had quickly collected Rs 9,060; the Hunphun[62] Society, Delhi, had collected Rs 2,000 and the Tangkhul Church another Rs 2,000. Sebastian and his cousin Linda paid for the air tickets. Many Tangkhuls made contributions of Rs 100, Rs 500 and some gave Rs 1,000. Someone had written it all down and looking back, Atim's heart filled with gratitude for her community which had been there to support her.

At the time, Atim was more worried about how she would inform her parents, but someone had already let them know. Her mother phoned and she was very calm. She told her that according to Tangkhul custom the body must be cleaned, and she instructed her on how to wash Ramchanphy. Atim said she could not do that because the body was in the hospital and had been embalmed. Then her mother said to at least wipe her with a wet cloth, and Atim managed to do so to the extent she was able.

Yaronsho dropped the brother and sister at the airport. At

---

62. The Tangkhuls call Ukhrul Hunphun.

the airport in Imphal many relatives had come from Ukhrul; Atim saw Ramchanphy's boyfriend looking grief-stricken. She did not know who had arranged for vehicles to take the body home. A senior government servant had arranged for lunch for everyone. There was a bandh call,[63] so special permission had to be taken. The funeral procession, led by the vehicle carrying the coffin with a black flag fluttering on top, slowly made its way up the hills to Ukhrul. At Ramva, the army stopped the convoy and insisted on checking the coffin.

Atim had expected her mother to be as calm as she had been on the phone. But she hugged Atim, and then she fainted. From the corner of her eye, Atim saw Lemyaola shooting the proceedings with her video camera. Hundreds of people had turned up; there was genuine shock, but some had come out of curiosity. The family had to make tea for the people who sat all night singing and keeping vigil. By the morning at least a hundred people had gathered and Atim arranged for tea and samosas for all of them. When the condolence service began many more people turned up.

Atim and Yaokhalek stayed for fifteen days and then returned to Delhi. Huimila had promised to find them alternative accommodation, but she had not kept her word. Atim was really angry. She was forced to go back to A-60 Munirka, the scene of her sister's murder, and she had to pay the landlord two months' rent. It hurt Atim deeply that Huimila had let her down at a time like this. Atim shifted to Rose's place and Yaokhalek went back to Vasant Kunj Extension.

Atim had to start looking for a place to stay. She cursed

---

63. The bandh call was for one day in support of the demand for 3 per cent reservations for government jobs for tribals with disabilities. From January 2009 to October 2009, Manipur witnessed seventy-nine bandhs and ten highway blockades. In the previous year there were nineteen statewide bandhs apart from district bandhs, including eight in the hill districts. In 2005–06 there were 145 bandhs.

herself for not moving out of Munirka earlier. If she had, then perhaps Ramchanphy would still be alive. Atim had noticed that the electricity bill had been too high and the water supply in the shared bathroom was always in short supply. As a matter of fact, one day she and Ramchanphy had gone to look for a room. They had found one, but there were so many spiderwebs that it looked like a haunted house; then there was another one on the fourth floor up steep steps. Atim could not help thinking that it would have been wiser to have taken that room.

Finally, Atim found a room in Sunlight Colony in Ashram. Her niece, Yarimayo, was staying nearby. She had done a course on designing and was working in a boutique in Shahpur Jat. Yaronsho helped Atim vacate the Munirka room, while Yaokhalek paid the rent to the landlord.

The new room was located deep inside the colony. Atim had to walk through very narrow alleyways to get there; and at night the cab dropping her home could not go up to the house. She did not feel very comfortable walking back in the dark, even though many of the tenants were Tangkhuls. After Ramchanphy's murder it had become even more difficult for Atim to return to an empty room at night.

She often found herself looking at the file with the papers relating to Ramchanphy (see Appendix). Every time she saw the photo of Pushpam in the newspapers, she felt rage. Atim had preserved the invoice from the ambulance showing her sister's final journey back home. This was not how it should have been.

* * *

On the night of 24 January 2010, when Atim returned from Q'BA she found her mother well settled in her room in Ashram. She knew Yaokhalek had picked her up in the morning, but it was still a surprise to see her here in Delhi. Her mother had tidied up the room and had cooked smoked pork and rice for her daughter. It was so wonderful to have dinner together, but both mother and daughter were too tired to chat that night and they went to sleep right after eating.

Early next morning Atim woke up to see her mother trying to quietly open the door. She asked her what she was up to and her mother said, '*Kaphung kapha*', which literally meant 'look for the mountains'. The mother thought if she climbed to the roof she would get a view of the hills and mountains. Atim told her there were no mountains and hills in Delhi, only tall buildings. However, her mother decided that she had to see the view in any case.

Shimtharla thought Atim's room was lovely; at least her daughter had an entire room to herself, and a small kitchen and bathroom. She even had a tiny storeroom. In Ukhrul, the entire family had to squeeze into a room slightly larger than the one Atim stayed in by herself. But she missed the fact she could not walk out and breathe fresh mountain air and look at the distant hills under a pure blue sky.

Atim took her mother to the kitchen window. She opened it and called out. Across the narrow alley another window opened and out popped a Tangkhul face. Her mother's face lit up with happiness. The rooms were so close that the girls could step into each other's homes through the window. Atim introduced her mother to the two sisters: Horyaopam who was doing a course in textile designing, and Wonyophi, her younger sister who was studying. Then she introduced her mother to Vareishang, the young man, and Thanyo, his sister, who lived next to them. They all greeted Shimtharla as 'aunty' and welcomed her to Delhi. And so, when Atim was away at work, her mother could call out to these young people and have a chat.

In the evening, Atim took her mother to meet Yarimayo who was her father's granddaughter, like Lemyaola and Mayori. Her mother liked their accommodation better, because it had an open terrace where she could sit and watch people. In contrast, Atim's room was stuffy.

At that time Yarimayo's sister Ringamphi was not working and she was happy to look after Atim's mother. In the evenings, she and Shimtharla would go for long walks; both enjoyed the hustle and bustle of the local markets. They would walk to the place where fresh fish was sold. One day they walked along the railway tracks of Nizamuddin and Shimtharla expressed her horror at seeing the dogs. She declared she would never eat a Delhi dog; they looked so dirty, as if they had eaten dead bodies.

Yet it was a Delhi dog that helped her when she got lost in Ashram. One day Shimtharla wanted to buy some vegetables so Atim took her to a nearby shop, just a lane away from her room, before she went off for work. After buying the vegetables, Shimtharla tried to find her way home but she got so confused that she just could not locate the right turn. She went to a shop where she had seen Atim buying things and tried to ask for directions by using gestures. She did not know any English or Hindi. No one tried to help her and some shooed her away as if she were a madwoman. Finally, after almost four hours, when she had given up and sat down, she saw a dog she had seen wandering around in the same lane where Atim's room was located. She followed the dog and it led her straight to Atim's house.

Inside the room her son was lying down, sound asleep. Yaokhalek had not even noticed that his mother had been away for so long. She was really angry with her son, but by the time Atim returned they all had a good laugh.

* * *

Lemyaola came to visit Atim's mother; she took her to North Delhi by metro. It was a hair-raising experience getting her to ride the escalator. She jumped off and announced that she would never take those moving stairs again.

One day Atim took her mother to the Central Park in Connaught Place and pointed out Q'BA, the restaurant where she worked. Then she took her to Palika Bazaar where her mother chose a sparkling blue kurta that her daughter bought for her. When they returned home, Atim made her mother wear her jeans and her new sparkling blue kurta; she applied make-up on her mother's face and did up her hair. Shimtharla was transformed into a young woman again.

The highlight of Shimtharla's stay in Delhi was a visit to the Ambience Shopping Mall, just as it had been for Atim when she had gone with Aunty Nandita on Mayori's birthday. The mother and daughter went up to the Food Court and had McDonald's burgers, French fries and Coca-Cola. Her mother said, 'It is just like being in heaven.'

On another occasion, Atim took her mother to the Lotus Temple and later to the Qutub Minar. Yaokhalek had also accompanied them and this time they clicked many photographs with her new digital camera.

Shimtharla wanted to visit Nandita and Sebastian. She saw their two-bedroom DDA flat and felt it was a luxurious palace; she said it was 'kakashung' (perfect). They had dinner and later Sebastian drove them to India Gate where they all had ice cream. He then dropped them back at Ashram. She was surprised when Sebastian gave her Rs 5,000. She later asked Atim: 'Why did they want to help us?'

The murder trial had started and Atim had to go to court. Shimtharla insisted that she wanted to go as well. She said, '*Iwui naongalava li kashaipa*,' which translates as I want to see the man who devoured my child. Atim had wanted to spare her the trauma.

Atim had to yield to her mother's demand and took her to court. And there the mother set eyes on the man she believed had murdered her child. She lunged at him and Atim had to control her. She said she would throw her sarong at him, '*Iwui Kashan railaga Kathanror ra*.' It is the biggest insult to a Tangkhul man.

Atim hoped the judge had seen her mother. He should understand what it feels like to lose a nineteen-year old daughter to senseless violence.

Atim's mother stayed from January till May 2010. She said she wanted to stay forever, but her husband needed her and the younger children were missing her. Besides, it was getting hot. This time Atim booked two tickets, for her mother and herself. She wanted to see Ukhrul. Touch base. She could not bear to be alone in Delhi. In Ukhrul, this was the time the Shirui Lily bloomed and she had asked some friends to take her to see it. The climb to the peak was exhilarating, and she clicked a photo of the lily to remind her of home. Atim had to return to Delhi because she had to keep earning as well as follow the murder trial in court.

*   *   *

I had met Atim and Yaokhalek soon after they returned to Delhi after their sister's burial. They had no idea how a criminal trial was conducted. In Tangkhul customary law, the parents of the guilty person would have offered to pay compensation. Normally the family accepted it and the matter would be settled. Except that such senseless murders were unheard of in Ukhrul.

The two had sat close together, their eyes still filled with the horror of what they had witnessed. My heart went out to them. I knew they were about to discover how heartless the judicial system was.

Atim had asked, 'What should we do, Aunty?'

There was something about Atim's demeanour that appealed to me. She was serious, responsible and utterly sincere. And that was why I wanted to tell her the truth, the brutal truth about the criminal justice system. I told her she would have to make endless rounds of the court, meet the lawyers and the proceedings would be slow and painful.

'But he confessed in front of everyone at the police station that he had murdered my sister.'

It was true that the police did record the confessional statement of Pushpam Sinha. The investigating officer's report had said:

> 'Confessional statement of the accused was recorded, in which he stated that Ms Ramchanphy was not responding to his feelings and on 24/10/2009 when she was alone and was cooking something in the kitchen on gas stove he wanted to talk to her but she refused and started raising an alarm. He strangulated her with his hands and subsequently put upper portion of her body over the gas flame and kept there for sometime. Thereafter he threw the body on the kitchen floor and came out. In the meantime the brother of the deceased reached there and the police was called later on.' [sic]

I did not know how to explain why confessions to the police were not admissible under Indian law.[64]

I helped to get a Special Public Prosecutor appointed for the case. Although the lawyer was someone I knew, he lost interest because the government did not clear his bills and the publicity around the case was over.

The Naga students who used to attend the trial also stopped coming to court. In the beginning as many as twenty-five students would be there, but now no one came. Atim said she had stopped informing them and no one had bothered to ask how the trial was going. She said it was very expensive for them to travel from Delhi University to Patiala House; she had to offer to pay their auto fares. Then she would have to give them a cold drink and all the expenses added up to quite a bit.

Atim attended court regularly, even if she did not always follow the proceedings. Her dream of working abroad had been put on hold. She did not bother to apply for a passport.

---

64. Such statements are admissible in some other countries, but in India such confessions are usually extracted after torture, so they are presumed to be unreliable evidence under the Indian Evidence Act.

She said she had to follow up on her sister's case even though it was a drain on her finances. Her parents could not understand how painful it was for her.

She asked, 'How long will the trial take?'

I told her that if Pushpam was convicted, he could appeal to the High Court and then all the way to the Supreme Court. If he was acquitted, she could appeal. It could go on and on and on. I advised her to follow up till the end of the trial in the Sessions Court.

I asked Atim to shift into my place if she felt more secure doing that. She took up the offer and in July 2012 came to stay with us; soon Yaokhalek moved into our home in Delhi as well. They felt safer, especially after they heard that Pushpam had been granted bail by the court. It is now 2016, seven years after the murder, and the court has still to give its verdict. The man accused of the crime roams free. This would not happen if he were being tried in accordance with Tangkhul customary law.

Chapter Seven

My Songs Sacrificed to the Winds

Atim wanted to tell her story, but her brother Yaokhalek was very hesitant. It took me a long time to persuade him to tell his story and to allow me to write about his struggles in Delhi. His hesitation was primarily because his story is inextricably linked to the stories of many others who did not want their names revealed as they were working in illegal call centres involved in numerous scams.[65]

Like Yaokhalek, most of these the young men had dropped out of school. For many, the lessons in school did not offer the promise of a bright future. They wanted to start earning as soon as possible, partly to support their families, but also to taste the freedom that comes with having money. They all came to Delhi with the dream of getting rich quickly.

One of Yaokhalek's friends, Worthing Shimray from Chinjaroi village, told me his story. He had passed twelfth standard from Pettigrew College in Ukhrul. His father worked as a driver for a local NGO in Ukhrul and Worthing sometimes

---

65. A call centre is a location or place where customers' telephones are answered by trained customer care agents (CCA) using sophisticated computer software applications. Call centres are also officially called ITES-BPOs or Information technology-enabled services-business processing outsourcing. In 2000, 500 foreign companies outsourced work to about sixty call centres in India; by the end of 2003, India had 800 call centres (*Economic Times*, June 19, 2001). Illegal call centres are set up to steal databases and use them to make false calls to the USA and other Western countries, to cheat people, often those from vulnerable sections of society, like the aged, refugees etc. They pretend to offer a service and illegally divert the money to the call centre.

earned a little by painting people's houses. He did not go for further studies because he had been contacted by agents who promised to send him and six others to Australia for a job involving fruit packing. This was in 2011.

Worthing said there were three agents: Shangamla Khansu who was from his village—she was married to an Indian, a man called Surjit who was a Meitei; and a Tangkhul man whose name he did not recall or perhaps did not want to tell me.

The agents took Rs 50,000 each from a group of ten men: seven were Tangkhul, two were from the Kom tribe and one was a Maram Naga. After they had paid the money, they were told they had to go to Delhi for medical checkups and that they would have to pay for their own travel. Surjit accompanied the ten men to Delhi where they were taken to a clinic near Ashram. They were not made to pay for the medical checkup. Worthing could not remember the name of the clinic.

After the medical checkup, they returned to Ukhrul. After a few months, they were all brought back to Delhi with the assurance that they would be given some training in food packaging. This time they found themselves in Gurgaon and were told to do construction work. They all refused, since it had nothing to do with fruit packaging. The three non-Tangkhuls returned to Manipur, but the seven Tangkhuls stayed on in Delh for another four to five months. Then Surjit informed them that another agent had run off with their money. Except for Worthing, the other men returned to Manipur, determined to get their money back. The Tangkhuls tried to phone Shangamla but she did not answer the calls. They tried to reach her through her parents, who lived in Imphal, but could not.

Then they contacted the Tangkhul Katamnao Sak Long or the Tangkhul Students Union and asked them to pursue the case. Worthing did not know what the TKS did, but he heard that some people even contacted the underground and asked for their help.

Worthing had been staying in Surjit's house at Mahipalpur in Delhi, but then Surjit told him to move out and found him another room. Worthing had no money for the rent and it was Surjit who first offered him a job at a call centre. Worthing knew many people who worked in call centres, but had no idea what they were about or what the work involved.

He moved into his cousin Ngaransing's place, which was also in Mahipalpur. The cousin was working at a call centre and he took Worthing for the interview. Worthing was thrilled when he was selected and offered a monthly salary of Rs 7,500; he was also promised an extra Rs 1,000 if he achieved the target. The manager even promised to give him a bonus if he attended regularly.

Worthing walked to the call centre; he was delighted because he thought he was going to be working for a US company called Payday Loan and would be talking to Americans in America.[66] He was told he would have to take on an American name like Bill, Cody or Kevin, and learn to talk with an American accent. It all sounded really exciting.

Worthing called himself Kevin and learnt to speak to Americans with an American accent, which he mimicked from the action movies he watched on television. It was only much later that he discovered it was an illegal call centre which was involved in cheating Americans. At first, he felt bad for the

---

66. Kiran Mirchandani has documented how Indian call centre workers live and work in India, but are required to organize their lives in terms of American times, celebrations and communication styles. Workers are expected to speak with American accents, take on American names, and adopt American holidays and greetings. In the West, these jobs are regarded as repetitive and mindless but among the Indian call centre workers, especially from the Northeast, it is looked upon as a privileged occupation. They would be shocked to learn that call centres are called new-age sweatshops and captive units of cyber coolies subject to depersonalized bullying.

people who were being deceived, but he also thought the Americans were stupid to fall for the scam calls.

* * *

I asked Worthing whether he knew of any agents in Ukhrul who were involved in trafficking young men or women to Goa, where I lived. He said he did not. Yaokhalek, who was sitting there, asked why I wanted to know. I told him of the time when Sebastian and I along with members of the Northeast Association of Goa were involved in an operation to rescue fourteen men who had been trafficked from Nagaland. They were all between the ages of seventeen and twenty-four.

It all began on 20 August 2012 with one Lanumeren Jamir sending an e-mail to the President of the Northeast Association, Goa, saying that his brother Ponsunep was being held by a mining company against his will. He alleged that his brother was being 'forced to work in mines under inhuman conditions'.

Ponsunep Jamir and thirteen other young men, accompanied by an agent, had got off at the Tivim railway station on 5 August 2012. They were put into a vehicle and they found themselves being driven on a slushy road which led deep into a forest.

They were made to wear the uniforms of the Nair Security Services and guard the equipment of the illegal mines. There was no toilet or kitchen, and they found themselves sharing a portacabin with men from distant parts of India, including Assam, Bihar and Orissa.

The men were from different Naga tribes and had been contacted by an agent of Nair Security Services who had promised good salaries and work in five-star hotels on the beaches of Goa. Each of them had dreamt of a new life with good food, their own accommodation and money to send back home, perhaps even to spend on a cold beer or two.

They were all shocked to find themselves living in a forest without access to the outside world. They had panicked and managed to send a SMS message to Lanumeren before their mobiles conked out because there was no place to charge them.

I told Worthing and Yaokhalek in detail about how we had rescued the men on August 20th of the same year. Eleven of the boys had managed to escape and we found them in Ponda, but two had been admitted into hospital and one of them had stayed behind in the mine. He wanted to wait till the end of the month so he could get his salary. When I went with the police to the site of the mine I found him; he said two boys from Assam wanted to leave as well. So we had rescued sixteen of them.

Some of the young men turned out to be drug addicts; we had sent them back home by train. The police managed to force the Nair Security Services to shell out money for their train tickets and to return their identity cards. The two from Assam and the youngest man, an Ao Naga, insisted on remaining, so Sebastian and I took them home.

We found them jobs with another security service. They were paid Rs 5,000 with accommodation and food; their work was to salute and wish guests at a five star hotel. But they did not get even one day in the week off. We learnt later that the three had left their jobs soon after and the Naga boy had taken to alcohol.

I was also disappointed because no case had been registered against the agents—one was from Kerala and the other was a Naga— although we had actually got their names and mobile numbers and the Goa police was keen to prosecute them. They told the Naga boys to file a FIR, but the boys refused and said they would do so once they reached home. They never did.

Yaokhalek and his friend murmured something to the effect that it would have been of no use to file a case against the agents. Perhaps they were right. Their top priority was to get jobs, not to prosecute criminals.

* * *

When Yaokhalek moved into my flat he had no job. He spent the entire day and much of the night either sleeping or watching violent Korean movies[67] on the large-screen TV they had bought.

The murder of his sister had affected him deeply and he was probably in depression. Only on Sundays did he go out of the house to the Tangkhul fellowship. There he got a chance to sing and hear music.

Atim asked whether there was a way of getting him a job that involved using his musical talents. She remembered how he loved music even as a small child. She said that when she was in fifth standard, she got some money and with it she bought a Walkman for Rs 250 and two cassettes. One cassette was called 'Ningshat' and it had songs by a Tangkhul singer from

---

67. Duncan McDuie-Ra observes in his study that Korean popular culture is phenomenally popular in the Northeast and among Northeast migrants. He writes, 'the so-called "Korean Wave" refers to the production and export of Korean culture—mostly film, television, and pop music…The Korean Wave is a crucial element of the cosmopolitan identity of Northeasterners…In the early 2000s, it was still uncommon to see Korean films for sale in the markets of the Northeast. In the second half of the 2000s, Korean popular culture had taken such a hold in the Northeast that fan clubs were established in Kohima and Imphal…Young people throughout the region started sporting Korean hairstyles, makeup, and fashion.

'At the Hornbill Festival, the flagship festival in Nagaland that attracts tourists from all over the world, there is a Korean Pavilion where Korean bands perform and where other exhibitions of Korean culture take place, including a Korea-Naga wrestling match in 2010.

'The rejection of mainstream film and television is not just aesthetic but bound up in questions of identity…The moral certainty of Korean movies was compared to the "immorality" of Bollywood films. Some respondents mentioned that as Koreans are Christians, they felt a bond with the characters and the problems they face in life.' See Duncan McDuie-Ra (2012) p. 170.

Shirui called Diana; the other had the songs from a Hindi film, *Kabhi Khushi, Kabhi Gam*. The brother and sister would sit side-by-side doing potty and listening to the music with one earphone each. They did not understand the Hindi words, but could hum the tunes. It was one of her most endearing memories.

* * *

Atim said Yaokhalek was like Tarzan in the jungle. He dropped out of school and would go off into the jungles to hunt for crabs. He brought them home and gave them to his mother who sold them in the market. That was how they could buy Colgate toothpaste or soap. Sometimes his friends would also go with him.

Once, Yaokhalek was away for two days and he brought back a pangolin, or saaham as they call it in Tangkhul. The shell is expensive and it fetched Rs 500; they cooked the meat and shared it with their father's friend who was very sick. Atim's mother cooked it in the traditional way by boiling the meat with salt and smoked chilli powder.

Yaokhalek also caught rats and Atim remembered him giving them to Mayori to cook for her father who was very ill. It is believed that soup made from wild animals is good for the sick. Yaokhalek also caught waterfowl, and sometimes when Atim went with him they would eat a pink fruit that was very sweet. They called it chinithei (sweet fruit). It tasted like custard apples.

One day, Yaokhalek and Atim, along with two friends, went into Somi's orchard and stole his peaches. While they were eating, the owner came and caught them. Yaokhalek had run off and hidden himself. But when Somi called out, 'Yaokhalek,' her brother appeared looking sheepish. The owner beat up the other two, but Yaokhalek got away with a reprimand.

Atim remembered the times they had spent in their maternal grandparents' home in Kalhang. She remembered their grandfather sitting by the fire with a bamboo mug of rice beer made by their grandmother. Atim and Yaokhalek loved to go to Kalhang during the Luira Phanit or seed-sowing festival. In Kalhang village they celebrated it on 27 January; Ukhrul celebrated it in February. There, it had become more of an official festival and had lost its traditional flavour.

On Luira Phanit, they would wake up early in the morning to the wailing of the pigs and smoke coming out of homes as the pork was being cooked. Everyone knew that the Raphei (northern) Tangkhuls were the best at cooking pork. Yaokhalek would run out with the other boys to collect the gall bladder. They would spend hours cleaning it with a bamboo stick, then washing it and rubbing salt on it. When it was ready, they would blow into it and it would swell up into the size of a football. Then the boys would play football and it would be impossible to call them away.

It was mandatory for the youth to wear their traditional clothes for the festival and Atim and Yaokhalek too wore their traditional Tangkhul dress; if any youth was caught without it they were fined. Atim wore a kashan[68] and the traditional necklace called kongsang and the boys wore a mayong pasi, a headdress made with bamboo dyed red. The sister and brother took part in the singing, dancing and traditional games. The boys got to compete in climbing a tall bamboo pole that had been rubbed with lard, making it slippery. The reward that year was a kettle tied right on top!

A year after Atim left for Delhi, Yaokhalek had accompanied his uncle to Burma. It had taken them two days of hard

---

68. A kashan is like a sarong. There are different kinds of kashans and some have been named after women who were raped or killed by the Indian security forces such as the Luingamla Kashan. Luingamla (1968–86) was shot by Border Security Forces in 1986. Her friend Zamthingla Ruivah designed a kashan in her memory. Luingamla was from the same village as Mayori's mother.

trekking through the jungles to reach a Tangkhul village across the international border. They had bought a piglet from a village for Rs 1,000, taken it back and sold it for Rs 3,000.

* * *

In Delhi, the first job Yaokhalek found had allowed him to continue living a life like he did in Ukhrul. He started working in March 2009 with friends living in Vasant Kunj Extension where they were making the famous black pots originally from Longpi. The pots had become very popular with sophisticated Delhiwalas.

The pots are made of dark grey rock which is powdered and mixed with a special kind of clay. In the late 1980s, my husband was a part of a project to introduce the potter's wheel to Longpi potters. He had taken two of the best award-winning potters, including Machihan Sasa, to a village in Himachal Pradesh where a NGO had hosted them.[69] They found that the potter's wheel could not help them, because the Longpi pots are made with clay which is too heavy to yield to the wheel. Machihan's talents were recognized and he was given several national awards.

Machihan's sister's daughter was Atim's friend. Her name was Chandi, but she preferred to be called Elvina; she had accompanied Atim on her first interview in Q'BA when Atim was selected and Elvina came back disappointed. Later, Atim recommended her, and the two worked together at the restaurant. Elvina's brother, Sochihan Luiram, had quite a name as a singer.

Yaokhalek had seen Elvina's grandfather make pots in Joyland, a village near Longpi and Kalhang. It was a pretty village with orange and lemon trees. Yaokhalek had learnt a

---

69. Sebastian was working with a project financed by the Ministry of Science and Technology and the Delhi Science Forum. They had a pottery project in Himachal Pradesh and it was there that Sebastian took the Tangkhul potters.

little about the pottery-making process and knew how to pick
up a pot with sticks when it was red-hot after the firing and
rub it with special leaves which gave it the famous black sheen.
Now Machihan's son, Mathew, along with other friends were
bringing the raw material to Delhi and fashioning the pots at
the back of their flat in Vasant Kunj Extension.

Yaokhalek got a job with them and earned Rs 4,000 a
month along with accommodation. In his spare time, he would
wander off into the surrounding woods where he could catch
small animals, and occasionally a peacock, to supplement their
diet. He worked with the pottery project till October 2009
when his sister was murdered. After that he gave up his job.

* * *

For nearly a year Yaokhalek did not work; then at the end of
2010 he got an opportunity to learn music from a Christian
organization. Yaokhalek, unlike Atim, attended church
regularly. He went to the Tangkhul Baptist church in Delhi; he
even helped with their activities. That is how he heard of the
Discipleship Training Course (DTC) being offered by Youth
with a Mission.[70] Atim paid Rs 18,000 as fees for the three-
month course. In addition, she bought him toiletries. He felt
grateful to his sister who had given him the opportunity.

Yaokhalek joined a hundred and fifty youth for the Bible
lessons being held in Hudson Lines, Kingsway Camp, in North
Delhi. One of his first assignments was to write something
about his life. He was not used to expressing himself in words
and found the assignment difficult. He confessed that the
worst moment in his life was when he had seen his sister lying

---

70. Youth with a Mission started in 1960 and has branches in
180 countries. It is an inter-denominational Christian organization
involved in evangelizing. Sarah Diamond, a US sociologist and
attorney, has written that the role of the movement is to be an on-
the-ground combat force against liberation theology. See her book
Spiritual Warfare: the Politics of Christian Right (1989).

dead in the kitchen. His words were much simpler: 'The most unhappiest moment is the day I saw my sister murdered.'

And the happiest day of his life was when his father bought him a toy gun.[71]

He enjoyed the classes and felt a sense of purpose; he loved the singing and play practice. The lessons on evangelizing gave him a sense of power he had not known before. The theological perspectives offered were based on a fundamentalist variety of Evangelical Christianity that emphasized solely questions of personal sin, morality and salvation. If only people could follow the Bible and avoid committing sin, they would achieve great happiness and fulfillment. There were no lessons on the causes of oppression and injustice in the world.

After he finished the three-month course, he was sent to Ladakh in February 2011 for the outreach programme. He was paid a stipend of Rs 5,000 and given free accommodation and also got to drive around the villages. His work was mostly singing and teaching the people Gospel songs. He also went to the Nubra Valley where they distributed small rice mills. The mills could grind other grain as well. It was Yaokhalek's first experience of camping and he loved it.

In the ten months he and his team worked in Ladakh, they succeeded in converting almost seventy people. This work gave Yaokhalek immense satisfaction and he wished he could continue, but Atim could not afford to pay the fees for the advanced courses. And now Yaokhalek just stayed at home. He often expressed a desire to have a guitar and dreamed of being in a band. As a teenager, Yaokhalek played guitar in a band of his own. His friend Worthing was also in the band and it was

---

71. In December 2015, the Diocesan Social Service Society in Ukhrul called for concerted efforts to dissuade parents from buying toy guns for their children through its sustained 'Anti-War Toy Campaign', saying the use of such toys help breed a culture of violence among children.

he who named it Zeitgeist; Yaokhalek could not remember what it meant.

Whenever I asked him what he wanted to do, he would say, 'music', so I challenged him to go out and earn Rs 5,000 to buy himself a guitar.

One day he said he had been offered the job of a sandwich man at Pragati Maidan. Of course, he did not use the words 'sandwich man'; he said he would have to roam around as a human billboard. He said he would feel ridiculous going around like that and he had refused the work. I told him that he should accept any job as long as he could earn some money to buy a guitar.

* * *

Then, one day, Yaokhalek announced that he had been called for an interview for a call centre of the Payday Loan Company. He was excited because he thought he would be working for an American company. Yaokhalek asked whether I could help him with the interview. He produced a piece of paper with some questions and statements that he had to learn by heart. He did not understand many words, including the word 'loan'.

Here are the questions and statements Yaokhalek and I practised for some three hours till the time he was confident he could reproduce them without my help.

1. Hi! My name is Bill. I am calling from Payday Loan Company. How are you doing?
2. I believe you have applied for a loan through our website a few days ago, is that right?
   OR
3. I am calling from US Payday Loan. You will be happy to know that our company has approved of your request for a loan of ___ amount with a monthly repayment of ___.
4. You will be glad to know that the finance department has extended your loan limit to $1000, so Ma'm/Sir can you please confirm your request for a loan from our company?

5. You do not need to give us guarantees or go through complex paperwork in order to get the loan. Would you like to increase the loan?

6. I need to inform you that the loan money you will be receiving will be through the Western Union. Do you have a Western Union store nearby?

7. The advantage of transferring the money through the Western Union is that we will be able to transfer the money in a few minutes; a transfer of money to your bank account would take much longer. It could take more than an hour.

8. If we transfer the money into your bank account the bank will take 11 per cent commission.

9. In order to get the loan you need to have proof of identity. A driving license will do.

10. You need to just pass one credit check by depositing a small amount so that our company is satisfied that you will pay back our loan.

11. As soon as the deposit is done the security deposit will be refunded to you.

12. So Sir/Ma'm, are you ready to pay your transaction fee?

13. Sir/Ma'm please grab a pen and paper so I can give you some details of how you can contact our senior accounts manager who will give you the loan approval number. He is the one who will release the loan.

14. As soon as you hang up you need to call our accounts manager who will release the loan today.

15. Have a good day Sir/Ma'm.

I have to confess that I did not really understand what this was all about. I thought it was an American company that had outsourced its work. Yaokhalek informed me that all his co-workers would be Tangkhul. That struck me as a little odd, but then I did not know much about the world of call centres.

Yaokhalek was thrilled with his job. He worked in a big room on the third floor in Mahipalpur. There were twenty-five computers and he was given telephone numbers of the people who had applied for loans. He enjoyed talking to foreigners and that too Americans, and best of all he could pretend to be one as well. He started making Rs 8,000 a month.

But over the days he began to realize that his employer, Vijendra Singh, was, in fact, involved in cheating the customers. Sometimes a customer would phone back and beg that his/her money be returned. That really disturbed Yaokhalek. He was beginning to understand that his employer was making them ring up people in America who had genuinely applied for loans, but instead of giving them loans, he was duping them into giving a transactional fee in exchange for a false promise of releasing the loan money. The fee went to Vijendra Singh and his call centre.

And then one day the office suddenly closed down and Yaokhalek was out of a job again. But now he had experience and so he got another job with the same company. This time their office was in Pitampura and his salary was Rs 16,000. He was given the rank of supervisor and he felt he had arrived. At the end of the month, however, he was not given any salary at all and the office closed down. He and the other employees never knew where their employer lived or any other details about the organization.

These illegal call centres changed locations all the time to avoid being detected. As a result, employees such as Yaokhalek did not usually know the name of the manager or owner or who their real employers were.

It took Yaokhalek time to start understanding the mechanism by which the illegal call centres made money. Even so, he did not really comprehend the enormity of the scam or the tragic consequences for the people who were being cheated.

The companies in India acquired databases on loan seekers in the US from online vendors. Their employees called US nationals under the garb of representatives from noted American loan companies like Paid for America and Net Loan.

They promised to provide loans without any bank credits or documentation. In order to get the loan, customers were required to pay a service charge of between $100 and $400.

They were also required to buy a Green Card Money voucher from Walmart to pay the service charges or to deposit money in Western Union. The customers then had to inform the call centre executives about the number on the card, using which the call centre in India diverted the funds to the company's account. After the money was transferred to the fraudulent call centre, the telephone numbers were rendered untraceable.

After listening to Yaokhalek's accounts I did a little research on the Internet. I was horrified to discover the extent to which this scam had reached. In Britain, these loan scams were found to be one of the biggest frauds carried out in the UK from overseas. It was estimated that sixty thousand Britons had become victims of a multi-million-pound Indian call centre and Internet scam. At the peak of the scam, from 2011 to 2012, more than a thousand people a day who had legally sought unsecured loans from banks and finance companies were getting calls from Indian call centres with a hundred of them actually paying a 'process fee' for non-existent cash. It was reported that the Delhi Police's Special Cell had been investigating this scam after receiving a request from the British High Commission and the Seus Organized Crime Agency in the UK.

I asked Yaokhalek whether he had heard of any arrests being made or police raids on any of these illegal call centres. He said he had heard of police raids and he had even heard that the FBI had come, but the owners of the fake call centres managed to get away by paying the police regular bribes. I told Yaokhalek that apart from it being morally wrong to cheat people, it was dangerous. He could land up in serious trouble. He said he would look for a job in a legal call centre. A few days later, he came to me to say that he had found a job that was absolutely legal, since it provided technical assistance to computer owners who had been attacked by a virus or some other such problem. This time he brought two sheets of paper on which his script was handwritten. They read:

> Hello, Am I Speaking with Mr/Mrs _____. My name is ERIC and am calling you from NTS Global, How are you doing today?
>
> Wait for an answer
>
> Actually, the reason of my calling is you remember last time you delt [sic] with our company there was issue in your computer and we resolve it for you and you paid us.
>
> Wait for an answer.
>
> Actually, last time you delt [sic] with us we installed some extra securities onto your network, which are everytime, anything goes wrong we get red alerts and we are receiving red alerts from last past 48 hours that there is some third party trying to enter into your computer. So we just have to analysis what the actual problem is, so can you please go in front of your computer so that we can check...

Then there are detailed instructions on how to use the TeamViewer to get access to the person's computer and scan it. The gullible person allows the conman to enter the computer and then pays for the service of a non-existent problem.

I told Yaokhalek this sounded like another scam and he said, 'No Aunty, it is technical help to people who have problems with their computers.'

I did a quick search on the Internet and showed Yaokhalek that Microsoft had filed a suit against a company dealing with technical support scams. Microsoft claimed that every year 3.3 million Americans fall victim to technical support scams and lose $1.5 billion. I read out to him what a senior Microsoft attorney, Courtney Gregoire, wrote on a company blog:

'These scammers claim to find non-existent computer viruses and infections then con people out of their hard-earned money for bogus tech support, in addition to stealing personal and financial information or even installing new malicious software.'

Microsoft said many of these scammers were based in India. Yaokhalek looked shocked. He said he had been told to say that their company had discovered that the Chinese had sent a virus into the computer and, on occasion to say, the non-existent virus originated in Pakistan.

Yaokhalek said a Mizo friend who had been working in an illegal call centre discovered that the man he had cheated was a fellow Mizo living in the USA. He called back and returned the money and warned him not to be taken in by such scams. Yaokhalek said he too had returned the money on occasion.

He had heard that some Tangkhuls had started their own illegal call centres. They had bought a complete database on people who had applied for loans, or those who were entitled to grants. One telephone number cost the owner Rs 15 and they needed to have a database with several thousand numbers.

Yaokhalek said he had been offered a job in one such company. The company had twelve agents (including three girls), two supervisors and one banker. He was offered five rupees for every dollar he made. He said the rate in other illegal call centres was anywhere from Rs 10 to Rs 13 per dollar made. I asked him how many calls did he have to make on an average every night, and he said up to two to three hundred. He said that on some nights he had made up to three hundred and fifty calls.

He realized that most people working in both the legal and illegal call centres did not make big money. Only a few conmen who had their own companies and took serious risks had made serious money. The rest, like Yaokhalek, just worked hard and often were not even paid.

* * *

I only recognized the terrible conditions in which these young men lived when Yaokhalek came home very late one day. He told me that Worthing's cousin Ngaransing had died the previous evening. Yaokhalek said he had gone to the room Ngaransing was sharing with two others. The four of them had cooked pork and had a hearty meal. The room was very hot and once they closed the door there was no ventilation at all. The landlord had not even given them a fan. Ngaransing said he was not feeling well; he lay down on the mattress and collapsed. The other three had not realized he was dead.

They had taken him to the hospital where he was declared dead. Yaokhalek and his friends had waited for the post mortem report and now Worthing would be taking the body home.

I remember the time I had seen the room in which one of Sebastian's nephews, Ikror, was living. It was a small, bare room with no ventilation. Just outside was a tiny kitchen in which two persons could not stand together. The kitchen and the room were absolutely empty, except for one mattress and a pillow. It was just one unit in a huge building with dozens of such rooms. Ikror had a job in Costa Coffee in Connaught Place; by the time his work was over it would be around two in the morning when there were no buses available. The company did not drop the employees home. Ikror would just sit or doze at a bus stand on a metal seat in the bitter cold of Delhi's winters. At six in the morning, he would catch the bus back to his room in Moti Bagh and sleep on the bare mattress.

Yet, when we met him, he looked well dressed and smiled and said he was working in a foreign company—the ugly reality well hidden behind his bright smile. If I had not seen his room I would never have known the reality of his existence.

* * *

Yaokhalek showed me photographs of his girlfriend on his mobile. He said he was now in touch with his friends through WhatsApp. Sometimes one of them would send a photograph of himself in a paddy field in Ukhrul and Yaokhalek could, for a few minutes, go back to the life he had once known; a life which was tough but simple.

Yaokhalek had made up his mind to give up working for these scams. He wanted to have a shop of his own or to run a guest-house. He told me that a few days after he had stopped working in the illegal call centre he had gone to visit an old friend. He had heard that the friend had made some serious money. He asked his friend to tell him honestly how much he had made and he confessed that he and his brother had made $70,000.

'Aunty, it's almost Rs 60 lakh rupees. It's all a question of luck.'

Yaokhalek said the scams would never stop; it was now getting even easier to transfer money. He tried to explain the world of digital money but I could not understand.

I asked Yaokhalek why he had still not bought a guitar. He said that every time he had saved money, he had sent it home; then he had bought a smart phone. Now he had given up the idea of singing; he wanted to open a shop.

Chapter Eight

In Our Hearts Is a Dull Deadness

Atim's heart was no longer in her work. It was true that everyone in Q'BA had been good to her; the employers had not cut her salary even though she had been away for so many months after her sister's murder. They had even kept her share of tips and service charges. The staff had also contributed Rs 5,000 towards the funeral expenses.

On her return to the restaurant, Atim found that many of her older women colleagues had left. She missed them sorely. Still she did have some companionship since Elvina was now working at Q'BA. But the work had lost its glamour. Besides, there was a continuous shortage of staff and the management had started making the hostesses do extra work—the work that the waiters used to do.

In the past, they could leave by 11 p.m. after the last order had been placed. But now they had to do the 'mizza'. Atim had no idea that what they had called 'mizza' was actually *mise en place*, a French phrase meaning putting things in place. By making the hostesses do extra work, the management could avoid paying overtime wages. Atim leant about overtime wages many years later.

The 'mizza' in this restaurant meant that the hostess had to sit and wipe all the plates, forks, spoons and knives. It could be some five hundred pieces of cutlery and some hundred and fifty small plates. This was in addition to wiping the tables and tablemats. The management told them that in this industry '*Aane ka time hai but jaane ka time nahi hain.*'

One day, the three hostesses were sitting together when suddenly Atim felt a surge of anger. She took the small plates called the B&B plates and, raising them above her head, sent them crashing down. Her friends joined her. It gave them a sense of satisfaction to see the plates lying in small bits. The managers were downstairs and the loud music drowned the sound of falling plates.

These late hours were stressing the women out. There were many fights among them; they even had catfights and these vitiated the atmosphere.

But the final straw was the lack of security when they were being dropped home by the taxis engaged by the management. On one occasion, the cab driver was drunk. The women told him to stop but he would not listen. Atim was sitting in front. The car swerved and then hit the divider and stopped. The women at the back jumped out, but before Atim could get down, the driver had re-started the car and driven off with Atim sitting beside him.

Atim started shouting till he stopped. He opened the dickie, and another man jumped out. Atim was terrified and ran and hid. By this time the other women had appeared. They had called the manager and he came with some waiters on their bikes and dropped the women home safely.

On another occasion, the taxi broke down in the middle of the road. They called the manager but he did not answer their desperate calls. The women were forced to take an auto. They saw three men following them on a bike. It was really scary, especially since it was around two in the morning. Luckily they reached home safely that night.

Atim demanded that the women be provided security when they went home at night. She said that she had to walk down a gully to reach her home in Ashram since it is too narrow for a car and she felt really scared walking by herself. But the manager shouted, 'If you don't want to work, don't work.'

It was in December 2010 that Atim handed in her resignation. She had worked at the same restaurant from 2006.

* * *

Atim was confident that she would get another job, so she was not worried about giving in her resignation without having another one in hand.

She had worked in Q'BA for four years and had about Rs 40,000 in savings in the form of her provident fund. Now she could buy some land for her family and they could start building a house on their own property. She told her father that he should start looking around for land.

Ramyo, Atim's father, found a plot in Greenland with a small pond. He bought it from a man called Victor for Rs 20,000, which Atim sent. But then there were objections to the sale since it was public land belonging to the church.

When the Tangkhuls first converted to Christianity in 1901, they were thrown out of the old village settlement, Phungcham. In compensation, they were given land in the Phungyo area, which is why the first church is called Phungyo Church. The land Victor had sold belonged to the Phungyo Church and, according to the law, it could not be sold. Victor was on the church land committee and had sold the plot illegally, which was why it had been so cheap. Now Ramyo had to give it back, but Victor did not return the money. He said he would give it back in installments.

The loss of Rs 20,000 was not a small amount for the family. Atim's father still did not get his full pension because it had been pawned during his illness to a man called Somi (not the same man from whom she and Yaokhalek had stolen peaches). Atim had noticed that Somi had the pension papers of many pensioners; it seemed to be another scam. Atim did not know what usury meant or whether there was a Tangkhul word for it. She did not know that Moses and Jesus fought against the evil of usurpation and debt slavery. But then, she had seen many pious people lend money at exorbitant rates of interest.

Atim knew that she would have to work hard and earn

more money before her dream of building a home for her family could come true. She was still living in the room at the end of a warren of gullies in Sunlight Colony in Ashram. She needed a job and Rose found her one at a coffee shop in Hauz Khas Village. It was owned by a woman called Dolly, who had returned from Australia and had incurred a huge debt and wanted to pay it off by starting a restaurant.

When Atim walked into the café there were hardly any customers, only a few sharing a hookah. The waitress on duty asked Atim in a condescending way whether she knew how to carry a tray. The kitchen was small and the staff ate food which was bought from outside; they sat on the stairs to eat. It was all really very unprofessional. She also discovered that the owner did a bit of prostitution to supplement her income. Atim was not even sure whether the owner could actually afford to pay her a salary.

* * *

Atim did not return to her job the next day, which was a Sunday and Yaokhalek persuaded her to accompany him to the Tangkhul fellowship in Ashram. There was a Tangkhul church in Lodhi Colony, but often the men and women did not have the time or energy to go all the way there on their one day off. Instead, they had organized their own fellowships in the localities in which they lived. Although Yaokhalek was a regular, Atim had never felt inclined to go for worship.

Her ambivalence was partly because of her suppressed resentment against her parents for converting her from a Catholic to a Baptist. Her mother had been brought up as a Catholic but after marriage had converted to the Baptist church. Atim, however, liked the nuns who had taught her in the Holy Spirit School at Longpi. As a small child she would pretend to be a nun by dressing up like one. She went for the catechism competition in Imphal where she did well in the oral part but not in the written segment.

When her family had moved to Ukhrul town she went to the Savio School run by Catholic priests. She would walk alone to the Catholic church and was baptized there. She loved to take the Communion. But her parents said it would be better if she converted to the Baptist church because it looked odd to have one family member going to a Catholic church. Thus in 2000, she had been forced to have a second baptism into the Baptist church.[72]

There was another reason why Atim did not like to attend church. She found it awkward because the women came dressed in stylish, branded clothes and looked down on anyone wearing a simple Tangkhul kashan. But then Atim missed out on the socializing that went with the occasion.

That Sunday, however, she decided to accompany her brother. There were around twenty people at the fellowship. She met Mahawon, a Tangkhul woman who told her that she had recently been selected for a job in the five-star Radisson Hotel in Noida. She did not want the job as she had got one in Le Meridien. She offered to recommend Atim to the manager at the Radisson.

Atim did not want to go on her own for the interview and took her neighbour, Horyaopam, who was also looking for a job. When the two women stepped into the hotel, Atim gasped at the opulence. She could not help comparing it to her home in Ukhrul.

Atim was first interviewed by the Human Resources Manager about her experience and family background. After the interview was over, she was sent to the Food and Beverages

---

72. There have been underlying tensions between Baptists and Catholics; Catholics have been thrown out of villages and there have been incidents of their churches being burnt down. The Baptist church does not allow marriage between Catholic and Baptists, while the Catholic church allows it. A Catholic converting to Baptism is baptized again.

Manager. He turned out to be a Christian and she liked him. He asked about her work as hostess in her previous job and just when she thought the interview process was over, he sent her to the General Manager, who sat in the office on the next floor.

Atim and Horyaopam were given coupons for the cafeteria in the basement meant for the staff. It was very well equipped and there was a coffee machine from which the staff could take as many cups as they wanted. They were shown the rooms where the staff could rest and change into their uniforms.

Next, the two women were sent for medical checkups and after the formalities were over, they were given their appointment letters and assigned to their new jobs. This was in April 2011.

Horyaopam was selected to work at the Chocolate Box, the patisserie, while Atim was appointed as hostess at S 18 Café. Horyaopam found herself learning the names of a bewildering number of cakes, all carrying exorbitant price tags. She had to manage the shop by herself and if the cakes were sold out, she had to rush to the bakery to place the orders.

When she got her appointment letter, Atim was thrilled to find that her basic salary was Rs 4,998, with a Special Allowance of Rs 5,694. This allowance was given because the hotel did not levy any service charge; with it she would be getting a total of Rs 10,692 in addition to the tips. She would also get a bonus and gratuity, which she had not even heard of so far. This time she was determined to save so that she could send money to her father to buy another plot of land.

Atim wished that the Radisson provided accommodation for the staff. Although the hotel in Noida was not very far from her home in Ashram, she had to reach before 6.30 a.m. because breakfast started early in the morning. She would go to the basement where she changed into her uniform, grabbed a cup of coffee and got ready for work. Her job was to record whether the guest was entitled to a complimentary breakfast or had to be billed.

Breakfast lasted till ten in the morning and immediately afterwards she had to prepare the small labels to describe each dish that would be part of the lunch buffet. Atim had not seen such a variety of cuisines: the buffet included Indian kebabs, Mediterranean salads and Lebanese mezze. She had to go to the kitchen and ask the chef to tell her the ingredients of each dish; she noted them all down and then went to the back office to type them out on the computer. She found the spellings confusing and learnt to spell-check by doing a Google search. Then she printed out the labels and put them in front of each dish.

Each time she went down to the kitchen, the chef would pass some sexist remarks. It became so unpleasant that she complained to the Human Resources Department and they took up the matter. After that the chef was silent.

Atim longed to taste some of the dishes, but the management was very strict and the staff had to be very careful when they sampled the leftovers. The Food and Beverages Controller was always on the lookout to catch them. Even the managers were afraid of being caught by him.

For Atim, the sheer wastage of food was appalling. She asked the F&B Controller what happened to the leftovers since the staff was not allowed to take anything home. He informed her that the food was given to the pigs.

On one occasion, the manager told Atim that the Rare Eastern Dining or RED restaurant on the first floor was going to have a Thai food festival and they wanted her to dress like a Thai woman. She was sent to the spa and for forty-five minutes Atim was subjected to a beauty treatment. She emerged looking radiant, dressed in a Thai silk dress. The manager took her around introducing her as a Thai.

Atim said the stewards and managers often profiled the customers, and that they preferred the Malhotras, the Chopras and Sharmas. She said that these people were much better mannered; they knew how to order the food and did not drop anything on the table. Whereas the Aggarwals, she noticed, were not always so sophisticated. They tended to ask for more onions, hold the glasses with the hands used for eating and then wipe their hands on the napkins. She said she could tell what kind of person the customer was the moment he or she walked into the restaurant.

The two customers she remembers most from the time she worked in the Radisson were an old woman and a young man who sat together at one table. The old woman, who could barely walk, would sit for long hours with the young man. She had thought they were mother and son, and was really moved by the way he looked after the woman; he really cared for her. Then one day when she made a remark about the two, the manager told her they were lovers. It was a shock that Atim never really got over.

Then there was a guest who was part of the Formula One racing world. He asked Atim for Black Label whiskey and she showed him the bottle. He said he knew how hotels cheated by putting cheaper liquor into bottles of expensive alcohol. Atim just smiled because she knew that it was true. She knew that after the guests were drunk, they could not make out what they were drinking.

Atim noticed that the hotel always seemed to be short of staff. This meant that in addition to her duties as a hostess, she would also have to serve the customers at the table. The workload had become much heavier and by the time she went home her legs pained. She had muscle cramps almost every night.

* * *

Horyaopam had decided to leave. She was keen to join a cruise. In fact, it was Atim who gave her the business card of Miss Mohita who was working in Carnival Cruises. The chef at Q'BA had given it to Atim when she still dreamt of joining a cruise liner. But after Ramchanphy was murdered, she had given up her dream because she had to attend to the trial in court.

Horyaopam contacted the cruise and was called for an interview in Chennai. Later, she told Atim she had to raise Rs 2 lakh for the training, but she was confident she could repay the loan amount within six months of working. There were many other women from the Northeast who were with her in the training. Once the training was over, they had to apply for visas from the US Embassy; although Horyaopam got her visa, nine of the other women were refused. They were devastated.

At the US Embassy, the question they had asked Horyaopam was, 'What will you do with the money you earn?'

And her spontaneous answer had been, 'Send it home.'

The others had said they would like to spend it on travelling.

* * *

Atim met Horyaopam when she came to meet her sisters who were staying in Ashram; one was working in a call centre and the other was studying. They were meeting after six months. Horyaopam said that she found the work very tiring. There was only one other Tangkhul girl while the rest were Filipino with whom she did not get along. Horyaopam saw that many of the women had an easier time by giving sexual favours to the managers and sometimes sleeping with the guests. Since she did not want to do that, she found support from the Indian staff and managers who did not encourage such behaviour.

Horyaopam complained that she was earning only Rs 60,000 a month. The only time they made money was on New Year's Day when the guests were very generous with the tips. That day, the staff was allowed unlimited drinks, but Horyaopam did not drink. The money she earned was not enough, and she did not even go out to see places because it was very expensive; even a packet of biscuits was beyond her means. Sometimes she made do with Moreh sunflower seeds for lunch.

This was because she was repaying her debts. However, she had managed to pay back everyone and had saved enough to buy herself a laptop.

Despite all the problems Atim was hearing about, she still wished she could join a cruise. But for the time being she was happy that Radisson had agreed to give her twenty-five days off because she needed to go to Ukhrul urgently. She had booked her tickets. But when she went to get official permission, the management refused to sanction the leave and so she was forced to resign in December. They also refused to give her a letter of recommendation when she returned, because she had not given them one month's notice. They said she owed them a month's salary.

She hated the idea of losing her job at the five-star hotel; she had worked in the Radisson for nine months, from April to December 2011. If she had worked for a year she may have got a bonus…but she had no choice.

* * *

The reason she had to go to Ukhrul was because it was her father's Ara-aza or gathering together of all the descendants. Every year all the descendants of her father, his sixteen children and their children and grandchildren got together. Last year Ninghor, his eldest son from his first wife, had financed the get-together; this year it was her turn as the eldest child from Ramyo's second wife. Strictly speaking, only sons were expected to bear the costs but now she was the eldest and sole earning member of her father's family.

Atim had to organize food for fifty people. She planned the menu and cooked the iromba with hanahun, sour leaves grown in the paddy fields. The leaves are mixed with mashed theirathei, a kind of lentils, ngari or fermented fish, and umrok, the Naga chilli (said to be the hottest in the world). The neighbours prepared the ooti or dried white peas cooked with ash; Ramyo's sister cooked the fish, while Atim's mother made the Raphei-style hoksa or pork of the northerners, a specialty of Longpi and Kalhang. The pork pieces are very large, and after rubbing each piece with lots of hand-crushed smoked red chillies and salt, the pork is roasted over slow fire. There were, of course, the usual boiled vegetables and loads of rice—the sticky rice which is available only in Manipur.

Atim placed the food on a big table outside their home, like a buffet. The family liked it very much and her father's youngest son by his first wife, Somaya, appreciated Atim's contribution and skills.

When it was time for Atim to leave, her mother asked her to inform Ninghor. Atim did not want to go to meet her stepbrother; she still held him responsible for much of the suffering her family had to endure. He had made her father leave their lovely home in Kalhang because he felt his father should not stay in his wife's village. He never helped when Ramyo was sick and now the family was in debt; she could not finish school and the family had… She forced herself to put aside those painful memories.

Ninghor had come for the Ara-aza and he had said grace; he had urged the family members to forgive each other for the past mistakes and remain united as a family. But then he said the same thing on every such occasion.

Atim knew that her mother had only asked her to meet Ninghor because if she did not, he would make snide remarks about her mother and the way she had brought up her children. To save her mother from such comments, Atim went to Ninghor's home and informed him she was leaving. In response, he told her that he did not approve of her going to Delhi; she should stay with her parents and work in the paddy field. He said she would achieve nothing by working in Delhi.

Atim could not stop herself from answering back, 'Masowon and Sochuila have made money to build a house.' She was referring to her nieces who were working in Dubai.

And he had replied, 'They are just wasting their time. When they come back they will not be able to work in the paddy field. You too will become fat.'

Atim was really furious, but she kept quiet and murmured goodbye and left.

* * *

Atim wanted to build a home for her family even though she knew that after her father passed away, the house would belong to Yaokhalek, the eldest son from the second wife. In other words, the home she was working so hard to build would not belong to her under Tangkhul customary law.

Many Tangkhul women were facing serious problems because of this law. For instance, her friend Rose had bought a plot for Rs 7 lakh with the money her partner had given her. She wanted to build a house for herself so that she could come back to Ukhrul when she was old. She was furious when she learnt that her father had sold half the land and bought a Scorpio or a Bolero, Atim did not remember which. The vehicle was being used as a taxi by Rose's brother. She had told her father that he would never have dared to sell the land if it had belonged to her brother.

Rose was angry because her parents had not allowed her to go to school and had made her work in the fields; now she was deprived of her land bought with her money. After her protests, her father did return a lakh from the three and half he had spent on the vehicle.

Atim's nieces, Sochuila and Masowon, had built a house with the money they had earned from working in Dubai. They had even signed a Family Agreement by which it was agreed that the brothers had no rights to the house. Atim also said that the two sisters were thinking of getting another house so they would not have to share the one they had built, since joint ownership between two sisters may cause problems later between their children.

Tangkhul women had started asserting their rights and challenging the customary law practices; often, parents supported them. For instance, Atim's friend Jajo had demanded a share in her father's property and he had given her a good plot right near the road in Phungyar village.

For Atim, the dream of owning her own home was very distant. She had seen the conditions in which her family was living. Now her sisters had got married, but one of them had returned with her two small children after her husband had started beating her. There were seven to eight people sleeping in one room. She had to build a home for them and then think of herself.

Finally, in 2012, Atim did manage to send some money to her parents to buy land. Ramyo had purchased it from Scotphill, whose father was in the Indian army. He said he would sell the land for Rs 60,000 if they gave the money in one go, but he would charge one lakh if they paid in installments. Atim could not contribute more than Rs 30,000, but this time Ninghor had helped and had given his father Rs 30,000 and so they were able to buy the plot at a cheaper rate. Ramyo, however, could not begin construction until the land was cleared since he had no money to employ people to chop down the trees and shrubs growing on it.

Atim knew that she needed to earn much more before the dream of a family home could be realized.

* * *

While she was in Ukhrul, her mother had told her that many parents living in Greenland had sent their children to Jaipur where a Christian couple ran a hostel and provided free education. Mayori's aunt's daughter, Philathing, had come to ask if they would like to send their youngest daughter Wonmipem to the hostel there. Shimtharla asked Atim whether this was a good idea.

Atim's little sister had been admitted to Savio School but

did not like it and was now studying in the Government Higher Secondary School. She was more interested in sports than in her studies and she could sing very well. Atim's parents thought that perhaps their daughter would get an opportunity to develop her talents in Jaipur. Atim intuitively said it was not a good idea. Later, Philathing herself advised them against sending the girl to Jaipur. She did not give any reason.

Atim told me this while we were sitting in my home in Goa in July 2015. I asked her whether she had not seen the news about the Jaipur home and how fifty children had been rescued and the pastor arrested. Almost all the news channels had reported the story. Atim had not seen it. I told her that it was in March 2013 that the rescue had taken place.

'Thank God I told my mother not to send my sister to Jaipur.'

I showed Atim a brochure brought out by the Tangkhul Shanao Long Delhi (or Tangkhul Women's Association Delhi) in June 2013. It carried the details of the rescue operation. What had shocked me was that the idea of the organization came up when the three children who had been trafficked way back in 2005 had been rescued in 2012. There were no details about that case.

* * *

Tangkhul Shanao Long Delhi was formed in June 2012 and was a unit of the Tangkhul Shanao Long Ukhrul, which was the apex body of the Tangkhul women.

The idea of forming the Delhi unit had come in response to the needs of young Tangkhul women from Ukhrul who faced the challenges of living in an unsafe city, where they encountered both racial discrimination and racial prejudice. The problem of children being trafficked was an additional concern.

My first visit to Ukhrul (when I went to Atim's mother's village Kalahang) with an all women's fact-finding team in

1982, was on the invitation of the East District Women's Association (EDWA). At the time Ukhrul was still called East District; soon after our trip, it was renamed Ukhrul District. Later, EDWA was renamed Tangkhul Shanao Long.

The president of EDWA in 1982 was N. Ruivanao; she said the organization had started way back in 1974 after a young woman, Rose Machuii, was raped by two men of the Border Security Force in March that year. Rose was then twenty years old. She had felt her rape would bring shame to her family and had committed suicide by hanging herself. Tangkhul women had designed a special kashan in her memory called the Rose Kashan.

I had written about the organization and it had been published in the Sunday magazine of the *Hindustan Times* dated 7 November 1982. The title of the article was 'Amazons of the East District'. It was a part of a larger article on the human rights violations committed by the Indian army after the first ambush by the NSCN. That article was entitled: 'Terror in Manipur'.

At that time the Tangkhul Shanao Long had focused on cases of rape and torture by the Indian armed forces. But now the Delhi Shanao Long had to take up cases of violations of a totally different kind. The old EDWA had been involved in human rights issues. They were challenging the state, not their own society. But by taking up the case of trafficked children, the Delhi Shanao Long had challenged both Tangkhul society and the church, in ways they had perhaps not anticipated.

I heard of the rescue of more than fifty children from two homes run by Christian missionaries in Jaipur when the news was broadcast on national television in 2013. Later, I learnt of the details from Felicita Shongvah, the then Chairperson of the Tangkhul Shanao Long Delhi. The association was not dealing with the Indian army or mayangs, but members of Tangkhul society and the Baptist church who were involved in the trafficking and exploitation of children.

A member of the Shanao Long Delhi wrote after her return from Jaipur that the 'saddest and worst revelation' was that 'our own people' were involved in the trafficking and this had left her sad and speechless. The writer, Seema Awungshi, named the Tangkhuls involved in the trade:

> 'Nganingmi Vashi and his wife, Anderson and his wife, these four people had served as wardens at the children's homes; in addition there were people who had served on the staff, including: Wonshim, Leiyashim, Leishipem.'

What also shocked a lot of Tangkhuls was that the children's homes were being run by a pastor. His name was Jacob John and he was from Kerala; his younger brother was married to a Tangkhul woman from Tuinem village. She was assisted by A.S. Worthingla of Khamasom Khullen village. Tuinem village had been affronted by the accusations that people from their village were involved in trafficking.

Skyrim Zimik, the treasurer of the Shanao Long in Delhi, wrote:

> 'For the first time in my life I felt ashamed of my religion. It was especially appalling that it was a missionary who was indulging in such reprehensible activities of exploiting children. After meeting these young, innocent children, I realized there were Christians hurting other Christians.'[73]

Many leaders of the Tangkhul Baptist church and the other Tangkhul social organizations had been critical of the Tangkhul Shanao Long Delhi for exposing the ills of Tangkhul society in public. A Tangkhul lawyer even threatened Felicita with a defamation suit!

Jacob John was in jail in Dimapur. He was there on 15 March 2015, the day when a mob had taken out Farid Khan

---

73. Quotes on reaction to the rescue operation taken from the brochure brought out by Tangkhul Shanao Long, June 2013.

from the jail and lynched him to death. Farid Khan was accused of raping a Naga woman. He was dragged through town, executed and his body hung by the clock tower in Dimapur. Although isolated Nagas did condemn the violence, there was no massive mobilization against the lynching.

On that day, as I watched the barbaric mob, my one thought was that why did the Nagas not feel the same anger against Jacob John? Could it be that Farid Khan was condemned as a Muslim and a Bangladeshi, while Jacob had to be protected because he was a pastor? Felicita said that there was no real public outcry against Jacob and the trial in Nagaland was not even being followed.

Tangkhul men and women do not always recognize the patriarchal basis of their society. None of the social organizations, such as Tangkhul Long, Tangkhul Katamnao Saklong, or clan heads have ever included women in the top leadership. The same can be said for the other Naga tribes. Naga women often justify the patriarchy as an aspect of their culture. Many times Atim would say, 'But Aunty, you don't understand. It is our culture.'[74]

She, like many Naga women, thinks patriarchy is a unique aspect of their culture. And when, for the umpteenth time, I tried to explain that patriarchy is a feature of societies all over the world, she would smile; she thinks Aunty does not always understand her society.

---

74. There are, of course, some Naga women, especially independent intellectuals, who are challenging this patriarchy and demanding equality within their society. Some are fighting for 33 per cent reservations in the Assembly. But they are individuals and to the best of my knowledge there is no Naga women's organization with feminist understanding of patriarchy.

Chapter Nine

What We Know Now
Is Not What We Want

Atim was back in Delhi in her Ashram room in April 2012. She needed to find a job urgently otherwise she would not be able to pay her rent. On impulse she phoned Shishi Changloi who had worked with her in Q'BA. She had heard that Shishi was now working in a restaurant in the posh DLF Promenade shopping mall in Vasant Kunj.

Shishi said there was indeed a vacancy for her at Kainoosh, but she would have to do break shifts[75] sometimes. Atim did not realize the implication of this at the time. She said as long as she was paid well she would join. Shishsi said she would get a salary of Rs 15,000 but with the tips she could expect to earn at least Rs 20,000 a month.

Atim went for the interview and was immediately selected. The restaurant was owned by the celebrity chef, Marut Sikka. She joined Kainoosh in May 2012.

---

75. Also called a split shift. According to the California Restaurant Association, in California, for instance, a split shift is a work schedule that is interrupted by a non-paid, non-working period established by the employer that is not a rest or meal period. If an employee initiates a break in his or her work schedule for personal reasons (for example, to accommodate childcare or personal business), that interruption is not considered a split shift, since the break was not established by the employer. When an employer requires an employee to work a split shift, the employer must pay the employee a split shift premium, which is one hour's pay at minimum wage in addition to the employee's regular earnings paid for that shift. It should be noted that the labour law in California does not set a required minimum length of time between split shifts. In India there is no clear law on the subject.

Very soon she found the shifts killing. She had to report for work at 11 a.m. and work till 3 p.m.; if some guests lingered on, it could even become four in the afternoon. And the next shift would begin at seven and last till one in the morning. This was worse than the Radisson where she could at least leave by eight at night. Besides, in the Radisson there were rooms in the basement for the staff to rest between the shifts, as well as clean toilets and hot showers.

At Kainoosh, Atim had no place to rest between the shifts. The bus ride would take too much time and energy and it was just too expensive to go back to Ashram and return by an auto. Atim started feeling so tired that she finally asked the cleaning staff whether they would allow her to rest in the toilet meant for the disabled, which was more spacious; it was right next to the restaurant. That was how she and a woman from Assam called Beauty managed to find a place to sleep in between shifts. They just spread out a sheet and slept on the floor of the toilet meant for the disabled.

Atim asked the management to find a room where the women could rest during the break shift. The manager said he had asked for a room in the basement for the staff, but the owner of the mall had refused to provide the space. In fact, after a month, Atim put in her resignation. Already many of the women from the Northeast had left because of the break shift. For two days she did not go to work. Then the management called and promised that she would get break shifts for only three days in a week; Shishi would do the other three days.

Unlike Q'BA, the staff food in Kainoosh was quite all right but there was no place where they could eat with dignity. Sometimes they would eat outside, but if it rained they would have to have their meal standing near the place where the dishes were washed. It was very crowded and smelly.

After Atim moved from Ashram to Nandita's place in Vasant Enclave in July 2012, she could occasionally go home and rest, but it cost her Rs 150 by auto even for the short distance. Buses did not ply on that route.

At Kainoosh, Atim had to learn about Indian cuisine. She had to know the ingredients of each dish; the management spent an hour before the evening shift giving brief lectures on the dishes being served. Atim had a notebook full of recipes that she was expected to learn by heart.

It was here that Atim acquired a taste for laal maas or red meat, the leftovers of which she had tasted. The dal makhani was also absolutely delicious. She wished she could learn to use all those spices and cook for her mother.

A few days after she joined Kainoosh, she found three pieces of Chicken Peri Peri when she was clearing the table. They looked quite nice. She was about to throw them away when she decided to have a taste. Just as she was putting a piece into her mouth, the F&B Controller appeared and caught her. He charged her Rs 700 for this offence. Later, he changed his attitude and would look the other way when the staff sampled some delicacy and, after a buffet, they were allowed to take the leftovers home.

Atim found that serving Indian food was much more difficult than any other type of cuisine. Two people were needed to serve five guests. First, the small plates had to be put along with small onions in vinegar that were served with roasted papad and mint chutney. Then the plates had to be cleared and the starters were served. The starters had their own chutneys—there were six kinds of chutneys. Many times the guests had dirtied the water glasses, so they had to change them. If there was a shortage of staff, Atim would have to wash and dry the glasses herself.

Then the drinks had to be served, followed by the main course, and the cutlery changed. A small plate was kept beside each guest for the rotis, along with two bronze katoris, one for the dal and the other for any dish with gravy. Sometimes the guests demanded another katori for the raita. Many guests demanded extra onions, mint chutney, chillies and papad.

Once the guests had finished, the table had to be cleared quickly; Atim could pick up the dirty dishes of three guests at a time. The bronze thalis and katoris were very heavy and it was difficult to pick up more.

Next, she would rush to get warm water for the finger bowls, clear the finger bowls and place the small plates and special small spoons for the dessert.

The most difficult part was handling the innumerable complaints from the guests. They would complain that the roti was cold, the a/c was not working properly, the fish was not fresh or the water in the finger bowl was not warm enough. The worst was when the waiters got the orders wrong and the customers would be irate; as a hostess she would have to deal with these complaints calmly and politely.

Serving at the tables was in addition to her work as hostess. As hostess, she would have to stand at the entrance to the restaurant on the ground floor. Her job was to manage the seating. Many times there were too many guests and she would have to seat them outside in a small garden and serve them drinks. On top of handling the rush, Atim also attended to phone calls and took down requests for reservations.

Fortunately, Atim had experience and she could do her duties with a certain panache that earned her the nickname of 'Miss Multi-Task'.

Her father's daughter's daughter, Rinyaola, was working in the Benetton showroom on the first floor. She was Huimila's younger sister, the niece with whom she had stayed in the early days when she arrived in Delhi.

Sometimes Atim visited her niece and she would give Atim and her friends a discount. One day, Rinyaola saw Atim standing outside the entrance of the restaurant and she came downstairs and asked why she did not work in a better restaurant like Kylin.

A few days later, Atim received a call from her mother. She sounded really anxious and asked what kind of work she was doing in Delhi. Apparently, Rinyaola had told her mother that Atim just stood outside the entrance and wasn't doing a proper job; it was just a way to avoid living in Ukhrul. This was the reason why her mother had phoned.

Atim felt deeply hurt and angry with her niece for causing so much pain to her parents by spreading false information. In her anger she told her mother, 'Even if I clean shit I would do it professionally and people will respect me.'

Atim explained to her mother that she was earning far more than her niece, who had to stand all day folding clothes without tips and not even a lunch break. Her mother felt a little reassured, but it was difficult for her to defend her daughter's honour when she did not really understand the work.

* * *

Many times Atim felt hurt by the way the guests behaved; the way they looked through the staff as if they did not have human feelings. For instance, Atim once came across a diamond earring on the floor; she quickly found the guest's phone number and informed her. The guest's husband came rushing back and took the earring without as much as a thank you. Shishi said he should have given Atim a tip.

On another occasion, Atim along with a steward called Rana were in charge of the private dining area. There was a beautiful cake in the middle. It was a New Year's Eve party. Just as the clock struck twelve and people were exchanging wishes, a guest turned to Atim and said 'Water'. Atim went to fetch a glass of water but she could not help the lump in her throat. The customers often ignored her as if she were of no consequence; but that day, being New Year, it hurt more than usual and she rushed to the bathroom to hide her tears.

Atim was quick to add that not all the guests were insensitive and there was a couple who always talked to her nicely; they wanted her to serve them. There was also a woman journalist who asked Atim where she was from and when Atim said she was from Manipur, the woman said she had been to Imphal and had interviewed Irom Sharmila.[76] Atim had no idea who Sharmila was. The woman was so kind that Atim found herself telling her how her sister was murdered and how the trial was taking so long. The woman gave Atim her business card, but Atim lost it so she could not remember the name of the kind journalist.

One day, the manager told all the women to wear saris because some Americans were coming and the restaurant wanted to give them a traditional Indian welcome. Atim did not have any saris or even a kurta. As usual, Shishi was the resourceful one and found several kurta-pyjama sets. Atim dressed in a green kurta while Shishi wore a cream one.

By the time the American tourists arrived in two Volvo buses, the women were ready. Shishi put the vermillion tika on their foreheads while Atim tied jasmine flowers on the women's wrists. The Americans were given a thali lunch and so the rush was not the same as it was when guests ordered from the à la carte menu. Atim said they had a good profile; the party was calm and the guests did not complain about anything.

One day, when Atim was standing at the entrance of Kainoosh, a Nepali woman who worked at the Smokehouse Grill came up to her while on the way from the toilet. She was feeling really upset. The manager had been propositioning her and insisting that she go out with him. But she had refused and now he was 'giving pressure', the term Atim and the Tangkhul women used to describe sexual harassment. Soon after, the Nepali woman left the job; Atim said women could not work

---

76. Irom Sharmila is a Meitei woman who has been protesting against the Armed Forces (Special Powers) Act, and in support of her demand to repeal the Act she has been on hunger strike since 2 November 2000. She finally broke her fast on 9 August 2016.

in the Smokehouse Grill at the DLF Promenade because of sexual harassment.

She said that in Kainoosh she had witnessed an incident of sexual molestation, which had shocked her. One day, an electrician, by mistake, brushed his hand against the bum of a Tangkhul waitress who was bending to take out candles from a cupboard. When the bartender asked him what it was like, the electrician replied, 'Very soft.' Thereafter the bartender started calling the woman 'softy'; what had shocked Atim was that the woman responded when he called her that. Atim said she had never ever greeted the general manager, Premjit because he too had called her colleague 'softy' and once she had even shouted at the bartender for passing sexist remarks.

She was furious with her Tangkhul colleague because she had refused to protest; instead she said she preferred to grant Premjit sexual favours in order to get a few benefits. Atim had seen some of her Tangkhul workers go out with managers; often the women received a few advantages in exchange for sexual favours.

Atim could not bear the break shifts and she was not compensated with big tips. This was partly because a large number of the guests came through companies like Dine Out, Bite Quest or Zomato and were given heavy discounts; they did not leave tips. Besides, there were men from the police and excise department who came daily and expected complimentary food. They too did not give tips.

Her only 'tips' were the expensive lipsticks, Gucci dark glasses, Christian Dior lip-gloss and other costly cosmetics left by the guests in the bathroom. This was a treasure the women shared.

Fed up of the long hours and lack of tips, Atim walked into the Harley Davidson showroom which was next door to the restaurant. She had heard there was a vacancy. The manager told her right away that they did not give jobs to 'chinkies'.

Atim called a former co-worker, a Nepali woman called Bhumi, and asked whether she knew of any vacancies. Bhumi said she had heard there was a vacancy in Underdoggs, which was also in the same shopping mall as Kainoosh. Atim called and got an appointment.

* * *

Atim walked into Underdoggs Sports Bar and Grill in her uniform during the break shift. She had taken along her bio-data. The manager took her into the private dining area for the interview where she met the owner. He asked how much salary she expected and she said Rs 15,000. The manager said it was not possible at present and offered Rs 13,000. Atim said then it should be at least Rs 13,500 and the matter was settled.

To Atim's relief, the timings were from three in the afternoon to eleven at night, when a cab dropped the women home. She was also not given any appointment letter, but her salary was as promised and if she had to work beyond her shift, they paid overtime.

Atim handed in her notice at Kainoosh and joined Underdoggs in April 2013. The atmosphere was relaxed and the guests were usually young people interested in playing the games on offer. Music played all day long and there were also huge television screens showing sports news and games. It had a fun decor; in one corner some two hundred pairs of Adidas shoes could be seen hanging right over the heads of the guests like a canopy of sorts.

Many of the men came to use the pool tables, but there were also traditional board games such as carrom and table football. In addition, there were some funky games like beer-pong where table tennis balls had to be aimed at glasses filled with beer. If the player got the ball into the glass he or she was given a free beer. Then there was Bladder Blast: for Rs 499 a person could drink unlimited beer until he needed to empty his bladder. The event that Atim enjoyed most was the

Chilly [sic] Challenge. In that, the guest was given twelve pieces of chicken wings rubbed with bhoot jhalokia, the hottest chilli in the world (the Meiteis call it umrok and in Nagaland it is called raja chilli). If a person could eat all twelve wings s/he would not have to pay. In a corner was a Fire Fighters' Hall of Fame where the photographs of three winners of the chilli competition were pasted: a Sardar, a Naga man and a slim German woman with shoulder-length hair. Atim, who could not eat any meal without chillies, found the bhoot jhalokia too hot.

In Underdoggs, Atim discovered she had to be very careful while letting in the guests; the owners were very strict about not offering alcoholic drinks to minors. Some bars, where kids from rich families went and drank themselves silly, had been raided and had been closed down after the bad publicity.

Here, she worked only as a hostess, greeting the guests and escorting them to the tables, or if they wished to play a game she would call the steward in charge of the games. She had to tell the guests the various promotions on offer and go back to her station at the entrance. Often, when there were private parties, Atim had to make sure there were no gatecrashers.

While working in Underdoggs, she was tempted sometimes to walk into Body Shop,[77] which was right across. She bought herself a cream for pimples for Rs 800 and a bottle of vanilla perfume for Rs 300. She got them at a discount because the woman at the counter was a Nepali acquaintance. Once, she had spent Rs 3,000 for cosmetics, but the pimples stubbornly remained, and her hair never became as glossy as the hair of the models she saw in advertisements. She could not understand why.

On 13 August 2013, Atim was delighted when she was chosen as the best Employee of the Month: 'In recognition of

---

77. Body Shop was started in the 1970s by Anita Roddick, but later it was taken over by L'Oreal. It has stores in sixty-one countries.

your efforts towards providing excellent customer services and showing leadership among your peers'.

She was given Rs 500 as an incentive and a certificate. During the lunch break she spent the money on buying ice cream for her fellow workers and a shampoo for herself and a bar of chocolate for Aunty Nandita. As she was returning to the sports bar, she got a call from one of her co-workers to say that there had been a raid and Underdoggs had been closed down. She took an auto and went home to Vasant Enclave. She had worked there for barely five months. Atim never did find out why the restaurant had closed down. Later it re-opened in the same mall, but at a different location.

* * *

Atim went back to working for Kainoosh in November 2013. This time she was assigned to working in Keya, owned and managed by the same people as Kainoosh. Keya was a bar with an extensive selection of wines; it claimed to have the largest selection in a stand-alone bar all over India.

I had read about this bar; it had been in the news for all the wrong reasons. On one occasion, after Atim had left Keya, the bar had not allowed a disability activist, Nipun Malhotra, entry. He had come with his parents and had lunch at Kainoosh and after that he had wanted to have a drink in Keya with his parents, but they were denied entry. Atim said the bar did not allow old people entry because 'they will not be comfortable.'

Several months after that incident, Atim accompanied Sebastian and me when we went to check out Keya; we had visited all her work places as a part of the research for this book. We were warmly greeted by a Tangkhul man, Mayo Khamrang from Somdal village in Ukhrul. Having heard all about how guests are profiled from Atim, I told Mayo that we were thinking of coming to the bar one evening. He replied with a smile, 'You won't be comfortable, the music is too loud.' There were no formal rules barring senior citizens from entering the bar, but Atim said the management strictly controlled the entry of guests by 'profiling'. Atim was not at all uncomfortable with the word or aware of the implications. She said that in the restaurants she had worked in, the Sikhs were charged higher rates for parties because they ate more heartily.

On the weekends, there would be a rush and the managers would carefully look through their CCTVs at the guests to prevent entry to certain kinds of people; they would tell the security personnel to stop those people who they thought might cause trouble. They checked to see if the guest had been there before and had created a scene, not paid his bill or misbehaved. But, according to Atim, apart from those people who had behaved badly in the past, the management also did not allow government servants, senior citizens or young people below twenty-five. Atim said the Keya management did not generally allow 'Black people [that is how she described Africans] or the Chinese looking ones.' This meant that people from the Northeast were also barred, unless the guest was known to the management, like a famous designer from Nagaland who came regularly to Keya.

The bar basically catered to young, rich couples with money to spend on expensive alcohol. And it was at Keya that Atim learnt all about wines and alcohol. She learnt to distinguish between red and white wines, the names of sparkling wines and the different kinds of liqueurs.

Atim saw young men ordering bottles of Moet and Chandon champagne costing Rs 33,000 in the same way people ordered Coca-Cola. I asked her to tell me the names of the most popular drinks and she reeled off names like Grey Goose vodka, Chiroc vodka, which she told me was the only vodka made with grapes, and Johnnie Walker King George whiskey which cost one lakh for a bottle. She said the most popular drink with the customers was Jagermeister, which was created with fifty-six herbs, roots and spices and took a year to make.

I asked if she had managed to taste some of these. She said one of the employees had a bottle (it was not clear whether he had stolen it or bought it) of King George whiskey and they had all sampled a bit. It was the excitement of tasting such an expensive alcohol that she remembered rather than the actual flavour.

Atim discovered that many of the guests did not really care about the taste, because once they were high they would not know when the bartender had substituted their drink with something much cheaper!

I enquired that if a customer asked for her recommendation, could she handle the request? She said no she could not. The captain dealt with that aspect. However, she did know about the availability of the alcohol, though she had to go for extra briefings to learn about the extensive menu on offer. Atim showed me the four-page list of dishes; she could proudly recite most of it: kilted sausages with mustard mayonnaise, Lebanese platter with lahem meshwi, sish taouk, hummus, babaganoush and spaghetti puttanesca. Not only did she know the names, but also the ingredients of each of the exotic dishes. She had acquired a taste for pan-fried noodles but not for tofu or goat's cheese.

Keya did not have many tables, and Atim said it was really difficult to manage the service in the constricted space crowded with young people enjoying their expensive drinks.

On any given evening, Atim and one other steward would handle six tables. She would escort the guest to the table; place the B&B plates and wipe the table if necessary and hand them the menu.

She also took orders and then punched them into the computer. First, she would punch the table number and number of guests; then go to the drinks menu and punch in the drinks and later the food orders. In Keya, she would have to give the bartender the KOT (the Kitchen Order Ticket) in addition to the token for the drinks. After doing so, she would return to the entrance, ready to escort the next guest to the table.

By that time, the people at Table One would have discovered that their friends were at the bar and would have moved to sit with them. Then at Table Three, when she went to take the drinks order, the man and woman were obviously having a fight. The woman asked for a large whiskey and the man said she should not have any more. In such a situation, Atim would wonder whose order she should take; from the point of view of the restaurant it was better to take orders for more drinks. She would then punch in the orders and take the KOT to the bartender.

And by then, Table One would be ready to place their orders for dinner, but soon after they would call her because they wanted to cancel some of the items. Meanwhile, on Table Five there were two women. They came every evening. They were well-dressed but always ordered orange juice and water. Then they would demand a straw for the juice and call out again for more ice. Atim suspected they were call girls trying to pick up some customers.

Apart from escorting the guests and taking orders, Atim also had to offer Shisha pens or e-shishasticks or electronic cigarettes. There was a steward who dealt with the orders; each stick was sold for Rs 1,500 and came in a variety of flavours—apple, peach, mint, grape and cappuccino. Most times, the guests would just take a puff or two and leave them behind like cigarette stubs. She had gathered them and had quite a collection. When she went to Ukhrul she gave them as presents.

When it was time to pay the bill, Atim noticed that the Indian customers often fought with each other over the privilege of paying; in contrast a group of foreigners, even if they had come together and were sitting on the same table, all paid their own bills individually. Some guests who were not regulars managed to leave without settling the tab. On one occasion, Atim and a steward were working at the table and the bill ran up to Rs 4,000 but the customers had managed to slip out. It was the captain's discretion whether to make the waiters pay the amount; Atim was not asked.

During the weekends, the crowd was so big that there wasn't enough space to accommodate them inside the bar, and so customers hung around outside. On such evenings, she and the women would serve the outside customers while the male waiters, or stewards as they were called, would be sent into the crowded bar.

There were, however, times when Atim had to serve the customers inside the bar. She said it was a nightmare with the crowd swelling up to three hundred on Fridays and Saturdays, when the bar lounge turned into a nightclub. The guests did not stay at one table, but moved around and Atim would forget the face of the customer and not know who had ordered the food she was carrying. She said that to her all mayangs looked alike. After all these years in Delhi, she still thought of the local Indians as mayangs or 'outsiders'.

I remember a Naga student leader who had come to Delhi for the first time. When I asked him how he liked the city, he said it was nice but there were too many mayangs. I told him that he was the mayang in Delhi. He had never thought of it that way, he said, surprised.

Every weekend there were guests who got so drunk that they had to be escorted out by the bouncers. And often, things could take a nasty turn. Atim recalled one guest who used to come frequently for hookah and drinks. He would turn up with a group of his friends, all male. On one occasion, the manager did not allow them to enter. The next day he arrived with a whole contingent of his friends, many of whom had their own personal security officers. They sat in Keya and demanded to talk to the manager. They ordered a bottle of champagne worth Rs 30,000 and shook the bottle before opening it, so that the champagne whooshed out and sprinkled the other guests.

Atim said even high-profile guests behaved badly, though not with the staff. The rich young men were generous with tips and did not take the change, even if it was a couple of hundred rupees.

While serving the guests in Keya, Atim caught snatches of conversations: the men and women talked about London, Paris and New York as if they were Mumbai, Kolkata and Chennai. They flew all around the world and came to Keya to relax. They were not showing off; this was their life. At night, when they drove back home, it was in foreign cars. There was one guy who had a yellow Lamborghini; Atim knew it was an Italian sports car that cost some crores. Others too had slick, posh cars, and these people always came in designer clothes, and the accessories they wore would cost more than Atim's annual earnings. She did not resent it; she too dreamt of buying such clothes and accessories one day.

Chapter Ten

The Poetry Is Dying Within Us

The long hours in Keya and the weekend rush had stressed Atim out. She was feeling very frustrated. Life was passing her by. She felt she was getting old. Soon her age would bar her from applying for jobs on cruises. She finally left Keya in March 2014 and went back to Ukhrul where her father was trying to complete the house. While she was there, Yaokhalek had phoned: he had received a summons from the court and the police had said that the two of them were required to give their evidence again. Atim felt angry at the injustice of the legal system and how it seemed to have imprisoned her, while the man who she was sure had murdered her sister was out on bail.

She tried not to compare her life with the lives of others who had been with her in the final year at Alice Christian Higher Secondary School. But something would remind her of one or the other friend and she would curse her fate.

I asked her to make a list of the students in her class and tell me what each of them was doing. She said she could not possibly remember all of them; there had been a hundred students in each section. Nevertheless, she started writing down the names as she remembered.

The first name she wrote was Singchon Muivah. I asked her what she was doing. Atim said Singchon played the bass; she along with her two sisters had formed a band called Minute of Decay or MOD. Thotyaphy played the drums and Worshon was a vocalist and played the guitar. They now lived in Delhi. I asked whether Singchon had called when her sister had been murdered and Atim said she could not remember.

MOD was formed in 2011 and their first album was titled 'Finding Betsy'. Betsy was a niece who had died after taking an overdose of drugs. The Muivah sisters said it made them realize that 'on the inescapable fate of man, MOD challenges not nor attempts to alter that fate'.

Another song they sing is called 'Lifesong'. The words, written by Shelmi Sankhil,[78] could have been for Atim:

From land afar I have come
Leaving green, blue sky and cool streams all behind
I carry dreams in my heart
And live each day remembering guns and tears.

* * *

By the beginning of 2014, Ramyo had started clearing the land to build the house. It had been a tough job getting people to cut the trees and now he was ready to start on the construction. Atim wanted to ensure that the job was completed so that she could plan for her own future. Since she had been living with Nandita and Sebastian she had saved the rent money; even so, she needed to have more money before she could go to Ukhrul. She borrowed from friends; most of them gave her interest-free loans while others gave the loans with interest, but at lesser rates than she would have got in Ukhrul.

She booked her ticket to Ukhrul; she was keen to make sure the house was built before the rains started. This time she had bought a one-way ticket. She intended to return to Delhi only after the house had been constructed.

When she arrived in Ukhrul in May, she discovered that her mother had started a chilli business. She used to buy a kilo of dry, smoked chillies and pound them by hand to make a fine powder, which was then put into small packages. She could pound five kilos of chillies in a little more than half an hour. The value of the hand-pounded chilli powder was Rs 240. She sold her powder cheaper than others, so people started phoning and asking her for it.

---

78. Shelmi Sankhil belongs to Lamkang Naga tribe. At present, he teaches in the School of Liberal Studies, Ambedkar University, Delhi.

Atim's mother would walk to Haotang, Viewland and Wino Bazar to supply women who had small shops and who bought from her. One day, Atim's mother decided to enlarge the scope of her business. She enlisted her sister and the two women bought Rs 2,500 worth of chillies. They started pounding the chillies and kept at it till the neighbours started to complain about the fumes. That day, Atim's mother and her sister made Rs 2,000 each and they were very pleased.

Sometimes Atim's mother would take her chilli powder all the way down to Imphal to sell there, and then she would buy some snails and bring them back to Ukhrul.

The chilli business was a welcome addition to her father's pension. Since they were still paying interest on the loans taken during his illness, Ramyo's pension paid for two bags of rice—a hundred kilograms each. But every day there were seven or eight members of the family, including the children; in addition, relatives from Kalhang came to Ukhrul for work. Atim noticed that there were sometimes ten people and they had two meals, which meant that three koktah (two-and-a-half kilograms) of rice was cooked every day.

They still did not have a vegetable garden and so they had to buy the vegetables. If they cooked meat, then the expenses went up really high.

By June, everyone in Ukhrul was excited about the FIFA World Cup. Atim decided to visit her friend in Sinakeithei village so that they could watch football together for three days. The girls cheered for one team and the boys for another. The girls' team won, so the boys made Maggi noodles and tea for everybody. She could not remember the name of the team she had cheered for. When she left, she bought fresh beans from the village for her parents in Ukhrul.

On the way back to Ukhrul, the Kuki underground stopped the bus. When the driver tried to avoid stopping, a militant fired in the air to warn him. But nothing else happened.

A few days later, she visited another friend's paddy field. She discovered that instead of cultivating paddy, they had used the entire field as a fishpond, filled with more than six thousand fish. She and her friends tried to catch some big fish but could not; instead, they got small fish and snails.

Atim went to meet all the members of her marup, the Meitei word for friend. A group of people, usually women, pooled in money or sarongs, and then each month there was a lottery and one of them got the whole lot. Unlike a yarnao, the marup was only for one purpose: pooling money. She had joined a marup a year ago with ten girls who had studied in the same class in Holy Cross in Greenland. The boys had asked whether they could join but they had been refused.

It had all started when one of their friends, Thotyachan, was getting married to a pastor, and the girls had contributed Rs 1,500 each to buy her one tola of gold. It was then they decided that they would do the same for each other—it would be a tola of gold, whatever the price at the time of the wedding. The ten of them started contributing Rs 1,500 three times a year, but soon they decided to contribute every month so that all of them would benefit equally.

Of the ten women, three were working outside their homes: Somipen, a schoolteacher; Wonshangla, a trained nurse; and Atim. Leishichan was studying for her PhD while the other six were married—Yuimiwon to an officer in the Indian army; Pamchuichan's husband owned a small pharmacy; Thotyachan was married to a pastor; Chonreiphi was married to someone in the security forces; Thanshim was married to a Hongray and Leingamphi to a man making pottery in Bangalore.

It was in Leishichan's home that she had seen an enticing poster of the Taj Mahal, and wished with all her heart that she could one day go and see the glittering white monument to love.

Atim had come a long way from the day when she had

sat for her ninth standard exams almost ten years ago, when she was given a pink card. When they checked the cards she discovered that only students with yellow cards were allowed to sit for the exams. The pink cardholders were those who had not paid their fees and, therefore, could not sit for the exams. She had felt so humiliated. How could a Christian school show so little compassion, she had wondered.

Now she could buy herself clothes, shoes and, more important, support her parents. She felt that once the house was built, it would restore her family's self-respect.

* * *

Later, in September, her nieces Sochuila and Masowon came to Ukhrul from Dubai for a short vacation. They had a huge paddy field near Leishipung, and the three young women decided to spend the night at the hut there. They bought five kilograms of chicken, which they cut up and marinated with soya sauce, ginger paste, vinegar, crushed fresh green chillies; then Sochuila's mother fried the pieces. They also took some sticky maize, rice, and boiled squash. They had quite a feast that night, sitting under the clear sky with a canopy of stars, surrounded by silence.

Atim was eager to hear stories about life in Dubai. Masowon said it was easy and safe for women. The best part was that they could dress simply, unlike in Ukhrul where people noticed if they did not wear branded clothes.

Masowon had another story. She said she had bought something with her credit card. Apparently, she had won some lottery. She kept getting calls on her mobile which she ignored, but at last when she answered, she was told that she had won a trip for the World Cup Final and she could bring one more person. So the two sisters had gone to Brazil and had found themselves being treated like VIPs with a room in a five-star hotel and a car at their disposal; and they were given £800 for shopping.

Sochuila's mother and the two nieces told Atim that she should also try to join them in Dubai. They were quite serious and, for the first time after many years, Atim saw a flicker of hope. She could dare to dream again of a more comfortable and secure future for herself.

Sochuila had worked very hard. Like Atim, she had done housework for a Tangkhul woman married to a German and living in Chennai. She had mopped the floors, swept and cleaned their house and with the wages managed to support herself and do a course in business management from Indira Gandhi National Open University (IGNOU). Thereafter, she had got a job in Dubai and even managed to rent a house on her own, despite the strict rules about women staying alone. In addition, she had helped her younger sister Masowon, who now worked in a watch shop in a posh shopping mall. And their younger sister Ningshichon had followed; she worked at a coffee shop at the airport.

Atim told me that their brother, Wungreingayung Zingkhai, would be coming to Delhi on his way to Dubai. She brought him to my house on his way to the airport. He had been in Dubai earlier, working at a construction site, but it was a tough job and he had left it. The rules for entry to the UAE were strict and he had to return to India before he could go back to Dubai and try for another job.

When I asked Wungreingayung how he liked Dubai, he said it was nice, and he did not have any problems. Often he had been mistaken for a Filipino. He said he had no occasion to talk to the 'Pathans'; for some reason he thought the Arabs were Pathans. He was not sure in which country Dubai was, but he complained about the fact that he could not live with his girlfriend in the same house.

He said it was more difficult for men to find jobs than women. But that seemed to be true for men in India as well. Atim translated an account written by a Tangkhul man on

Facebook in which he recounted his ordeals while trying to get a job in Delhi.

The man was from a very poor family and he spoke of the difficulties he had trying to finish his studies; he finally graduated in 2005. And then began his search for a job. He did not have the money for the bus fare for the interview at a call centre; the consultancy agency gave him the cash. But he still had no money to go back home after the interview, so he walked all the way from Nehru Place to Munirka.

For six years he looked for a job, any job. In those six years he lost all hope and his courage. He felt God had abandoned him, and started questioning his very existence. But the Tangkhul pastor in Delhi, Dr Mathnami Zimik, gave him encouragement and prayed for him.

The man felt very disappointed each time he was refused at an interview and that made him despondent. He made four attempts to enlist as a soldier in the Indian army but he failed the exams on each occasion. There was no possibility of his returning to his village because he did not have any land or home; his father was elderly and he himself felt he was getting old.

And then one day he was called for an interview and he was selected and appointed as a sub-inspector of Delhi police.

Atim wondered what would happen to Yaokhalek. He too was an adult. He had not found a stable job, and was now dreaming of opening a shop. But he needed money to be able to pay the hefty deposit a landlord would ask.

In the midst of all these worries, Yaokhalek had phoned to say that the court had sent summons and that they were expected to give their testimonies again. Her heart was heavy when she booked her ticket back to Delhi.

In any case, it was time for her to return to Delhi. She had been in Ukhrul for six months and the house was nearing completion. It had three big rooms and a kitchen, but they did not have the funds to make a bathroom or a septic tank. The house had been constructed with tin and plywood. Atim had planted a myriad flowers and told her sister to take photos when they bloomed and send them to her. She planted begonia, geranium, lilies of different varieties.

It was October and the cold was getting quite intense. Atim could not bear the sharp, crisp cold of Ukhrul winters when the temperatures could go down to below zero on some nights. They had to depend on small maiphu, stoves run with charcoal and build fires to keep warm. Firewood had become very expensive and people went to bed by six in the evening because often there was no electricity.

* * *

It did not take Atim long to find herself another job. Her two friends, Chonreiyo Jajo and Pemreichon Alongnao (Apem), with whom she had worked before in Q'BA had joined a new Japanese restaurant called En; they were keen that she join them as well.

En, which means synchronicity, was housed in an old renovated haveli, with a grand wooden staircase and wood-panelled doors and a dark rich wooden floor. It was a part of a complex called Ambawatta One, in a trendy area of Mehrauli. The magnificent Qutub Minar could be seen from the terrace and from some of the rooms.

Atim had heard that in the past the complex had been an asylum for mad people, others claimed it had been a sub-jail. Now it had Manish Malhotra's boutique with clothes that cost lakhs. Atim had not dared go inside. Next door was Aayana, which advertised itself as 'a temple of beauty', where the rich and famous could get all kinds of treatments to hide their age and lose their weight. A billboard claimed it could make you beautiful from inside and outside.

Atim found herself entering a totally new world—the world of Japanese cuisine, culture and etiquette.

* * *

As a hostess, Atim had to stand outside in her uniform of black trousers and a red top designed to look like a mini-kimono. She was taught to welcome the Japanese guests with her left hand holding her right hand and bowing. She learnt to greet in Japanese: konnichi wa was a general greeting, and a more formal welcome was irashaimase.

The Japanese manager, Imuara, handed her a page with points on Japanese etiquette. Atim showed me the paper. It was written in English and Japanese. The opening paragraph read:

'When you went to the restaurant, how often did you feel to go there again?

'The factor that you feel to go again depends on the satisfaction you got at the restaurant. I think people feel to go to the restaurant again when they feel excitement. Excitement in this case means that their satisfaction is more than their expectation. And I feel this excitement depends more on your service than food itself or inter decoration.' [sic]

And the definition of good service was to provide the customer with what he would want before he had requested for it. The menu card was always given opened and the staff was instructed to be ready to take orders the moment a customer had 'lifted his face from the menu'.

The manager taught the Indian waiters and waitresses the Japanese protocol for seating, and while serving, the guests must be served before the host. There were strict rules about the cutlery and crockery. For instance, the spoon in the saucer is placed under the cup handle facing the guest. Atim noticed that the Japanese did not drink plain water; they had tea instead.

Atim would serve the Japanese guests because they were expected to know the items on the menu; the Japanese manager insisted that only those who knew the ingredients of each dish should take the orders from the non-Japanese customers who wanted to know about Japanese food.

The Japanese manager said the waiters should learn to describe each dish and tell its story as well as any trivia related to it. And they were to 'try to start a conversation with the customer with any topic. It will be the opportunity to reduce the distance between you and customers.' And the bill should be put gently on the table. If a customer asked for the washroom, they were instructed, 'Do not say in voice as: "This is Toilet," guide in the gesture'.

The Japanese manager said that when taking the orders, or answering questions and saying goodbye, the waiters must smile. For the three Tangkhul women it came naturally; it was a part of their upbringing. I often had to warn Naga women that in mainland Indian culture we do not smile at strangers.

Atim would bid the guests goodbye with arigatou gozaimashita, which is the thank you used for people of higher status. Often, the Japanese took her for a fellow Japanese and were surprised to know there that were Indians who looked liked them.

One night Atim came home late at night; I was waiting up for her. She had brought a box of sushi for me to try with soya and wasabi sauce. She took out a pair of disposable chopsticks and deftly mixed the sauce and lifted one piece for me to taste. I asked how she had learnt to use the chopsticks. She said Jajo had taught her.

On one occasion, the former chief minister of Nagaland came to dine at En. He had come with his wife and daughter. Atim placed the chopsticks before them, thinking that the family would know how to use them, but she found the wife did not know and the father and daughter struggled with them. Atim said it took a lot of practise to learn.

And then there was this Meitei woman who came with an Indian. Atim noticed how elegantly she ate with the chopsticks while the Indian could not. She knew Japanese food and ordered mushrooms. Atim told Jajo in Tangkhul how she loved the taste of mushroom. When the woman asked Jajo to clear the table, Atim noticed that she had left half the mushrooms. Obviously she had understood their conversation and left the mushrooms for the two waitresses.

Atim felt a rare happiness working in En. First of all, there was no pressure. Most people came for the sumptuous buffets or ordered the fixed five-course meal. There was no tension in serving the guests. And even when the Japanese ordered à la carte, serving was not difficult; they were always polite and never dropped food on the tablecloths or dirtied the napkins. But then they also seldom left tips.

At En, the three Tangkhul women could have fun and chat. Now they all had smartphones and could listen to Tangkhul music while waiting for the guests; often there were none during the weekdays. The chefs, the Japanese as well as the Indian, were also polite.

One of the Japanese chefs had even asked Atim what she would like from Japan and she had asked for seeds of flowers. She wanted to grow them in Ukhrul now that they had a proper house and a garden. When he returned, the chef brought her the seeds, along with especially sharp knives for the Tangkhul chef and Japanese sticky rice for Jajo and Apem.

* * *

Among the nine chefs there was one Tangkhul called Phungreingam Ramsan. He had begun by working at a spa at the Delhi airport after his Bible studies. Then he had found a job at a Japanese restaurant in Rajasthan and after that he had joined En. There were very few Tangkhuls who worked as chefs, and Atim and Ramsan became friends.

I asked Atim about her relations with the Indian waiters and other co-workers. She said it was always professional. Only once when she had been working in Q'BA, had she and the other Tangkhul girls accepted an invitation to a waiter's home on the occasion of Diwali. The family had been very warm and welcoming and they had enjoyed the vegetarian meal and fireworks. But the invitation was only because he was going out with a Naga girl.

Atim said, 'If they are good to us, we are good to them.' She said they (the Indians) trusted them (the Nagas). For instance, one of the waiters gave Apem and Atim his debit card and even told them his pin number. He wanted them to buy him jeans and shirts from Sarojini Nagar market. Another time, when one of the waiters got married, he asked Atim to buy panties and bras for his wife. Atim had asked what colour. He had said any but not white or black.

The trouble with a job as a hostess was that there was no promotion to look forward to. Those who were serving started off as assistant trainee steward and then moved on to assistant steward, senior steward, then trainee captain, captain, and if you did well, you could be promoted to assistant manager. The lucky few became F&B Manager or Operations Manager. The men got more opportunities than the women. Everyone just ended up dreaming of opening their own restaurant...

One day, when Atim came to work, she found Jajo totally involved with something on her smartphone. Atim had noticed that she had been distracted of late and she asked what it was. Jajo told her of a new video game which she had downloaded, called the 'restaurant game'. The game allows you to own your own dream restaurant in the virtual world. You can choose the dishes you will serve and put them on a stove for cooking. The idea is to have enough food for the customers who enter the restaurant. As they eat, the number of available servings for the food they've chosen will go down—which means you'll need to stay in the kitchen and make sure there's always something on the stove to replace the current meal.

Happy customers bring in more customers; the more people coming in, the more quickly you run out of seating. Once there are no seats, angry customers start to storm out and your popularity begins to drop. The game continues to play even while you are away or sleeping, so you have to ensure there is enough food to serve when you're not there.

Atim soon got hooked on to the game. She was busy decorating her restaurant, buying beautiful red chairs and wall clocks. She ran out of money to buy the more expensive decorations but she managed to keep the restaurant running. She was living in this beautiful dream world where she was the owner of a restaurant, cooking spaghetti and baking cakes. She soon realized she had become an addict, not sleeping at night and not being able to concentrate on the job. She stopped herself from playing and forced herself to face the real world.

* * *

Atim soon began to dream of having her own restaurant in Ukhrul. She dreamt of making sushi but with a Naga twist. She said she would put smoked pork and chillies. Her friendship with the Tangkhul chef had deepened; Ramsan confided that he too dreamt of opening a sushi restaurant in Shillong. Why sushi? Atim said the youth had seen people eating sushi in Korean films and they too wanted to try those dishes.

Chapter Eleven

Money, Money, Money

'Aunty, now I just want to make money!' Mayori announced when I met her in June 2015. 'I am not interested in politics or anything. I just need to make money.'

It was her first visit to India after she had got married to an Englishman in November 2014; she had come loaded with presents for everyone. She had bought a fancy pair of boots for Atim and video games for people back home in Ukhrul.

'We all do. But the question is that you all seem to want to make it very quickly.' I responded.

I had often tried to sell the idea to young Nagas that it was possible to make money by hard work and saving. But Atim and Mayori both felt that only Indians could save, it was not something Nagas could do. They felt it was a part of their national character and not a skill they could learn!

When I looked around I could not find any story to disprove them, but there was a story in the making. Livingstone had contacted me to say that the owner of the restaurant in which he was working as a waiter was leaving and there was a possibility he could buy it from him. It was a a fine dining restaurant rated as one of the best for Thai food; it seemed that only the other day he had gone home with his legs aching from standing so many hours working as a waiter. I told Mayori and Atim his story.

* * *

It was October of 2008 when Livingstone set off from Bengaluru to Panjim, the capital of Goa, accompanied by his friend Ayo. Livingstone remembered the bus ride from Bengaluru to Panjim as the worst journey in his life. As it got dark, he felt something moving on his back, then on his legs and soon he felt it all over. He put on his torch thinking he would see ants but instead he saw bugs, hundreds of them crawling all over the seat. On top of that, the mosquitoes kept up their relentless attack and there was no escape for fifteen hours.

Once they reached Panjim, he felt better. Panjim looked smaller than Bengaluru and he noticed that there were a lot more trees. From Panjim, they took a bus to Mapusa. Livingstone remembers crossing a bridge over a beautiful river. From Mapusa they took another bus to a place Ayo called Tivim. Instead of going towards the sea, he found the bus going through jungles and up a hill.

Tivim, for Livingstone, was like a village. He saw a lot of Tangkhuls and he was told there was a man called Yangmi who was from his father's village, Mapum. But Yangmi was not there at the time.

Ayo's girlfriend was pregnant and he was in no hurry to look for a job, but Livingstone wanted to begin looking for one straightaway. It was October, the beginning of the tourist season when restaurant owners recruited employees.

After a few days, Ayo took Livingstone to Mapusa and from there to Calangute by bus. From the bus stop they walked to a bylane where a lot of Tangkhuls lived in rented rooms. It was hot and many of the men were not wearing anything except their underwear. There was no road between the houses and they walked on sand, going from room to room, stepping over sleeping people. Many people seemed to be living in each room. Livingstone was shocked to see how easily Ayo walked in and out of people's rooms and even more shocked to see the conditions in which his people were living.

Ayo was collecting information about the availability of jobs. In one room Livingstone met a woman from Mapum, his father's village. He was shocked that she did not invite him for a meal. But here no one behaved with the same warm hospitality as they did back in Ukhrul. The season had just begun, so most people did not have money and when someone offered them lunch, Livingstone did not feel like eating. He felt embarrassed about having a free meal.

Ayo knew the Candolim, Calangute and Baga area like the back of his hand. The two men walked from one end to another. They checked out some of the restaurants where they had heard there were vacancies, but Ayo refused each one because he did not like the terms. In one, the tips were not good; in another, the tips were all taken by the senior waiters; in yet another, they wanted someone with experience in serving alcohol.

The walking in the heat was tiring and neither of them had money. Livingstone had a one-dollar-note which someone had given him as a tip when he was working in Pizza Hut in Bengaluru. He gave it to Ayo who exchanged it quickly and with the money they bought a bottle of water and cigarettes.

Eventually, there was just one other place on their list, the Oriental in Calangute. It was owned by a German called Henry Pfeifer who it was said, did not pay well, but he allowed the waiters their fair share of the tips. The Tangkhuls had told Ayo and Livingstone that the tips were good, but Henry shouted a lot at his employees and never accepted his own mistakes.

Henry interviewed Ayo and Livingstone. He seemed pleased with Ayo since he had experience and Henry offered him a job right away with an incentive of 10 per cent of the tips. Henry did not promise anything to Livingstone, but he said if no one else came he might get the job. Henry promised to phone Livingstone within two days. But there was no call.

Ayo and Livingstone went back to Tivim where Ayo's girlfriend was staying. After spending two days there, they picked up their meagre belongings and appeared at the Oriental again. Henry was interviewing some Tangkhuls but when he saw Livingstone he told him to join.

Livingstone joined the Oriental on 28 October 2008 but he was not given an appointment letter; Henry told him that his salary would be Rs 3,000 with food and accommodation. Livingstone deposited his belongings in the staff quarters, which turned out to be a big hall almost opposite the restaurant within walking distance. He shared the space with sixteen other men: three Tangkhuls, eleven Nepalis who worked in the kitchen and two Bengalis. There was just one bathroom.

He had to report every morning at eleven and work till 3 p.m. He had two hours off before turning up at the restaurant again at 5 p.m. Work continued till one in the morning or till the last customer had left. Saturdays were off, since on that day many of the Oriental's usual customers went to visit the famous Ingo's Saturday Night Market started by a German hippie.

Livingstone had heard Henry shouting at Chawee, the Thai chef who had left the Taj Hotel to work with him. She had two daughters from a previous marriage and struggled hard in the kitchen. Henry had married her and they had a son. Together, they had registered a company in July 2001 called Eastern Delicacies Private Ltd.

Ayo did not always stay in the staff room. He rented a bike and went back to Tivim to be with his pregnant girlfriend. He would be late for work and this angered Henry, especially since he was giving him a good salary and tips. Finally, Henry threw Ayo out of his job.

Henry had noticed that Livingstone worked hard and willingly, even though he was paid the least, and in the next month he increased his share of tips. Henry did shout a lot but he was fair about paying the salaries and giving overtime.

Livingstone learnt the menu by heart and also the ingredients which went into making each of the forty to fifty dishes on the list. It had not been easy because he was not familiar with Thai spices. Livingstone enjoyed the work, especially the opportunities it gave him to chat with the customers. Although he could take orders in English, he found it difficult to respond when he was asked anything outside the menu.

An elderly couple from Britain made friends with him and gave him some lessons in English. He would ask them how he should respond to customers in various circumstances and they patiently taught him.

There were twenty-three tables and when Livingstone joined, all of them would be occupied during November and December, and from January to March there were long queues of people waiting to get a place in the restaurant; it was impossible to get a table without reservations. Henry warned the waiters not to serve a customer who came only for drinks and starters.

Most of the customers were foreigners. Henry had told the waiters to discourage Indian customers by putting the reservation sign on the empty tables. At the time Livingstone thought Henry was very clever. He internalized Henry's attitude towards the Indians.[79]

Livingstone was surprised that they were given incentives for selling seafood and wine bottles: Rs 20 for wine, Rs 20 for a seafood platter, Rs 40 for lobster and Rs 30 for tiger prawns. He managed to earn around Rs 60 to Rs 100 every day. In those days, Livingstone did not drink alcohol and so could save a lot of money and send it home. The incentives he earned were enough for his daily expenses; he could even afford to occasionally have a meal of tandoori chicken and roti at a fast food joint. Soon, however, he began to enjoy a glass of Kingfisher beer with his dinner.

The food for the staff in the restaurant was also good. In the mornings, it was always dal and rice, with either fish, chicken or pork. In the evenings, it was rice and dal because the chef did not have time to make anything else. But Livingstone and the other waiters could always supplement their meals with the

---

79. This practice is common in many restaurants in Goa and Indians, including the local Goans, are made to feel unwelcome.

leftovers. He liked the Thai food because it had some chillies, even if it was not as hot as the curry back home where they used umrok, the Naga chilli. However, when he first tasted western food like steaks and spaghetti he did not like the bland taste.

Livingstone did not mix too much with the other Tangkhuls because they drank. He was good friends with Ngathingpam (or Apam for short) who was also a waiter at the Oriental, and on their free days they often stayed back in the staff quarters watching television or listening to music. They had each bought a guitar from Mapusa; Livingstone had spent Rs 5,000 for a cheaper one, while his friend bought a more expensive instrument. But Livingstone found his fingers were not flexible enough to play the guitar well, even though he did try quite hard.

Livingstone was pleased and proud of his achievements. He remembered Ramtawon and her friends telling him repeatedly that he would take a long time to catch up with them. She used to earn Rs 16,000 and she said it would be difficult for a man to earn that much immediately. He called her in Bengaluru and announced that he was already earning Rs 11,000. He told her he was managing his daily expenses with just his incentives. He had not touched his salary or tips. Ramathawon was suitably impressed; still, she advised him to keep the money properly. In Tangkhul she said, '*Na Khamahaile zang haira khahe nawui hotkhana wuivang einana*'—You are lucky, that your hard work has paid off. Livingstone told her he would soon be earning as much as she did, but she said he still had a long way to go.

At the time Livingstone had not paid attention to the warning, but later it seemed that Ramtawon had a premonition of the things to come.

* * *

The season ended by April and the Oriental closed down. Livingstone decided to go to Bengaluru in the hope of finding a job. He met his old friends and roamed around the city, but he knew he could not get used to working there after the casual and relaxed working atmosphere in Goa and so he returned.

In the off-season months, from April to October, the staff had to find their own accommodation. Apam and Livingstone rented a place in Calangute for Rs 5,000 a month and five other men from the Northeast joined them. In addition, there was Livingstone's younger brother Yarmi who had recently arrived from Ukhrul.

Livingstone had asked Yarmi to come because he had identity papers and a school certificate from the Open School; Livingstone did not have any identity papers and so he had to work as Yarmi.

There were eight of them staying in one room and no one was earning. Apam's family had sent him some money and so had Livingstone's father. On one occasion, his brother Donald too had sent some. Livingstone did not like taking money from his family but he had no choice. However, even after putting together what both their families had sent, the money was still not enough to pay for the rent and food. To avoid their landlord, the men would come to the room late at night to sleep and leave very early and roam around.

Livingstone did not have money to buy his cigarettes and if he did manage to get some, the others would all demand a drag. He noticed that although his other roommates never had money for the rent or food, they always managed to find some for alcohol— even if alcohol was cheap in Goa and easily available, it still cost money.

Livingstone remembers one day well. The day he felt really angry and very helpless. Apam and he had got up early in the morning and were sitting on the beach. It was too early to even look for work. They had no options and the situation seemed so hopeless. Finally, Livingstone and Apam went to a Kuki acquaintance by the name of James to ask for a loan. James readily lent them money with which they bought a bag of rice to take home. Livingstone remembered the Naga-Kuki clashes and thought how ironic that a Kuki should have come to his rescue.

What had made them really angry was that the whole ten-kilo bag of rice had been consumed, because the roommates had invited their friends over. Sometimes Apam and he would go to the beach to wait for the fishermen to bring in their catch and would pick up the fish they discarded. One of their roommates had cooked a really delicious curry. But in the monsoons the fishermen did not go to sea. There was nothing at all to eat. Livingstone felt especially responsible for his younger brother.

When Livingstone had first arrived in Goa he did not drink. The Baptists were forbidden from touching alcohol and back in Ukhrul it was difficult to get any and it was very expensive. But he had started relishing a glass of beer, and by now had started drinking heavily.

Henry usually drank after ten at night and soon after he would take Chawee and her daughters back to their home. The moment he left, the barman, a Goan, would announce that the 'bar is open'. Then the staff could have as much to drink as they wanted; they helped themselves to the alcohol left unfinished by the customers, including the complimentary brandy that Henry offered to all clients. Livingstone had already learnt the names of the different kinds of alcohol from the barman, who also enjoyed his drinks hugely.

* * *

When the season started, Livingstone and Apam did not move into the staff accommodation because it was not very spacious and there were a lot of mosquitoes. They continued to live in the same room with their friends who were all addicted to alcohol as well.

None of them bothered to keep the room tidy expect Yarmi who tried to stop Livingstone from drinking. But now they were all earning; between the seven of them they earned a combined salary of Rs 80,000 a month, but none of them saved. All their money went into buying alcohol.

Every night, the other waiters carried Livingstone back to his room, dead drunk. In the mornings, he came to work with a massive hangover and by evening he was drinking again and his colleagues would cover for him, hiding him from Henry. A Goan woman near their rented room had started selling alcohol to Livingstone and his friends, which meant that they did not have the bother of walking to a liquor shop; they could buy it on their doorstep.

Livingstone had stopped sending money home, but this was not just because he was spending it on alcohol. He was upset with his father because he had been discouraging Livingstone from marrying his girlfriend, Ruth.

Ruth and Livingstone had met in Ukhrul in 2007, but she left for Hyderabad soon after their meeting. Ruth had started working when she was very young, barely out of her teens. Both her parents had passed away and she had to support her four younger brothers (she had no sisters). Ruth had come to Goa from Hyderabad in 2005; she did not know about Livingstone coming to Goa in 2008. Then, in 2009, Livingstone got a call from Ruth. It had warmed his heart just to hear her voice. He realized that he had not had any female company for more than a year. They had started living together and wanted to get married, but Livingstone's father had objected.

Then, early in the morning on 3 January 2010, Livingstone received a call from Ukhrul. His father had died. Henry gave him an advance and some other friends also gave him some money. But there was not enough for both him and Yarmi to fly to Imphal, so Livingstone flew alone from Goa to Kolkata where Donald met him and then they took the flight to Imphal. From there they drove up to Ukhrul in a car.

Donald and Livingstone went to the Seipet Ramlung

Church where their father's body lay in a coffin. On the way, people shook hands with them. Livingstone looked down at his father's face; it looked really calm and serene. But he could not look for too long, as tears welled up in his eyes. He felt a profound shame; he knew that his father had heard about his drinking. It must have pained him. And he felt guilty about exchanging angry words with him over Ruth. Now he could not even apologize. He wanted to stay by the coffin, but the sun was setting and people had been keeping vigil for two nights. Donald made a short speech and they took the body to the cemetery for burial. Before they lifted his father's coffin, Livingstone made a silent promise that he would stop drinking and take full responsibility for the family.

Livingstone was surprised at the number of people who came for his father's funeral—the neighbours, the relatives and the youth. It was a comforting feeling to be with his people. Livingstone's mother told him that the neighbours had cooked food for all the people and had fed them for a week; they had also contributed money for the funeral.

Livingstone's mother's relative Apila had come from Shimla where she lived with her Himachali husband. She offered to take the two youngest children back with her and admit them to an orphanage run by Catholic priests. Livingstone's mother had no choice because she knew she could not support such a large family on her own. Although three of her sons—Donald, Livingstone and Yarmi—were now working, none of them were earning enough to send back money to support the nine children still with her. That was how Livingstone's youngest brother, Machinmi, and sister, Soshimla, went to live in Shimla. To this day, the children and their mother have not been able to see each other.

* * *

In 2013, Livingstone sent a friend Yangmi to fetch Machinmi and Soshimla from Shimla to Goa. It felt really strange to meet his siblings who spoke Hindi and English, but who could no longer speak Tangkhul fluently. But they had been brought up well and were much politer than children back in Ukhrul; they added 'ji' to people's names to show respect. Most importantly, they had been getting a good education.

When Livingstone asked his little brother and sister what they wanted, they said they only had two wishes: one was to fly in an airplane and the other was to see their mother again. Livingstone promised them that he would fulfill their wishes one day.

* * *

Livingstone turned over a new leaf when he returned to Goa after his father's funeral. He moved out of the room that he had been sharing with his alcohol-loving friends and found accommodation in Calangute, where he, Ruth and his brother Yarmi could live together. Their apartment had a large balcony.

In the meantime, Livingstone's father's brother and cousin had contacted Ruth's family, since she did not have parents, and had spoken to them about a 'compromise'. This is what is done when a man and woman elope and start living together. The families come together and reconcile and then the couple go to church and confess to their sin, after which they are taken back into the church.[80]

Once the season was over, Ruth and Livingstone went to Ukhrul and confessed, one by one, before the congregation that they had been living together in 'sin'. This was on

---

80. Nowadays couples decide to elope and save the expense of a church wedding and feast. In a case of genuine elopement, the girl's brothers will give serious chase to the man and if he is caught before the negotiations, he can be seriously harmed. After the 'confessions' in church, Ruth and Livingstone's relationship was looked upon as legitimate, but legally speaking they did not have any documents to prove their marriage. This makes it more difficult for them to apply for a passport etc.

17 April 2011. But they did not have enough money for a feast to celebrate the occasion. They went back to Goa by train in May, the hottest month, and had to travel in a compartment without air conditioning.

It was still the off-season when they returned to Goa and the Oriental was closed. Livingstone found a job at Pulse, a restaurant owned by Mervyn Wong, the nephew of Nelson Wong who owns China Garden in Mumbai.

* * *

It was during this period that the members of the Tangkhul Welfare Union contacted Livingstone to ask permission to have their meetings on his balcony.

Livingstone had heard of the Union when he first arrived in Goa. He had heard that it had been inaugurated on 12 May 2009, and that the chief guest was Sebastian Hongray and his wife Nandita, who, he was told, was a Kashmiri.

The founder of the Union, James Muinao's term was over in 2010 and Soreingam had been elected President of the Tangkhul Welfare Union. He spoke English fluently and had been active in the Youth with a Mission movement.

From this time onwards, the meetings of the Tangkhul Welfare Union began to be held in Livingstone's rented room, and that was how he got the opportunity to closely observe the functioning of the Union. This also gave him the chance to learn how to run an organization. Livingstone actively participated in the Union's activities, including sports events— the Tangkhuls had four football teams and held matches on the beaches. They also organized entertainment programmes like singing, fashion shows, debates and culinary events.

What Livingstone admired most about Soreingam was his ability to handle the non-Tangkhuls, the Goans and the other Indians. He invariably made a distinction between the two. Soreigngam seemed to always win in the arguments he had with the locals.

* * *

In the meanwhile, James was trying to start a Fellowship for the Tangkhuls. He wanted to be a pastor,[81] but it meant full-time work and the Tangkhul community in Goa would not have been able to support him financially.

James ultimately did succeed in becoming a pastor on 9 January 2011 with the backing of the Tangkhul Baptist Fellowship in Bengaluru, which sent him Rs 8,000 a month. The Tangkhul community in Goa also managed to raise enough money to support Yangmi Pangrei from Mapum (Livingstone's village) as assistant pastor. Yangmi had been to a Bible school in Rajasthan. The community also had to pay the rent of between Rs 5,000 and Rs 8,000 for the space where they held their weekly service.

James had done an excellent job of organizing the Tangkhuls and the incidence of alcoholism came down substantially. The Tangkhuls had learnt to discipline themselves, which was no mean achievement under the circumstances they found themselves in. Livingstone too started attending the Tangkhul Fellowship and he found that more and more people were coming.

James had even converted one of the Meitei migrant workers to Christianity. That person was called Sword; his father was a Meitei and his mother a Tangkhul. His father died when he was very young. His father's family was educated and his uncles were engineers and advocates, while his brother had joined the

---

81. Pastor is a term used in the New Testament (while priest is used in the Old Testament). A pastor is chosen by the congregation and is considered the leader of the local church. Only a licensed and ordained pastor can administer sacraments. There is stiff resistance to ordination of women, but in 1992 an Ao community ordained a woman pastor; even so they do not have equal status as male pastors. James had the requisite degree to act as a pastor, but not a reverend, which would allow him to preside over marriages. The pastor must be financially supported by his own congregation. James finally became a reverend in 2016.

Manipur police. Sword had run away from his family after a
fight and when he came to Goa he had no money. He found
a job in a shack in Arambol. His employer was a Goan who
offered him a salary of Rs 1,800 for eighteen hours of work.
His day began at 7 a.m. and after a quick wash, he would start
peeling six to seven kilos of potatoes; then chop three kilos of
onions, three kilos of garlic, a kilo of green chillies, and clean
half a bucket of fresh coriander. All this had to be finished
by eight in the morning when the cooks began the cooking.
Sword then had to wash the dishes and this went on till late
in the night until the last guest had left. After the tables had
been cleaned, he could sleep on the mattresses on the floor of
the restaurant. They were full of sand and he got barely three
to four hours of sleep. Although the owner provided food, he
found the curry unpalatable and could not get used to the taste
of coconut.

Sword looked for another job and soon found one in a
restaurant in Calangute where he worked as a cashier for
a salary of Rs 3,000. He said that the owner treated the
employees from the Northeast badly. Sword also felt that the
Tangkhuls were very undisciplined, but he lived with them and
felt a sense of belonging. He converted to Christianity under
the influence of the Tangkhuls and James baptized him in a
pond near Tivim.

The Tangkhul leaders were strict about imposing a moral
code among their followers. Once, a man beat up a woman
very badly and Soreingam sent him back to Ukhrul for a period
of three years.[82] When Livingstone was in Ukhrul, he saw the
man who had been banished from Goa. Ruth and he were
out shopping in Wino Bazaar and saw him settling a dispute

---

82. Duncan McDuie-Ra's observation about how crises enable men
to take roles and responsibilities and enact traditional masculinity in
tough times are relevant here. The Tangkhul organizations are deeply

(Contd...)

between two men involved in a fight. They watched from a distance and had a good laugh.

* * *

Soreingam's two-year term as President of the Tangkhul Welfare Union came to an end in 2012. The members wanted Livingstone to be the next president, but he was hesitant. Unlike Soreingam, who had devoted all his time to the organization, Livingstone had a full-time job during the season and besides he could not speak Hindi or English as well as the previous president. Moreover he was going to be a father. But the will of the members prevailed and he was elected, through a show of hands, the President of the Tangkhul Welfare Union in May 2012

One of the first cases Livingstone had to deal with, as president, was a death. He could not remember the date, but he remembers that one of the Tangkhuls had received a call from the Calangute police station saying that they had found a dead body on the beach early that morning; he had been identified as Thotreingam from Mapum, Livingstone's village. The man had not come home, so his friends had reported him missing to the police station. He used to drink heavily and they suspected he had fallen down while drunk and had drowned.

Livingstone decided not to reveal his identity as President of Tangkhul Welfare Union because it could create more confusion in the minds of the police who would not understand who the Tangkhuls are. He could not also involve the wife of the deceased since they were not legally married.[83] So, he said

---

(...contd)

patriarchal. The formation of these organizations outside Ukhrul allows masculine norms from home to be reproduced in the face of ruptures produced by migration. See McDuie-Ra (2012) p.139.

83. I have mentioned these cases of to illustrate how difficult it is for the migrant workers to get basic documents such as identity cards, marriage certificates and even death certificates.

he was a distant relative of the dead man who happened to be from his father's village.

The police asked him a series of questions: How did he know the deceased? Were they were related? Where would he be taking the body? If he was going to send the body to Ukhrul, who would pay for the expenses? After Livingstone told them that he would bear all the expenses, the police helped him fill all the necessary forms and got him the No Objection Certificate. The police then arranged for the release of the body.

Livingstone and the Tangkhul Welfare Union wrote out a condolence message for the family and raised between Rs 30,000 and 40,000 to cover the expenses for the coffin and airfare.

Livingstone met the family members when he went to Ukhrul in November 2015. He thought the parents would invite him over for a meal, but they did not even thank him adequately. He narrated this story to illustrate how people's attitudes had changed in Ukhrul.

* * *

However, in Goa, the Tangkhul community came together in times of emergency, illness or death. Livingstone felt deeply grateful to his community for their support during the time Ruth had their first baby.

Livingstone vividly remembers 27 May 2012, the day his son was born, not because it was a joyous occasion but a day filled with horror and frustration. He remembers it well as the day his newborn baby nearly died.

When Ruth was fourteen or fifteen she fell ill and one doctor told her that she would not be able to have children. When she became pregnant she was overjoyed, but the pregnancy turned out to be very difficult. She developed a skin disease but could not take any medication and for months she did not sleep properly. Livingstone could not bear to see her pain. He pleaded with her to take the medicine, saying that they could try for a baby another time. But she had been determined, and now the day had come.

They decided to go to a government hospital, Asilo Hospital at Mapusa. It was a big building and seemed very nice and fairly clean from inside. The baby was born, but there was a slight complication and the doctor decided to send them to the Goa Medical College (GMC) at Bambolim. Livingstone held the tiny baby as he got into the ambulance with two friends, two nurses and Ruth. Ruth was on oxygen and the cylinder was next to where Livingstone was sitting with the baby.

The moment the driver started the ambulance, Livingstone realized that he was absolutely unfit to drive. He drove at a breakneck speed with the vehicle swaying from side to side. At one time, he jammed the breaks so hard that Livingstone went flying and the baby's head nearly collided with the oxygen cylinder.

Livingstone and Ruth went through hell while both the mother and child were in hospital. But the Tangkhul community kept up their morale with their presence and their prayers. Every day at least ten Tangkhul friends would be with Livingstone and one day he counted seventeen mobikes that they had borrowed to come to the GMC hospital. Moreover, they had collected more than Rs 50,000 to tide them over their crisis.

The baby was still not well, even after they were discharged from the hospital, and one day 'he screamed like a man,' as the doctor at the clinic in Candolim tried to find his vein. This time, the ambulance was well equipped and very clean and the driver drove with care and took them to the GMC again.

The baby was diagnosed with a hernia and the doctors advised an operation. When they rang up home, their family said it would be better to massage the baby and put back the hernia. But where were they to get such expertise? There was no money and it was off-season. Somehow they borrowed money and Ruth took the baby to Ukhrul.

She went to a local traditional doctor who massaged the baby and suddenly, as if by magic, the baby started smiling and seemed full of energy. Ruth stayed through the rainy season and returned to Goa in October 2012.

* * *

In January 2013, Henry sent his family back to Germany. It had taken a long time to get visas for Chawee and her daughters, but finally they could leave and find schools for the children. There was talk that Henry too wanted to go back and wanted to dispose of his business. Livingstone heard the news and asked Henry whether he would give the business to him. Henry asked him whether he had the money and Livingstone said he had a plot in Ukhrul that he could sell.

Henry returned to Germany by end April without anything being finalized. In October, Henry phoned to ask Livingstone whether he had some money to invest so that he could open the restaurant; he would be returning at the end of the month.

Livingstone had told Henry he would manage but, in fact, he had no money. It was the beginning of the season and so none of the Tangkhul friends would have money. He prayed for some miracle, and it was then that he decided to contact Nandita and ask for money.

Livingstone invested the money in shifting the restaurant to a new location at Mira Hotel. By the time Henry returned, there was a functioning restaurant with good reviews on TripAdvisor.

Henry started to teach Livingstone the various aspects of restaurant management and on 1 March 2014 Livingstone took over the restaurant. On that day, they made the highest profit of Rs 70,000. Henry left three days later.

* * *

Mayori had listened carefully and then she burst out in her inimitable manner: 'But Aunty, Livingstone did not SAVE money to start a restaurant. He just borrowed it from you!'

Chapter Twelve

The Exodus Is Not Over

In January 2015, the Tangkhul community in Goa was outraged by the news of the murder of a thirty-year-old Tangkhul woman, Chongamla Zimik, in her home in South Goa. The news of the murder was itself shocking but what really shocked the community was that she had been murdered by her Tangkhul servant. He had hit her with a baseball bat.

Chongamla Zimik had a five-month-old son and her husband, Savio Fernandez, was away on a ship at the time of his wife's murder. The Tangkhul Welfare Union members rushed to Madgaon to find out what had happened, and also to be with the family of the woman when they arrived from Ukhrul.

It was such a strange case, because I knew that within Tangkhul society there were very few murders that were not related to the insurgency, that is, people killed by the Indian security forces or the militants.

At the time my husband was in hospital after a serious accident, so it was much later that I asked Livingstone about the murder. He had been to see the twenty-five-year-old Banner Keising who stood accused of the murder. Livingstone brought me the court papers and among them I saw a timetable made by Chongamla for her employee. The local newspapers had reproduced it on their front pages. The timetable was handwritten:

Everyday Schedule:

5.30-6.15—Wash Clothes/ Bring old clothes Back and Fold

6.15-6.45—Flowers and Staircase

6.45-7.15—Broom and mop/dusting

7.15-8.45—Baby Abraham Time [underlined]

8.45-9.30—Boil water/Bfast [sic]

9.30-10.30—Clean Master bedroom/ BFast [sic] and Bathroom

10.30-11.30—Wash Clothes/Bring old clothes back and fold

11.30-12.30—Prepare Lunch

12.30-1.30—Baby Abraham Time/Lunch [underlined)]

1.30-2.30—Wash Clothes/Lunch

2.30–3—Clean/wash kitchen

3.00-4.30—Cleaning duties [The timing was underlined]

4.30-5.00—Iron Clothes

5.00-6.00—Prepare Tea/wash/clean Kitchen

6.00–7.00—Iron clothes for the night/broom and mop

7.00–8.30—Prepare dinner

8.30–9.30—Abraham Time

On the other side of the paper was a day-by-day schedule for Banner Keising:

MONDAY – Wardrobe and Chest of drawers and Bed in Abraham's room

TUESDAY – TV Unit, Sofas, Dining Table, Showpiece

WEDNESDAY – All shutters, glass to be wiped (Bedroom, Balcony both)

THURSDAY – All (9) doors to be wiped down with damp cloth

FRIDAY – Bleaching of the whole house floor

SATURDAY – Car to be washed

SUNDAY – Off.

Banner had to work from morning to night for a salary of Rs 4,000 plus food and a separate room without a bed. He had told one of the Tangkhuls that the only bright spot in his life was the baby, and he was holding the baby when he was arrested and taken to a sub-jail in Vasco where he continues to languish.

From the court papers I gathered that Banner had got fed up with the way he was being treated and that morning he had exchanged hot words with Chongamla; she had hit him and he had hit back, with tragic consequences.

Abuse of domestic help is rampant. In Ukhrul, parents send their children from the villages to Ukhrul town or to their relatives living in other parts of the country. I remember that Sebastian's nephew Kokpan had been brought from Ukhrul to study in Delhi. He was around ten years of age and was living with his older cousin sister, Wormipei, who was married to Sunil Batra. Apparently Sunil had converted to Christianity and turned over a new leaf after serving a term in jail on serious criminal charges. But Kokpan was not sent to school, instead he was made to do the housework. He was so badly treated that he had run away and worked at tea dhabas till one day an army officer had taken him home, and Kokpan had looked after his son who was the same age. Kokpan had been missing for several months before he was finally traced. When Sebastian went to fetch the boy, he found he was happy with the Indian family and did not want to be rescued. However, his father had insisted on taking him back to Ukhrul.

Such inhuman treatment of domestic help was prevalent among Nagas, both in Manipur and in Nagaland. There were many Tangkhul children and youth working as domestic servants in Tangkhul homes who were well looked after. But many times the servants were small children from other parts of India or Nepal, or children belonging to other Naga tribes. These were often treated very badly.

One friend told me she had kept a little girl because she had found her husband sleeping with their maid. Another time, I had seen Sebastian's cousin treating a little girl who was barely eight as if she was a slave. He was a pastor and I could not understand how they justified making a little girl work from early morning to late night and then making her sleep on a thin mat on the cold floor. It was especially disturbing because this was happening in a tribal society which had earlier been far more democratic than the caste-based Hindu society.

In Goa, the Tangkhul migrant workers felt solidarity with Banner languishing in jail. They knew he had not committed the murder deliberately. They made it a point to visit him in jail and Livingstone had even talked to the lawyer handling his case. The lawyer seemed to be optimistic about his client's release and he had told Livingstone to pray for Banner. I was curious about how the lawyer communicated with his client who knew no Hindi, English or Konkani.

* * *

I wondered whether there were any viable options for these migrant workers. Could they find any other way of making money?

The only viable alternative to the life of a migrant worker seemed to be doing business, and most of them dreamt of having the money to start a business of their own.

Yaokhalek and Atim had once taken me to see the shops in Humayunpur in the Safdarjung Enclave area of Delhi. It was like walking through a street in Wino Bazar in Ukhrul! There were Tangkhuls walking up and down the narrow lane and there were shops selling all kinds of items from the Northeast. The largest shop was owned by a woman from Manipur. It was spacious and as soon as I walked into it, I saw vegetables that I had seen in Imphal's famous Ema Market or the women's market.

At that time, I had reminded Atim about her story of her mother's visit to the INA market in Delhi. She had come away unimpressed. She said it was not a very good market.

Diplomats from all over the world went there to do their shopping, but Atim's mother had not been impressed. She looked at the fruits, vegetables, fish and chicken, but she could not find any of the vegetables she used to buy in Imphal's Ema bazaar.

But here in Humayunpur, in the middle of Delhi, was a shop with fresh vegetables from Manipur. I recognized yongchak or the monkey rice which went into the making of iromba— these, of course, were Meitei names and part of Meitei cuisine but had been enthusiastically adapted by the Tangkhuls. There was awaphadigom, a special kind of coriander; khavathei, a bitter brinjal which was Sebastian's favourite; and thangjing or lotus fruit and tree tomatoes, my favourite.

When I asked how the shop owner managed to get all these vegetables, Atim said they came every Thursday by air. In a corner was a big freezer and there we found smoked pork and beef; I also saw dry fish of various varieties.

This was the kind of shop Yaokhalek wanted to open in Ashram but he did not have the money. Atim had said she could not finance such a big project. I asked her how the Tangkhul woman in Humayunpur had started her shop. She said she had a boyfriend from Nigeria and he had provided the finance. There were several relationships between Northeast women and men from Africa, many from Nigeria.

I asked Yaokhalek whether he knew how to run a shop; he was very confident. He said he had the skill but just needed the money. But he did not realize that business was not only about buying and selling. If it had been just that then Mayori would have been very successful indeed.

* * *

Mayori, like so many Naga women, had been seriously involved in direct selling of cosmetics. In fact, it was from her that I first heard about this direct marketing. Before she came to stay with us in Goa in 2002, she had sold cosmetics. Afterwards, while she was staying with us in Delhi, she had tried her hand at selling books. She took books from small publishers in Delhi and sold them in Nagaland and Manipur. She was excited when she made profits, but then she lost a large sum of money when someone in Kohima did not pay the amount that was owed to her. There was no way she could recover such losses.

When she returned to Manipur, she went back to the business of selling cosmetics. After trying her hand at various kinds of enterprises, she made lots of money selling Jafra Cosmetics between 2010 and 2011. She said she took a course with them on how to apply make-up. She gave me a quick lesson.

Mayori said it could all be summed up as CTM or Cleanse, Tone and Moisture. Never use soap; begin with a cleanser which opens the pores; then the toner that closes the pores. Then one should use the anti-aging cream or skin brightener for pigmentation. Only after that does one apply a moisturizer before putting on any make-up. Mayori regretted the fact that the primers were not sold in India, so one had to begin with foundation; then powder, blush, eye-liner, nose-liner for nose contouring, mascara, lipstick—and each of these cosmetics costs more than Rs 1,000.

In addition, there were the body scrubs and body polishes— and this could mean polish with gold! Each body spray and perfume costs anywhere from Rs 1,000 to Rs 4,000. What surprised me was that most of Mayori's clients were men who, except for the make-up, used all the same kinds of sprays, gels and creams. But then Prime Minister's Modi's Make In India policy affected the company and it closed down.[84]

* * *

After Jafra closed down, Mayori took to selling puppies. She made more money by selling puppies of expensive breeds such

---

84. In 2011, the US-based company directly imported all its products from America, but it has since started manufacturing in India.

as Great Dane, Labrador and Tibetan Mastiff. She was thrilled when she sold a Tibetan Mastiff for a sum of one lakh rupees. I showed her a news report saying that the opening price for a Tibetan Mastiff in Delhi was Rs 2.5 lakhs, and some fetched as much as Rs 10 lakhs![85]

She bought puppies online, cared for them, groomed them and then sold them to people in Nagaland. She said that at one time she had bought a puppy for Rs 28,000, but it fell ill and she had learnt how to give it injections. Once, it vomited on her hand while she was giving the injection, but she didn't let go. Then it shat on Lemyaola, who was also holding it, and Mayori shouted: 'Rs 28,000. Remember it cost Rs 28,000.' The puppy was saved and sold.

* * *

'Aunty I made seven lakhs! And then I lost it all.'

Mayori had started putting her money into a Ponzi scheme called Visarev. The investment company promised 25 per cent returns and in the beginning they got the interest and she invested that too. She bought a Bolero and used it as a taxi.

She not only invested her money but also got her friends to put in theirs. One friend put in Rs 10 lakh. Mayori was so successful that she had an air-conditioned office in Dimapur and was earning a lakh a month. Many people in the underground also invested their money in that Ponzi scheme, as did church leaders.

Mayori was thrilled. She was making more and more money. She had not realized that a Ponzi scheme is a fraudulent investment operation that pays returns to separate investors, not from any actual profit earned by the organization, but from their own money or money paid by subsequent investors. The

---

85. The canine pet population in India rose from 4 million in 2011 to 15.7 million by the end of 2015. India spent Rs 14 billion on pets in 2015.

Ponzi scheme usually entices new investors by offering returns other investments cannot guarantee, in the form of short-term returns that are either abnormally high or unusually consistent. The perpetuation of the returns requires an ever-increasing flow of money from investors to keep the scheme going. If there are no new investors, it will crash.

In January 2013, the company stopped paying returns. Mayori, along with many thousands of investors, waited till May hoping that the company would recover, but then she had to face the reality: she had lost all her money; so had everyone else.

Mayori described the catastrophic repercussions of the crash. One of her friends, who was a manager of a bank and had stood guarantor for investors, lost his job; one person who was in the underground had to sell his house to pay off the people who had invested at his behest; and Mayori sold her Bolero so she could pay the church leaders who had invested money in the company on her recommendation. She had nothing left. Her entire world had come crashing down.

Desperate to recover her losses, Mayori went for training in early 2014 with the Toyota company and got commissions for selling cars. She managed to sell three in Nagaland. But her heart was no longer in the business of buying and selling. Besides, it was not only the Ponzi company that cheated her. The Naga friend with whom she had opened a shop to sell accessories for pets also defrauded her.

She then discovered that she could buy second-hand imported leather bags, polish them up and sell them. She borrowed money from an aunt to buy them and managed to sell the bags to all her friends.

It was during those days that she made friends with a man she met online. He was an Englishman living in a small town in Britain. After a year of correspondence, she flew to the UK in July 2014. They spent a few months together before getting married in November of that year.

Unfortunately, it was becoming increasing difficult to get a spouse visa in the UK. Mayori's friend Miranda was also married to an Englishman and had lived in Britain. She had had a baby who was a British citizen, but the UK authorities had refused her a spouse visa twice. Migrants were not welcome. That was when Mayori and Brian decided to settle in India, and they both came to Goa in November 2015. Having seen them together, I realized that she had found happiness; both of them had.

* * *

Atim was faced with a choice between trying her luck in Dubai or getting married. She felt she had achieved what she set out to do; when she had arrived in Delhi she was penniless and in awe of the world she found herself in. But now she could say she had worked in a five-star hotel and 'happening restaurants', tasted all kinds of food, the most expensive dishes and enjoyed them 'more than the guests did'. She had supported her parents and she was an independent woman who could afford to buy shoes, jeans and nice T-shirts with her own hard-earned money.

Most important of all, she had helped her parents build a home on their own plot of land and restore their dignity. But one dream still remained unfulfilled: to have a small house on a plot of land where she could open her own restaurant. If she went to Dubai perhaps she could save enough money to fulfill that dream.

Atim's niece, Sochuila, had painted a rosy picture about life in Dubai. She had fired Atim's imagination with stories of jobs in five-star hotels. Sochuila had offered to organize Atim's work permit if she sent her the money. Atim tried to send the money through Western Union, but she was told she would have to transfer the money through a bank. When Atim went to her bank, the Jammu and Kashmir Bank, she was told that it did not deal with dirhams, the currency of Abu Dhabi.

Atim then found Benson, a Meitei who was an agent, and

he said he would help her with all the formalities. First, she needed a health checkup. She went to the designated doctors and got the report. It had cost her Rs 4,000. Sochuila asked her to send her CV, and I did some research on the Internet to make an appropriate one for a hostess applying for a job in Dubai. It was a real revelation to see that CV writing had become an art form in its own right, and I have included it in the Appendix.

Several weeks had passed. Atim was waiting for news, but neither the agent nor Sochuila contacted her. The niece advised that it would be better if Atim came through an agent, while the agent simply stopped answering her calls.

Atims's dream of going to Dubai was fading. And she was torn between the idea of getting married to Angam Ramsan, the chef she had met at En, or trying to run a business before she settled down to having a family.

Atim's father had found a plot for Rs 50,000 and I said I would give her the amount from the advance royalty of this book. But when I gave her the money, she said that her father had told her that the price of the plot had gone up to two lakhs.

Atim did not want to go back to the life of a migrant worker, so she decided to try her hand at business.

* * *

The first place she went to was her favourite haunt, Sarojini Nagar Market. She decided to buy tops and kurtas for Rs 100 and sell them in Ukhrul for Rs 300. However, she had not taken into account the cost of sending them from Delhi to Ukhrul.

She then thought she would begin with something in Delhi. She bought beef and shredded it, fried it with lots of chillies and put it into small packets. She also fermented soya beans and put them in small packets. She said her boyfriend's brother had a shop and she sold her packets there. She got some money, but she was not sure exactly how much profit she had made.

Atim announced that she was going to Ukhrul because her friend had sent her photos on WhatsApp of some shoes with big soles that were selling there for Rs 2,000; she could buy them in Delhi for Rs 200.

Before Atim left for Ukhrul, the agent finally called and gave her an offer from a five-star hotel in Dubai. It was tempting, but I think she no longer wanted the life of a migrant worker. She wanted to go home. She did open a small shop, but she gave it to her sister.

On 6 April 2016, Atim got married to Phungreingam or Angam (the diminutive of Phungreingam) at the Siraarkhong Church. I saw the beautiful wedding dress designed by her niece in a picture she sent to Yaokhalek on WhatsApp. Yaokhalek could not go because he had just returned after being with his grandfather in Kalhang. The grandfather had wanted to see his favourite grandson before he died.

Atim and Angam came back to Delhi. She was pregnant. Atim found a job in a restaurant called Imperfecto in a Gurgaon mall. She said the music was really loud and the menu had weird dishes such as spaghetti with rogan josh. She had not informed the management that she was pregnant.

Angam started working in a food van, but soon he had a quarrel with the management and left his job. Now Atim was the sole earner and they were sharing a flat with Angam's sister. She said they could not afford to have the baby in Delhi; it would cost more than Rs 50,000, whereas in Ukhrul it would be less than Rs 10,000.

* * *

Livingstone was still struggling to make a success of running the restaurant in Calangute. He was beginning to understand the problems of management, but had no one to turn to who could help him. Managing a fine dining restaurant was proving to be a much bigger challenge than he had imagined.

Before leaving, Henry had given him some quick lessons.

He had introduced Livingstone to the suppliers for dry rations, beef and seafood. Livingstone knew that there must always be at least 50 kilos of beef in the fridge because sometimes 100 to 150 kilos could be cooked in one shot in a day. They had to buy 5 to 10 kilos of chicken breasts every week, while vegetables were bought every day.

Chawee had taught Ruth how to make the special sauces. The recipes were their valuable trade secret. But without knowing much about Thai or European cuisine, Ruth and Livingstone could not innovate and modify the menu. Henry used to change it every season, but Livingstone had not done so in the three years he had run the restaurant. He had not even revised the prices because he was afraid a rise would result in losing his regular clientele.

Livingstone had been confident about handling customers. Many of the older ones continued to patronize the restaurant and he still got good reviews. But because of the economic crisis in Europe, customers from Sweden, Finland and Russia had stopped coming. Henry had never encouraged Indians and Livingstone had a similar prejudice against domestic tourists, whom he regarded as the hated mayangs.

He had also been positive that he would make money from the sale of alcohol. When he had come to Goa he knew only the name of one brand of rum, Old Monk. The barman at Oriental taught him about 'pegs'; a small peg was 30 ml; a regular peg was 60 ml, though sometimes it was called a large peg. There were twelve pegs in a bottle of alcohol; he found that a bottle could cost Rs 1,800, but a small peg was sold at Rs 200. He could not believe that customers were willing to waste so much money. But now that he was running the restaurant, he felt he would get profits from the sale of alcohol. Unfortunately, the profits were not that high.

One day soon after Henry had left, a man walked into his restaurant. Livingstone asked him who he was. 'I am the accountant,' he said.

He was about to ask why the accountant had come; after all he had a chartered accountant. (Henry had introduced him to the company's CA.) Livingstone had assumed that this person was the accountant Henry had been trying to fix an appointment with.

Livingstone thought it was wiser to remain silent. Instead, he asked the accountant the question that was uppermost in his mind, 'Do I have to pay you?'

The man replied, 'Yes, of course.'

'How much?'

'Rs 25,000 a month.'

Livingstone was shocked. He had not even known that he had an accountant to whom he would have to pay such a large amount to do the accounting!

Livingstone felt that the real problem was that the restaurant did not run during the off-season. But he still had to pay the salaries of the main chefs even when it was not open. They knew how to cook the forty to fifty different dishes listed on the menu and if they were to leave it would be disastrous. He also had to pay rent for a room to store their furniture and fridge and other items during the off-season months. This was apart from the need to have money for his family's expenses.

When the restaurant closed in April 2015, for the first time since he had taken over, Livingstone and Ruth went to Ukhrul. It was partly a family visit so that his mother could see her grandson; but it was also with an idea to make money so he could start a second branch of the restaurant which would run throughout the year.

I asked Livingstone whether he had thought of opening a restaurant back in Ukhrul. There was already one which had become very popular. It was called 25 Degree North. They had even advertised for a post of a waitress. Livingstone said the price of land had skyrocketed and he did not have the money to open a restaurant in Ukhrul.

Livingstone and his sister bought a piece of lampan land in her husband's village. Lampan land is village community land. The land itself is not sold; what is sold is the right to cut the trees for a season. Livingstone invested Rs 50,000 with the hope of making Rs 10 lakh from the firewood he aimed to cut.

I met him in November of 2015 on his return from Ukhrul. He looked very thin. He had lost 16 kilos chopping firewood, but had not made any money. The reason was that he had spent money in employing labour to cut the trees and then it kept raining so heavily that he could not cut enough wood to make any profit.

This was the longest time Livingstone had spent in Ukhrul after he had left for Bengaluru in 2008. He found that many young people had nothing to do all day; these were the people who had not left to work in cities and towns. There was no count of how many men and women had left Ukhrul in search of jobs; Livingstone felt there should be a census.

Livingstone had also witnessed the elections to the Autonomous District Councils,[86] which had taken place while he was in Ukhrul. He had seen the extent of corruption and the exchange of money.

* * *

In the past, the Nagas had a clearly defined enemy—the Indian state. Now the enemy was invisible and yet it was everywhere. It was a ubiquitous thing called money. I asked Livingstone whether he had heard of a song by Abba called 'Money, Money, Money'. He had not. I read out the lyrics:

---

86. The Autonomous District Councils in Manipur have been constituted in the tribal areas and are meant to ensure that tribal people have a fair degree of autonomy in the administration of their areas. District Councils get funds directly from the Centre.

Money, money, money
Must be funny
In the rich man's world
Money, money, money
Always sunny
In the rich man's world
Aha-ahaaa
All the things I could do
If I had a little money
It's a rich man's world

Livingstone laughed. I asked him whether he had ever asked himself why he remained poor even though he worked so hard; and why some Tangkhuls had become rich while others struggled every day. He said he had not.

While interviewing Tangkhul migrant workers, I had become aware about the total absence of class consciousness among them. It was their ethnic identity that defined their lives.

Livingstone said he felt that once Nagas achieved independence things would be better. I asked him how the people in Ukhrul had reacted to the Indo-Naga Accord signed between the NSCN (IM) and the Government of India on 3 August 2015.[87] He said everyone in Ukhrul was excited. They thought it was a step towards independence.

Atim had been in Goa with us on that day. She had come excitedly and said her mother had phoned to say Nagas have got their independence. She showed us the video of the signing ceremony on her smartphone.

I asked Atim and Livingstone what independence would mean for them. Atim said it would mean they would all have

---

87. On that day, the NSCN (IM) and the Government of India signed a framework agreement which they claimed had laid the foundation for a long lasting resolution to the Indo-Naga conflict.

water supply and homes. Livingstone was silent. He said he had never asked himself that question. I felt he thought it was a magic word which would mean the chance to live a life with dignity and self-respect. India had not been able to accommodate this little dream. But would an independent Nagalim be able to?

* * *

When I think of Naga society and how deeply divided it has become along class lines, I have come to realize how callous and cruel the rich can now be towards the poor. Now Nagas are being pitted against each other and the enemy is not visible. Years of military repression have not crushed the Naga unity and self-respect; instead the corrupting power of money has destroyed the Naga soul. It has eaten into the innards of Naga culture and society. Globalization has torn apart the society into the rich and the poor. More and more migrant workers keep arriving in cities and towns with the dream of becoming rich. They are dazzled by the glitz and glamour of the metropolis.

Globalization has packaged injustice and oppression in such a beautiful wrapping that it will take the migrant worker years before he or she can tear it open and see what it really is.

Afterword

In June 2016, Sebastian and I decided to go for a holiday to Norway; we were planning to first go to Oslo and then to the Arctic. It would be our first real holiday abroad. Yaokhalek was sitting in the room and he said: 'I have a friend in Oslo.'

I looked at him in amazement. How on earth did he know someone in Oslo? He said his friend, Sonang Raihing, was working there. Yaokhalek immediately contacted his friend on WhatsApp. It took a little time, but Sonang got back to him. Yaokhalek asked his friend whether he would have time to meet his uncle and aunty who would be coming to Oslo. Apparently, Sonang thought Yaokhalek was joking; how could an aunty and uncle be expected to be going to Oslo from Ukhrul!

Yaokhalek also gave us his friend's sister, Themreichon's mobile number. We contacted her and met Themreichon on a bright sunny Sunday morning in June 2016 in Oslo's famous Gustav Vigeland Park. She turned out to be exceptionally warm and charming.

I told her I was writing a book on the lives of Tangkhul migrant workers and would like to include her story. She was quite happy to let me interview her.

Themreichon had three sisters and two brothers. After her mother died, her father married again. That was when she felt she had to earn her own living and so she went to work with a Tangkhul family in Imphal. They helped her find a job in Singapore.

She said she had left Ukhrul ten years ago, in October 2006. Themreichon worked in Singapore for three years, after which she got an offer to work as an au pair[88] in Oslo through

---

88. 'Au pair' is a French term. which means 'at par or equal to' denoting that the person lives on an equal basis and reciprocal relationship with the host family; the au pair does light housework while studying the host country's language

a placement agency. She arrived in Oslo in November 2009 and found herself working with a Norwegian family, looking after their small children and a baby. She also had to do other housework, including shopping for groceries.

After two years, she left that job and took up odd jobs; she worked in an old-age home, then at a cancer centre and at various hotels. In each of these places she had to work for eight hours, from 7 a.m. to 3 p.m. After that, she would clean one, or sometimes two, homes.

Themreichon saved enough money to send money for her brother Sonang to be able to fly to Oslo. Now he was working in a restaurant there.

And now, what work do you do? I asked her.

She said she lived in a beautiful house overlooking the Oslo Fjord and her job was to look after a dog because the owner travelled frequently. In fact, he was away at the moment so she had locked the dog in the bathroom and come to meet us. But she needed to get back.

On the way, we stopped to have a quick lunch. We were passing Gronland which is a neighbourhood where many migrants and refugees live. It was the neighbourhood where Themreichon herself had stayed. She knew the area well, so she suggested we eat at the Panjab Tandoor, an Indian restaurant, where she and her friends ate sometimes. It was the cheapest meal available in Oslo: a plate of rice, two pieces of chicken with curry, a bit of salad and a big naan roti for 79 Norwegian Kroner, which would be around Rs 632 per plate. It did not seem very cheap to us.

Themreichon insisted on paying for the lunch. When I said she should not waste money on us, but save for her future, she said she had already bought land in Ukhrul. We could not argue any further. Since Sebastian had already paid for the lunch, she bought us huge ice creams on the way to her home.

We decided to drop her to her home in Nesoddin, an hour's drive from Oslo. She told us that many artists, painters, musicians and news presenters lived in the neighbourhood. The location of the house was truly stunning. She went inside the house and brought out a small dog. He was really friendly. This was the dog she looked after. And for hours, days and weeks she had only a dog for company. She said it was very difficult not to have anyone to talk to. On top of that, the neighbours got angry if the dog barked or she called out to him when he ran down to the sea.

What about her brother, I asked. Did they not meet? She said he worked and lived quite far from there. And he had to work long hours at the restaurant. There were two other Tangkhuls in Oslo; both women were married to Scandinavians and she met them on occasion. But her friends were some Filipino women who had come with her from Singapore. They would get together on their off days and wander around the city.

Themreichon still had a student visa and under that she could only work as an au pair. She was going for Norwegian language classes, and to our ears her Norwegian sounded quite musical. In addition, her employer had paid for driving classes. She said the next time we came she could take us around in her car!

Themreichon was worried because her student visa was about to expire. She said she could have got a better job if she had a work permit, but it was very difficult to get a work permit nowadays, with so many migrants coming to Norway from all over the world. We left her smiling bravely.

But we are in touch over WhatsApp and she sent an email to say she has got an extension on her student visa for another six months...

* * *

Back in India, Yaokhalek waited eagerly for us to tell him about his friends working in Norway. We showed him our photographs. I asked him whether he would like to work abroad. He replied: 'I don't even have a passport.'

I asked him to apply for one, but he said he had no identity papers except his driving licence. He said he had found it very difficult to open a bank account and he was hoping to get an Adhaar card soon.

Yaokhalek announced that Atim and her husband Phungreingam (or Angam) were in Delhi. Mayori too had come up to Delhi from Goa in connection with her husband's visa application. We invited Atim and Angam to dinner.

The first thing Atim asked was about this book.

Mayori teased Atim that when the book came out she would become a celebrity. But I was worried. I was afraid that her resolve to publish her story might be shaken now that she was a married woman, expecting her first baby.

I asked them whether she was worried about the reaction of the society to the book. Could it be misunderstood as an attack on Tangkhul society? Atim said the book told the truth and if people did not like the truth that should not be my problem. She wanted her children to know how much she had suffered. She wanted to make sure they did not have to suffer in the same way.

Atim had read the manuscript of this book before she had gone to Ukhrul for her wedding. When I first gave it to her, she said she did not like reading books; it gave her a headache. But once she started reading, she kept going till she finished. She looked at me and said, 'I find my life really interesting when I read about it.' Then on a more sombre note she said, 'It is the same story for so many of us.' She said that ever since her sister was murdered she had wanted to tell her story.

Mayori too read the manuscript. She had tears in her eyes. She said, 'I didn't realize how sad our lives are. You have understood us.'

Atim and Angam are still dreaming of having a restaurant where they can serve sushi. Atim said their sushi would have a unique Naga taste, with thin slices of smoked pork and a bit of umrok or Naga chillies.

* * *

Sebastian and I returned to Goa. I wanted to include the stories of the Tangkhul women who worked in the casinos. I wanted to know how they felt when they saw people gamble away lakhs of rupees every day, while back home, their families could barely afford to have two proper meals a day.

Goa and Sikkim are the only two states in India where casinos are legal. In both places there had been strong protests against casinos by local people but casinos are a source of income for the government.[89]

I had heard of a Tangkhul woman who had been working in a casino for more than eight years. I told Mayori about her and she found out that she knew the woman; she was Lemyaola's friend! She told me the woman, Chon, would be quite willing to talk to me so we met at Mayori's home.

I asked Chon to tell me her first reactions to the casino. She said it had came as a shock. 'Money does not have any value.'

She said there were now almost fifty Tangkhul girls working in the casino where she worked as a trainer. Chon said it took three months to train the girls to become dealers. They had to learn multiplication tables and learn to calculate quickly. And then they had to learn how to pull the chips towards themselves

---

89. 'According to an industry insider, each of the offshore casinos sees average net profit earnings of Rs 1.75 crore per day, while each of the ten-odd onshore casinos earn Rs 3.75 lakh to Rs 4 lakh per day. Official figures peg the turnover of Goan casinos at Rs 1,000 crore annually. The Goa government received Rs 135 crore in taxes in 2012-13, apart from Rs 17.96 crore from entry fees, Rs 57.5 crore from license fees, Rs 53.29 crore from entertainment tax, Rs 2 crore as VAT and Rs 2.2 crore as excise license fees.' Joseph Zuzarte, 'To have or not to have casinos: Existential dilemma facing Goa and Goans' in *DNA India*, 29 September, 2013. http://www.dnaindia. com/lifestyle/report-to-have-or-not-to-have-casinos-existential-dilemma-facing-goa-and-goans-1895379

after every round. 'It looks easy but it requires training. We cannot have long nails if we work as dealers.'

I asked her to share the reactions of some of these dealers to the life in the casinos. She said they too felt: 'Money does not have value.'

I asked her whether she had seen the special rooms kept for people gambling with Rs one crore or more. She smiled and said: 'Yes.'

I felt a rising impatience but checked myself. The lack of verbal expression was a part of the culture but how was a writer to write without words?

To provoke her, I asked Chon whether she would like it if casinos started operating in Ukhrul. Her prompt reply was an emphatic 'No.'

The armed groups in Manipur and Nagaland have in the past stopped the casinos and prostitution to some extent. But now it was all creeping into the Northeast; the power of money to corrupt could not be checked either by arms in the Northeast or democratic protests in Goa.

Studies of casinos in Sikkim showed that many of the dealers were involved in prostitution. I asked Chon whether the company encouraged the women to go out with the guests. Chon said the company did not, but many of the girls went off with guests to make some extra money.

Chon, like most Tangkhuls, saw the girls who went astray as morally weak, but did not seem to see that the people who owned the casinos as being morally corrupt. She thought the company was 'good' since it paid its employees, arranged for transport for them and provided accommodation.

* * *

Livingstone had some good news he wanted to share. He had found a very good location by the Baga River where he wanted to open a restaurant which he could run all round the year. I asked him how he would raise the money and he said two of his Tangkhul friends had promised to help him; one was a hair stylist and the other a manager at a resort. He had decided to serve Northeast food. He wanted to call it Onra—which in Tangkhul meant a resting place.

Livingstone and his friends came over to discuss the décor and menu. I showed them coffee table books on Naga culture. The three were absolutely amazed because they had never seen such books. Livingstone picked a picture of the Khonoma Gate and said he wanted that as the entrance to his restaurant. I asked a young Goan artist, Kalidas Mhamal to help us and he is now busy designing the Naga gate.

As we sat together to choose the motifs Livingstone confessed he still felt as if he was waiter in the restaurant. But here he hoped to feel like the real manager. I said: 'Not manager, Livingstone, you will be an owner and the CEO.'

* * *

Mayori was sitting in my home reading the manuscript of the book to check for spelling mistakes when I got a call from Wungchipem, the former President of the Northeast Association, Goa. He said some women working in the Snip Salon and Spa wanted to meet me to ask for legal advice. The Indian Spa Industry is worth around Rs 11,000 crore. In Goa, the spa industry plays a big role in tourism and local economy, generating a revenue of Rs 15-18 crore per year for the state. But the spa industry had acquired notoriety after police raids exposed flourishing sex rackets in several places.

Snip was one of the best-known spas in Goa but it had got into trouble with the police. In September 2010, eight Indonesian girls working at Snip in Goa fled to Mumbai, where they complained to the Indonesian consulate that they were brought to India with forged documents and bogus appointment orders. The women also complained that they were being made to work long hours and were treated badly. Three other women working in the Bandra branch in Mumbai had come to the consulate with the same accusations.

The women said that according to their agreement of February 5 2010 with the owners, Sumeet and Archana Bhobe, they were to work in Ajanta Medicals Private Limited and this name was entered in their visa permits also. However, they were made to work as spa therapists in three of the spas owned by the Bhobes in Panaji, Calangute and Bandra.

The Indonesian consulate in Mumbai filed a complaint with the crime branch in Goa. Acting on this, the Goa police raided Snip Salon and Spa in Panaji and Calangute. A case was registered against the Bhobes under sections 419 (cheating by impersonation), 465 (forgery), 468 (forgery for purpose of cheating), 471 (using as genuine a forged document) and 341 (wrongful restraint) of the IPC.[90]

Talking to some of the Tangkhuls working in Snip, I learnt that the Bhobes had continued to get girls from Indonesia; those girls were less educated than the ones who had run away, so even if they were treated badly they did not know how to register their protest. However, now a law had been passed making it difficult to bring women from abroad.

Almost 80 per cent of the Snip Spa and Salon's employees were from the Northeast. I had heard about Snip because the owners had offered the Northeast Association free accommodation just after the women at the Tatva Spa won their case in the labour court in September 2014.[91] To me it was clear that the Snip owners were buying the loyalty of the Northeast migrants to prevent future litigation.

The word masseurs had become associated with sleazy practices, so they were now called massage therapists; but in

---

90. Preetu Venugopalan Nair, 'Indonesian girls allege harassment at Goa spa' in *The Times of India* http://timesofindia.indiatimes. com/city/goa/Indonesian-girls-allege-harassment-at-Goa-spa/ articleshow/7039740.cms

91. See Chapter 4, page ___ for discussion of this case

India the therapists did not need to be certified. This time again it was the therapists, especially the women, who had found the working conditions at the spa unbearable. The women complained that the practice of women massaging men made them vulnerable to exploitation.

There has been a major controversy around the practice of cross-gender massaging. In 2010, the Goa Public Health (Amendment) Rules were amended vide Notification 49/4/2009-I/PHD, 15A(f) which requires:'Provision for male masseurs for the massage of males and female masseurs for the massage of females.' The spa owners, speaking in the language of human rights, argued that the rule encouraged discrimination! But the Northeast women working in the spas said that they did not like this practice because it made them vulnerable.

The thirteen women who came to see me were from Manipur, Nagaland and Mizoram, and were all employed as massage therapists in Snip. The immediate reason for their resignation was a dispute about working overtime, but their grievances went much deeper. The women were hesitant to speak, partly because they did not know English, but mostly because they had never spoken of the work they were forced to do. One of the Tangkhul girls, Mirinyo, from Ngainga village, said she had heard that I had helped the women at Tatva. Mayori, who was present at the time, told Mirinyo she too was from Ngaigna. Mayori acted as the translator, and soon the women opened up.

Mirinyo explained that the therapists had to report at 10 a.m. and work till 9 p.m. Each of them massaged five to six persons a day; some wanted a one-hour massage while others asked for the ninety-minute massage. The most popular massage was the ninety-minute aroma spirit massage for Rs 3,800. This is described in the brochure: 'The melting cream from an exotic wine and liqueur flavoured grapeseed moisturizer candle is used in this massage to reverse the skin's aging process. Pure luxury makes you feel top of this world.'

Valentina, from Senapati District, said it was very tiring work. Another therapist, who did not want to be named, said that whenever they tried to talk to the owners, they did not listen. She said: 'When we say a few words the manager talk big, big words.'

The women complained that they were often sent to massage the Bhobes' male clients in their homes. One therapist from Nagaland said she had been sent several times to a man who lay down on his double bed in a dimly lit room. On one occasion he refused to wear his briefs, and when she told him to wear them he said that the others had not insisted. The others were too petrified, as the owners would cut their salaries. Another therapist told me that she hated it when she had been sent to the Bhobes' friend's beach party and made to do foot massage for the guests. It was so humiliating. And one of them said she had refused to go, but then the Bhobes had cut their salaries.

Mirinyo said this time when they raised a dispute Sumeet said they were welcome to resign because there were many other women from the Northeast to take their place. Archana Bhobe threatened that if they tried to create trouble she would ensure that they would not get a job at any spa.

The women proved to be very enterprising and got a copy of the message circulated about them by the Bhobes (on the facing page).

The Northeast Association Goa had by now chosen another President, Aghato Awomi. The Snip employees contacted him and we also decided to contact the All India Trade Union Congress (AITUC) again.[92] The women told the trade union that all they wanted was an apology. On Wednesday, October 5, 2016 Sumeet Bhobe came to meet the AITUC lawyer along with his lawyer. After negotiations, the women said if he

---

92. See discussion of the Tatva Spa case, pp 99–101.

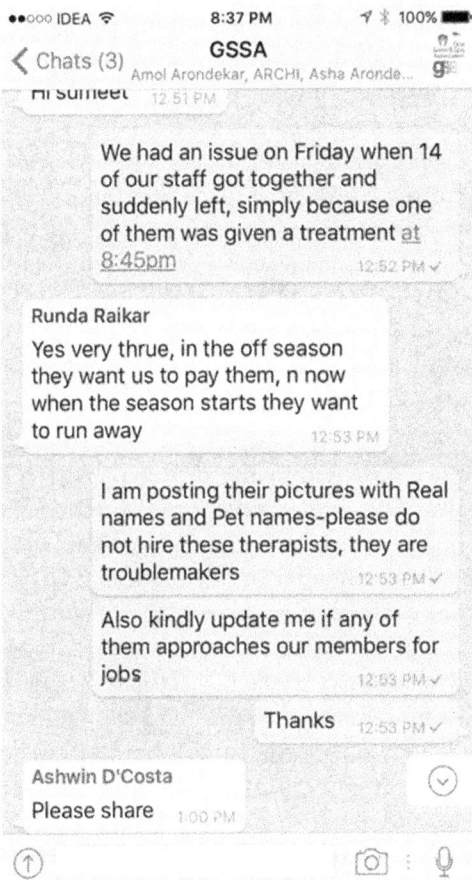

apologized and publically shared his apology on his WhatApp the matter would end. Bhobe agreed and said by Saturday he would do so. However, on Saturday he went back on his promise and said he had been intimidated by Mayori and the AITUC lawyer!

The Snip employees who had not resigned told us that the Bhobes had put up a notice inside their salon, stating that the employees who had resigned were trying to 'blackmail' the management into giving compensation. This was a lie, since the women had only demanded a written apology. The Bhobes promised an 'excellent loyalty bonus' for those who continued to work for them (see Appendix for full notice).

Sumeet kept harping on the fact that he had made generous donations for the Northeast Association. He said he had even paid for the funeral expenses when one of his employees had committed suicide. But the woman's sister's husband (who did not want to be named) said Sumeet had deducted the amount from his salary the next month. Others said that one of the reasons for her suicide was the working conditions, and the Bhobes had paid for the funeral in exchange for silence about this aspect.

The deeper I went into the matter the more facts were exposed. I was getting a glimpse into the underbelly of Goa. The women had taken Mayori and identified several of the houses where they were taken for massage. I was shocked to learn that one of the men who had himself regularly massaged at his home was one of Goa's well-known environmentalists, committed to 'living a green life'. I shared these facts with a Goan feminist, Sabina Martins, and she said, 'your study will not only help the Northeast girls but us as well.' She said she would support any campaign the Northeast women were planning.

The women said they wanted to fight. They wanted justice. If the Bhobes did not apologize, they would continue to fight for their dignity. On their intitiative, the Northeast Association called a general assembly meeting and a resolution was passed that they would continue to fight. Livingstone was at the meeting and he said he had never seen the women express their anger before. He said everyone felt a new respect for them because they had given the Bhobes a scare! Mayori and I exchanged smiles.

I could not help but hope that the Northeast migrant workers, especially the women, would organize themselves and fight for their rights, just as migrant women in the West had done in the beginning of the last century. Their strike is celebrated as International Women's Day. The former Snip employees were sitting in my home and I decided to tell them about the history of the women's strike. Thanks to YouTube they saw the images of the strike and heard the famous song that it inspired for the first time. They asked me to give them the lyrics so they could learn them and perhaps they would also organize a strike of all the employees in the salons and spas in Goa! We laughed, but at that moment even if the idea seemed preposterous it was a seed planted…

The song they are now learning as this book goes to print is 'Bread and Roses'. They said they would sing it at the release of the book:[93]

As we go marching, marching, in the beauty of the day
A million darkened kitchens, a thousand mill lofts gray
Are touched with all the radiance that a sudden sun discloses
For the people hear us singing, bread and roses, bread and roses.

As we come marching, marching, we battle too, for men,
For they are in the struggle and together we shall win.
Our days shall not be sweated from birth until life closes,
Hearts starve as well as bodies, give us bread, but give us roses.

As we come marching, marching, un-numbered women dead
Go crying through our singing their ancient call for bread,
Small art and love and beauty their trudging spirits knew
Yes, it is bread we fight for, but we fight for roses, too.

As we go marching, marching, we're standing proud and tall.
The rising of the women means the rising of us all.
No more the drudge and idler, ten that toil where one reposes,
But a sharing of life's glories, bread and roses, bread and roses.

---

93. James Oppphenheim wrote those words in 1912 during the women's strike.

Appendix

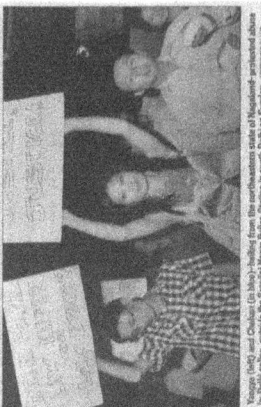

'We were racially abused'

NAGA COUPLE alleges harassment by drunk men and cops; Police deny claim

POLICE SPEAK South district police discuss issues faced by community with representatives

Delegation meets Sheila Dikshit over violence

'Incapable of a normal relationship'

Accused's parents 'not shocked, but devastated'

Media reports cannot capture the anguish and rage of Northeast migrants

BILL/CASHMEMO TEL.: 9350640858, 9350016581
9350119196, 9868476173

P.S. FUNERAL & AMBULANCE SERVICES PVT. LTD.
Regd. Off : 224, Ist Floor, Humayunpur, Safdarjung Enclave,
New Delhi-110029

S. No. 094

Date: 25/10/09

M/s H/R Ramchanphy Hongray

DATE	PARTICULARS	RATE	AMOUNT Rs. P.
	– Coffin Box ordinary polished		5000
	– Packing material		1500
	– Packing/handling and undertaker fees		1500
	– Ambulance charges Aiims to Airport		1000
Rs. Nine thousand only		TOTAL	9000

E & O. E.

For P.S. FUNERAL & AMBULANCE SERVICES PVT. LTD.

Ramchanphy's last journey home

30th Oct.'09 Friday
2 PM
Jantar Mantar - Parliament Street

Naga Students' Union, Delhi
beckons your presence in the
North East
Mass Protest Rally
Against
Murder, Rape, Atrocities and Racial Attacks

Crimes against humanity, especially the women and other vulnerable groups are increasing at an alarming rate in different geographical landscapes including the national Capital of India, Delhi. The politics of RACISM and HATE campaigns against different nationals in different countries is not a new phenomenon. The recent racial attacks and discriminatory treatment meted out to Indian nationals in Australia, a continuing debate, is a matter of serious concern in international and diplomatic affairs. The fear and the chaos created by such racial discrimination against the 'OTHERS', that is, the Indians who were students and employees, can seldom be applauded as it happened in a so-called civilised country. Whether it is direct, indirect or cultural, they are all different forms of violence. It may not be out of place to say that, people living in different metropolitan cities like Delhi are all facing one or the other forms of violence every day. Furthermore, victims of such violence have sadly been marginalised by the media, police and the judiciary alike. The level of discrimination does not end with the public in day to day interaction, but with law enforcers as well who discriminate them on the basis of race and cultural differences. North eastern people especially the women face myriad issues relating to the subject of this rally initiated by the Naga Students' Union Delhi, in wake of the recent gruesome attempted rape and murder of **Miss. Ramchanphi Hongray, a 19 year old Tangkhul Naga teenage girl from Manipur in the capital city, just 10 mins way from the Vasant Vihar Police station.** This rally has been demonstratively supported by various student bodies, women and other civil society groups of India and particularly of the north-east diaspora *in toto.*

The effort of the young students, job seekers and families trying to mingle with the culture of the people of mainstream Indian society has not been received well because of the lack of willingness to accept people from other parts of the country. Cultural pride and prejudices at play has been the major factor of discrimination against the north- easterners who have been repeatedly projected as people with loose morals by the media alike.

However, this particular incident requires utmost sincerity of each one of us to come out in support because it clearly shows the dignity of the deceased girl to save her modesty, ultimately resulting in her death. It is not the maniacal character of the accused as highlighted by the police, but this is only another attempt to cover up the crime which will not help discourage further hate crimes.

Unless we voice out together continuously about the countless other cases that could not see the light of justice, we cannot reach out towards equality. Unfortunate incidents like this, sadly, had to be the platform. But, in positive augmentation of sensitising the public towards positive mind-setting, let us show our solidarity to fight for our own-selves, other marginalised sections of the society and in particular for landmark JUSTICE to prevail for the soul of late Sister Ramchanphi.

The Naga Students Union, Delhi and the Rally supporters, seek your integrity and presence to voice for the North-East community towards EQUAL JUSTICE TO ALL.
****

But the protests continue

Naga Students' Union, Delhi

29 Aurangzeb Road, Nagaland House, New Delhi - 110011
E- Mail : nsu_delhi@yahoo.com, helpdesk@nsud.org
WEB: www.nsud.org

Mob + 91 9873237407
+ 91 9871549882
+ 91 9873835644
+ 91 9899419584

Motto : "Strength in Unity"

Date: 30-10-2009

Memorandum to the Honourable Prime Minister of India, Dr. Manmohan Singh, Representing the Anguished Security of the lives of the North-Easterners in Delhi, the Capital of India, Bracketing the Case of Attempt to Rape and Murdered of Late Miss. Ramchanphi Hongray in Munirka, on Saturday, the 24th of Oct. 2009 for being a mere Unprotected North-East Girl.

Sir,

While we learn to appeal the values of justice and equality, the conscience of India's democratic values shrink in our very face day to day. There are 90,000 to 1,00,000 North Easterners in Delhi struggling to find career windows in the capital of India. These are students and home-makers devoid of opportunities back in the North East. **However, we are being treated in the national capital not just as mere "others" but further subjected to subhuman treatment, without respecting our socio-cultural and geo-political differences.** And the worst, the law-keepers and the Delhi Police has never been the protector to these vulnerable sections of population. **Rather, they blamed** the North-Easterners **for being different,** and shamelessly issued pamphlets of **"Police Dik-Tats",** for these unprotected people in the year 2007, (about how to dress, what to eat, where to go, when to sit).

However, without losing confidence to the institute of Nation-State, we the students from North East in Delhi have been time and again sending representation to your office, registering our protest against Racial Profiling of North-Eastern Students, Constant Harassment to our womenfolk, Unhelpful Service of the Delhi Police to the North Eastern Communities, and etc.

Mr. Prime Minister, we would dearly invite your kind attention to ponder awhile again the democracy that India is investing all through these **"Discrimination, Racial Profiling, Devaluing the NorthEastern Cultures and Social Values, and Constant Abused to our Womenfolk."** It is now quite uncommon to find NorthEasterners being harassed, molested, abused, raped or murdered on account of being racially different once in a week in the capital of India. But unsurprisingly, most of the cases we have reported and complained to different police stations at different intervals remained unregistered. Only because, the state system has made

Naga Students' Union, Delhi

Mob + 91 9873237407
+ 91 9871549882
+ 91 9873835644
+ 91 9899419584

29 Aurangzeb Road, Nagaland House, New Delhi - 110011
E- Mail : nsu_delhi@yahoo.com, helpdesk@nsud.org
WEB: www.nsud.org

Motto : "Strength in Unity"

higher the authority of the state, the higher the discrimination it mounts for the NorthEasterners. **But the question that constantly appeals to all the NorthEasterners is "What made us Vulnerable or the Soft Target"? Is it because we are being racially different or is it because we are unprotected? And if the reason is that we are being racially different, the simple question that we ask Mr. Prime Minister is that, what is the commotion about in Australia?**

The Times of India, on 27th Oct. 2009 reported 50% of the molestation and harassment on women in Delhi involves girls from North East. And even more gruesome to the whole picture was that, the vulnerability of the North Easterners in Delhi is that, in the early 2009, on April 17th, a minor of 6 years old girl from Jalukie, Nagaland was brutally raped, ripped her private parts and murdered at her home in Mahipalpur, New Delhi. Followed by raped and murder of Ramchanphi Hongray (19) of Ukhrul, a Naga girl from Manipur, on 24th Oct. 2009 at her home in Munirka, New Delhi. Now, we wonder, **the Delhi Police might even issue codes for the North Easterners, "Don't Stay At Home".**

The rapists and the murderers, to quote the DCP of Delhi police HDS Dhalliwal, "a maniac" or the press and medias "pervert" "mentally unstable", but the main question is, **Are government and the Delhi Police really counting how many maniacs, perverts and mentally unstable in Delhi, looking for vulnerable victims?** Such redundant attitude to the security of the North Easterners does not only trivialize the issue but broods to major crime rates.

Chain of Incidents Happening In the Capital City

1. **On October 24, 2009,** late. Ramchanphi Hongray, a 19 year-old Naga girl of Ukhrul district of Manipur was attempted rape and brutally murdered at her home in Munirka village, under Vasant Vihar Police Station.

2. **On October 23, 2009,** another 21 year-old girl from Arunachal who is a Jamia Millia Islamia was molested again by a group of Government-run school boys in Bharat Nagar under New Friends Colony Police Station.

3. **On October 15, 2009,** a Mao girl from Manipur was molested in Naraina when she was returning home from work.

Naga Students' Union, Delhi

29 Aurangzeb Road, Nagaland House, New Delhi - 110011
E- Mail : nsu_delhi@yahoo.com, helpdesk@nsud.org
WEB: www.nsud.org

Mob : + 91 9873237407
+ 91 9871549882
+ 91 9873835644
+ 91 9899419584

Motto : "Strength in Unity"

4. **On October 11, 2009** a couple from Manipur, and girls and boys from North East were beaten up and harassed in Humayunpur, Safdarjung Enclave, New Delhi, by group of local goons and allegedly by the police.

5. **On September 21, 2009, a Moyon Naga girl from Manipur was molested after being beaten up blue and black by the neighbour in Munirka village, under the Vasant Vihar Police Station, New Delhi.**

6. **On September 20, 2009, a Chiru Naga boy from Manipur was badly beaten up with iron rod by some local goons just because of verbal tussle at Out Lines, Delhi.**

7. **On April 17, 2009,** Gaipuiliu Gangmei 6 year-old Zeliangrong Naga of Jalukie, Nagaland, was **raped and murdered** by local goons at Mahipalpur, New Delhi.

8. **On December 30, 2008,** an Assamese girl was **raped** in IT hub city in Gurgoan, Haryana.

On May 9 2005 a girl from Mizoram a student of Delhi University was abducted from Dhuala Kuan and **raped** on the moving car, subsequently, the students' organization and various civil bodies in Delhi requested the Delhi Police, but the response was to no avail. The crime rate on the North East population has grown unabated.

Therefore, we, the North Eastern students representing various organizations from the region, took this protest to the street of Delhi, to register our protest for the callous behavior of the Delhi Police and the Central Government on the North-Eastern Population.

Hereby, we undersigned representing different organizations from the NorthEast in one voice raised the following demands for immediate action.

1. Immediate arrest of all the culprits, involved in the rape and murder case, and compensation may be given to the kith and kins of the victims.

2. The Delhi Police "Zero Tolerance Policy" made the police truly intolerant to the NorthEast population, therefore, cases filed against Delhi Police personnels by the Students' Organisations from North East at different police stations may be immediately look into it, and take necessary steps as demanded on the complaints.

Naga Students' Union, Delhi

29 Aurangzeb Road, Nagaland House, New Delhi - 110011
E- Mail : nsu_delhi@yahoo.com, helpdesk@nsud.org
WEB: www.nsud.org

Mob : + 91 9873237407
+ 91 9871549882
+ 91 9873835644
+ 91 9899419584

Motto : "Strength in Unity"

3. Special Police Division and Control Room may be instituted under the capacity of Deputy Commissioner of Police (DCP), with special leverage power in the entire jurisdiction to attend the problems and complaints involving North Eastern Population. The division may be facilitated with PCR Van and Mobikes, etc.

4. Exclusive Delhi Police Recruitment may be facilitated for over 1,000 jobs for the North Easterners at the earliest. This will effectively help the North East Population and foreign nationals registering complaints for those who do not speak Hindi, as the majority of the present Delhi Police are ignorant about English language.

5. Immediate publication of A White Paper on the First Information Report of various incidents which have happened in Delhi and NCR.

6. Attention also may be invited in the Parliament for necessary discussion for dispensation of JUSTICE, EQUALITY and RIGHTS to the North Easterners without stereotypical biases and prejudices.

We remained confident to have addressed our grievances before your esteemed position.

Sincerely Yours,

1. Mr. Luikang Lamak
    President, NSUD

2. Zuben Ovung
    General Secretary, NSUD

Copy to:

1. P. Chidambaram, Home Minister o India
2. His Excellency, the Lt. Governor of Delhi
3. Ms. Sheila Dikshit, Chief Minister of Delhi
4. Governors of all Northeastern States
5. Chief Ministers of all Northern States
6. MPs. from 8 states of North Eastern Region
7. Commissioner of Police, Delhi
8. R.C. of all Northeastern States in Delhi

OFFICE OF THE JOINT COMMISSIONER OF POLICE;
SOUTHERN RANGE; NEW DELHI.

No. $|$ 4 0 9 6 /SO/SR(III), dated, New Delhi, the 7·11·   /2009.

To

         Shri Luikang Lamak (President),
         Naga Students' Union, Delhi,
         29, Aurangazeb Road,
         Naga Land House,
         New Delhi -110011.

Subject:-   Regarding S.O. No.383/2009 issued in respect of tackling the
           problems faced by students and others from North-Eastern States
           in Delhi .
                ....

Sir,

         Please find enclosed a copy of Standing order No.383, as desired by

Joint Commissioner of Police, Southern Range, Delhi.

                              Yours faithfully,

                            So to Joint Commissioner of Police,
                                Southern Range, New Delhi.

Encls:- <u>As above.</u>

Police Guidelines for dealing with violence against Northeast migrants

DELHI POLICE

REVISED STANDING ORDER NO. 383/ 2009

TACKLING THE PROBLEMS FACED BY STUDENTS AND OTHERS FROM NORTH-EASTERN STATES IN DELHI

The North-East M.P's Forum while addressing the then Union Minister for Home Affairs in connection with an incident which took place at Dhaula Kuan, wrote "..............it is generally experienced by the girls students in general and students from North-East in particular, who are pursuing their higher studies/ vacation in Delhi face a problem of eve teasing, molestation and many such instances of abuse and humiliation, go unreported. It is no secret that the girls/women coming from North-Eastern region are more vulnerable than others by virtue of their distinctive features, language and culture".

"The general perception is that the police are not sensitive and responsive when girls approach the police for help and term them as un-friendly. There is a general feeling that anti social elements indulging in such crime against women get away scot-free and as such encourage the culprit to repeat such heinous crime against women/girls and women from North-East become an easy prey".

II.   A news article captioned "Stalker makes girl's life hell" featured in the Mid-Day of 22.2.2008. It was alleged, therein, that an individual was stalking a girl from the North-East and kept following her wherever she went. He also sent SMSs to her. While the police did offer tea and snacks to the complainant, as per the report, they did not take any action as no cognizable offence was made out. It has been repeatedly emphasized that top priority needs to be given to complainants and their problems which should be addressed in a proactive manner. When the complainants are students/residents from the North-Eastern states, particularly women, the level of sensitivity and response should be of even a higher level. There has to be a clear 'Zero Tolerance Policy' as far as Crime Against Women in general and far North Eastern States in particular are concerned. Many problems including those such as stalking, sending SMSs etc. can easily be nipped in the bud if the person concerned is contacted and firmly advised to behave himself and not to harass the individual concerned. Where necessary, action as made under the law or preventive action under the Cr.PC can be initiated. When cases are made out, they should be immediately registered and investigated on a day-to-day basis and finalized. Quick action by the police would restore confidence not only of the victim but also of the community and send a clear message to the accused that such behaviour would not be tolerated. There should, however, be no scope for any complainant, particularly those from the North-Eastern States, to come to the police station and go back with the feeling that the police has not responded, at the time of their distress.

If there is any complaint or if any information is received that any girl from the North East has reported regarding any cognizable offence or eve-teasing, stalking or about indecent/suggestive/ unacceptable SMS messages and no follow-up action was taken, then a very serious view will be taken against the concerned police officer and also the SHO who is expected to lead from the front.

This aside, in all police stations in North and North-West Districts at and around the Delhi University including police stations Model Town, Mukherjee Nagar, Civil Lines, Roop Nagar, Timar Pure etc. there should be regular patrolling covering not only hostels where students live but also pockets in normal residential colonies in which North-Eastern students live in large numbers. The beat constables in such areas should be sensitized to establish close interaction with the community leaders of the residents belonging to the North-Eastern states so that he is aware of the problems, if any, being faced by them and can take appropriate action himself or inform the Division Officer/SHO for necessary action. The SHOs must have a regular quarterly meeting with the community leaders. The Area Security Committee which has been formed in the North District should meet regularly and interact with various stake-holders including the students.

The university aside, there are other pockets such as Munirka, Kotla, Satya Niketan near Dhaula Kuan etc. having a substantial residents belonging to the representative of North-East states. Here again, the SHOs must have regular meeting with the leaders of the Community. Such meeting should be held at least once in two months. This aside, the area should be covered by patrolling and the beat constables should be sensitized as mentioned above to take action in a proactive manner.

There will be three nodal officers – one for the northern range i.e. DCP/North, DCP/East will be the nodal officer for the North-East States Community living in Trans Yamuna area, while DCP/South will be nodal officer for the North-East States Community living in the Southern Range and New Delhi District for interaction with students and other persons belonging to the North-Eastern States.

The nodal DCsP should also send minutes of meetings held by them to the Joint CsP who may put up minutes, if necessary, to CP with their comments/ recommendations. Joint CsP must ensure that action is being taken in their ranges and if necessary, in other ranges, to address issues raised in a nodal meeting pertaining to other districts in Delhi. The Joint CP/NR should hold a six monthly meeting with all the district DCsP to ensure that there is proper co-ordination in the three ranges and all issues raised are being addressed by the concerned DCsP. Efforts also should be made to co-opt a member of the North Eastern state community in Thana Level Committees to ensure that there is another forum available to address issues at the Police Station Level.

This aside, the nodal officers would also also ensure:-

1. Liaison with the Resident Commissioners.
2. Ensuring that the Recruitment Cell keeps the Resident Commissioners, Doordarshan, All India Radio informed about the recruitment programs.
3. Regular meetings of the Area Security Committee should not be restricted to students only as, at times, they are not able to clearly express their problems and we should also include the representatives amongst the residents of North-East region.
4. Regular patrolling of areas in which there are pockets of citizens belonging to the North-East States.
5. Regular interaction with North-East Students by RWAs of the concerned area.
6. Liaison and interaction with the leaders, representatives of various student groups/residents or group of various North-East students/leaders. He should conduct bi-monthly meetings in this regard. In such meetings, leaders and representatives of the North-East States besides residents, RWAs office bearers should also be called.
7. In case, the nodal officer is contacted by any student or other citizen belonging to North-East States or in case of any such problem he must follow up the matter with the concerned DCP/SHO to ensure that appropriate action is taken.

Women from North-East can make use of help line No.1090 of the scheme 'Eyes and Ears' of the police, to give information, particularly when they want to keep their identity secret. This aside, they can also use regular women help line

No.1091, besides the PCR call centre No.100. In all such cases, a follow up action should be taken up rapidly and followed by the DCP/PCR and the District DCsP. A special sensitization programme be organized by the DCP/PCR to sensitize those handling Help Line No.1090, 1091, 100 and 23317004 or handling of calls from women or any other individuals from the North-East. This programme should be organized with immediate effect. The representatives from the North-East Group should also be invited to speak about the areas of their concern etc. etc. Wide publicity needs to be given to the availability of these services in addition to reporting in Police Station.

This Standing Order supersedes previous Standing Order No.383/09 issued vide Hdqrs. No.16551-16800/RB/PHQ,dated 18.3.2009, and corrigendum issued vide No. 17151-17250/Record Branch PHQ, dated 13.10.2009 on the subject.

(Yudhbir Singh Dadwal)
Commissioner of Police:
Delhi.

O.B. NO. !! ○/RB/P **HQ Dated 15.10.09**

No. 176 51- 9ʊ2/RB/PHQ, dated Delhi, the 15-10- 09

Copy forwarded for information and necessary action to the:

1. All Special Commissioners of Police, Delhi.
2. All Joint Commissioners of Police, Delhi
3. Additional Commissioners of Police, including P/PTC, Delhi.
4. All Deputy Commissioners of Police, District/Units, including FRRO, Delhi/ New Delhi.

5. SO to Commissioner of Police, LA to Commissioner of Police, Delhi
6. ACP/IT Centre with the direction to upload the Standing Order in Intra DP Net..
7. All ACsP Sub Division, Delhi including all ACsP in PHQ, Delhi.
8. All SHOs/Delhi Police through their respective DCsP with the direction to place the Standing Order in register No. 3 Part-I of the Police Stations.
9. All Inspectors/PHQ, including Reader to CP, Delhi.
10. Librarian/PHQ.

'Put on your best behaviour'

COP CIRCULAR Police chief wants his men to adopt a 'zero-tolerance policy' to crime against northeastern women

Vijaita Singh
▪ vijaita.singh@hindustantimes.com

HT 23.10.09

NEW DELHI: The Delhi Police chief wants his men to behave better with women from the north-eastern part of the country.

In a circular, police commissioner Y.S. Dadwal has asked his men to adopt a "zero tolerance policy" as far as crime against women from north-eastern states are concerned.

Even police control room (PCR) staff who answer helpline numbers (100, 1090) are being trained how to answer the grievance calls of women from north-eastern states.

Three district deputy commissioners of police have been appointed to deal with issues of the community.

"If there is any complaint that any girl from the northeast has reported about eve teasing,

minister saying "students from northeast in particular who are pursuing higher studies in Delhi face a problem of eve teasing, molestation and many such instances of abuse and humiliation that go unreported"

> It is no secret that girls/women from this region are more vulnerable than others by virtue of their distinctive features, language and culture.
> **NORTHEAST MPs' FORUM**

stalking, rape, SMS and no follow-up action was taken by the police, then a serious action will be taken against him so the concerned police on must also the Station House Officer (SHO) who is expected to lead from the front," said Dadwal in the order.

The police have been asked to identify the areas where people and students from the northeast live and intensify beat patrolling in these pockets.

"The beat constables in such areas should be sensitized to establish close interaction with the community leaders and the area SHO must have a quarterly meeting with them," the order said.

On October 18, two men reportedly tried to pull into their car a woman from the northeast in Sarojini Nagar area of south Delhi when she was on her way home.

On October 12, a couple from Nagaland alleged they were beaten up by drunk men in Safdarjung enclave area and the police did not register their case.

"A special sensitisation pro-

gramme be organised by the DCP-PCR for the policemen manning the help lines," said the order.

DCPs of north, east and south districts have been appointed as the nodal officers for the northeast/arm community living in north, trans-Yamuna and southern parts of the city.

"The nodal DCPs should also send minutes of meetings to the Joint commissioner of police with their recommendations and ensure that proper action is taken," said the order.

Many problems such as deleting or sending unwanted text messages can be tipped in the bud if the concerned person "is contacted and asked to behave himself and not harass the individual concerned," the order said.

Dear Associates,

You are probably aware that 12 therapists from [...] suddenly resigned in August.

They have approached the North East Association of Goa (NEAG) and All India Trade Union Congress (AITUC) and have started harassing us.

In spite of facing major losses due to their sudden resignation, We have paid every single paisa of their salaries and deposit, yet they are trying to blackmail the management for compensation which they are definitely not eligible for.

For the last 2 years, we have made huge donations to the welfare of North East Association of Goa, but in spite of our goodwill, their representatives are threatening us and trying to spoil our image. They have abused us and our company and said that

We request you to kindly avoid getting carried away by the false information and dirty politics of the NEAG and the AITUC. We are all a family and all of you are aware that we have always treated you fairly and equally.

Regarding your salaries and other benefits, we have already assured you that we are going to review them in November and we will also give an excellent 'Loyalty Bonus' on 1st January 2017 to everyone who has completed 2 years or more at Snip.

We look forward to your support. Kind Regards

Archana & Sumeet

Notice to employees posted by the owners of the Snip Spa and Salon in response to the North East Association's demand for the dignity of women employees.

(Reg. No. 854/Goa/2010)

NORTH EAST ASSOCIATION GOA
C/o All India Trade Union Congress
Velho's Building, (2nd Floor), Opp. Municipal, Garden, Panjim-Goa. Mobile No. +919890461212.
E-mail: northeastassociation.goa@yahoo.com
north.east.association.goa@gmail.com

Com Christopher Fonseca,   September 22, 2016

A.I.T.U.C. Goa

Dear Comrade Christopher,

Please accept our warm greetings from the Northeast Association, Goa. We still remember the help and solidarity extended by all our friends at the AITUC in getting us justice for the women working at the Tatva Spa. It greatly encouraged many of our people who continue to work for long hours without knowing our rights under the labour laws.

The working conditions for the girls and women at the spas and salons are shocking. We would like to bring to your attention the latest case that has come to our Association. Thirteen girls resigned recently from one of Goa's best known spas called Snip Spa and Salon. The immediate cause of resignation seemed rather small but our investigation revealed that the girls had been suffering under very difficult conditions.

We intervened on behalf of the women and they have been paid their dues but we discovered that the owners of the Snip Spa, Sumeet Bhobe posted the photographs of the girls on a WhatsApp group of Spa owners and they told them not to employ these girls. We got access to some of the correspondence and it seems to be unfair labour practices when the spa owners stop future employment of employees who have dared to demand their rights under the law.

We are reproducing a part of the chat in the WhatsApp so you can see for yourself

Hi sumeet

> We had an issue on Friday when 14
> of our staff got together and
> suddenly left, simply because one
> of them was given a treatment
> 8:43am

Runda Raikar

Yes very thrue, in the off season
they want us to pay them, n now
when the season starts they want
to run away

> I am posting their pictures with Real
> names and Pet names-please do
> not hire these therapists, they are
> troublemakers

> Also kindly update me if any of
> them approaches our members for
> jobs

> Thanks

Ashwin D'Costa

Please share

This impinges on the dignity and safety of our women.

We would also like to bring to your attention the following unfair labour practices being followed by many spas, including Snip Spa and Salon:

1. The workers are paid in cash salaries which are much below the minimum wages. For instance at the Snip the therapists are paid Rs 10,000 in cash without being given any provident fund, health insurance, uniform etc

2. The therapist are given commission for each massage done but when salary is deducted for absence of anything then the commission and salary is added together and then deduction is made.

3. Salary is never given on time and sometimes it is paid more then ten days after the first of month.

4. There are no fixed timings; often the women are made to work beyond the working hours which are from 10 am to 9 pm. Some salons even have night shifts working till one in the morning.

5. The Spa owners have a practice of sending the girls to massage their clients at their homes. This makes the girls and women vulnerable to sexual exploitation .In snip when the girls have refused the owner have deducted their salaries.

6. No one gets appointment letter and even after being trained the owners refuse to give certificates or letter stating that the employee can buy certificates for Rs. 500 for Ayurvedic massage when they do not get any training in that massage.

7. Cross massage must be stopped since that makes the women vulnerable to be exploited.

We hope you can guide us in getting the basic protection of labour laws for the employee working in Spas in Goa.

Thanking you for your support and solidarity,

Your Sincerely

Aghato Awomi

(President NEAG)

ATIM'S CV

Ngatalim Hongray
Vasant Enclave
New Delhi-110057
[email address]
[phone number]

• •

CAREER OBJECTIVES:
To obtain a waitress position in the Food and Beverage Industry with a challenging company that offers me the possibility of professional growth and career advancement opportunities.

QUALIFICATION SUMMARY:
- Extensive knowledge of principles and processes for providing customer service, including customer needs assessment, meeting quality standards for service, and evaluation of customer satisfaction.
- Wide knowledge of principles and methods for showing, promoting, and selling products or services, marketing strategy and tactics, product demonstration, and sales techniques.
- Strong communication and interpersonal skills and abilities.
- Leadership among peers

WORK EXPERIENCE:
Have been working in hotels and restaurants in New Delhi from 2006 to 2015; including Five Star Hotels and fine dining restaurants handling large parties and rush hours which included more than 200 guests. Her employers have appreciated her ability to multi-task even under severe pressure and has been awarded certificates of appreciation.

1. Q'BA located in heart of New Delhi i.e., Inner circle Connaught Place having two floors (Lounge & Restaurant) and two open air terraces offering multi-cuisine and wide range of drinks.

Worked as Hostess from 2006 to 2010. The responsibilities included:

- Greeted and seated guests at the same time as monitoring the flow of guests in keeping with seating chart and servers
- Gave quick and exact information and directions to guests
- Answered all questions regarding the menu and services
- Ensured coverage of the hostess stand at all times
- Answered phones, took messages and made reservations

2. S 18 the Coffee Shop at the five star Radission MBD Hotel at Noida

   Worked as Hostess in the Food and Beverage Service Department from April 20, 2011 to December 2011. Awarded certificate in recognition of good and consistent performance and integrity during work.

The job included decision-making and exercise of supervisory functions. The work of Hostess included:

- Warmly greet guests and bid a tender departure and invite to visit again
- Find out the seating place of guests as per requirement
- Present menu and hot deals of the day
- Run waitlist, gauge kitchen, servers and general dining room performance
- Ensure that requirements for all guests are met; including small children, disabled or food allergic guests
- Examine and maintain the entrance area, doors, windows in addition to menu covers and inserts

3. Keya-Kainoosh is a bar and fine dining owned by TV Celebrity chef Marut Sikka. Keya, the bar has an extensive selection of wines, the largest selection in a standalone bar all over India. It is located at the dlf promenade in Vasant Kunj, New Delhi.

Worked as Guest Relations Officer from 2012 to 2013 and the work included:

- Checking customers' identification in order to ensure that they meet minimum age requirements for consumption of alcoholic beverages.
- Checking with customers to ensure that they are enjoying their meals and take action to correct any problems, escorting customers to their tables.
- Explaining how various menu items are prepared, describing ingredients and cooking methods.
- Informing customers of daily specials, preparing checks, presenting menus to patrons and answering questions, making recommendations upon request.
- Active in removing dishes and glasses from tables or counters and taking them to kitchen for cleaning.
- Serving food and beverages to patrons, preparing and serving specialty dishes at tables as required.
- Stocking service areas with supplies such as coffee, food, tableware, and linens.

4. Underdogs, Sports Bar and Grill in the Ambience Shopping Mall. Given a Certificate in recognition of excellent service and leadership among peers. Had to leave Underdogs when it was closed down and went back to Keya-Kainoosh till 2014.

Worked as Hostess and the responsibilities included:

- Checking customers' identification in order to ensure that they meet minimum age requirements for consumption of alcoholic beverages.

5. En, a Japanese restaurant spread over three levels and divided into various areas is housed in a century old royal heritage Haveli. Appointed Guest Executive Service in November 2014 and working there till the present day. Given training in Japanese culture and etiquette.

Responsibilities included

- Collecting payments from customers.
- Writing food orders on order slips, memorizing orders,

entering orders into computers for transmittal to kitchen staff.

- Informing customers of daily specials, cleaning tables or counters after patrons had finished dining, filling salt, pepper, sugar, cream, condiment, and napkin containers, stocking service areas, and escorting customers to their tables.
- Prepared hot, cold, and mixed drinks for patrons.
- Describing and recommending wines to customers.

PERSONAL INFORMATION:

NAME: Ngalatim Hongray

DATE OF BIRTH: June 11, 1988

FORMAL EDUCATION: Higher Secondary School, 2004

LANGUAGES SPOKEN: English, Tangkhul, Meitei-lon and Hindi

MARITIAL STATUS: Single

NATIONALITY: Indian

Date: July 2015

Acknowledgements

Thank You!

A big Ningshilakhaira from the bottom of my heart to all those of you who have trusted me with your stories; most especially to R. Mayori, Ngalatim Hongray, Yaokhalek Hongray and Livingstone Shaiza.

Thank you to Ruth and Brian for your support.

It has been a learning experience to work with the Tangkhul Welfare Union and even more with the Northeast Association, Goa. I have especially enjoyed working with Wungchipem Pheirim, Aghato Awomi and Lunminlal Baite and Martin.

I have been truly inspired by the girls and women of Snip Salon and Spa who had the guts to speak out against their employers and fight for their dignity: Mirinyo, Valentina, Jenny, Toto and all the rest of you. Thank you for trusting me.

Thanks to Albertina Almeida for answering my calls even late at night and being so generous with her time; and to Sabina Martins and Ulka Lotlikar for always being there.

Thank you to Andrea Wright for her generous and prompt response.

Thank you Aruna Ghose for making this book read so much better, and Shalini Krishan for your sensitive finishing touch. And of course to Ravi Singh for agreeing to publish this book long before I was sure what shape the book would take.

And, finally, to Sebastian without whose care, love and support I would not be able to do anything.

Panaji
11 November 2016